BEYOND THE KILLING FIELDS

BEYOND THE KILLING FIELDS

WAR WRITINGS

SYDNEY SCHANBERG

COMPILED AND EDITED BY ROBERT MIRALDI

POTOMAC BOOKS, INC.
WASHINGTON, D.C.

302 9933

"The Big Picture," in chapter 1, is an essay from *Crimes of War: What the Public Should Know*, ed. Roy Gutman and David Rieff (New York: W. W. Norton, 1999). Used by permission.

The other articles in chapter 1, as well as those in chapters 2, 3, and 4, originally appeared in *The New York Times*, and to the extent they are reprinted here, they are reprinted by permission. Some articles have been abridged.

Chapter 5, "Pol Pot's Poison Legacy," originally appeared in *Vanity Fair* (October 1997). Reprinted by permission.

Chapter 6, "How John McCain Buried Information on American Prisoners Abandoned by Washington," originally appeared as "McCain and the POW Cover-up" in September 2008 on the website of The Nation Institute; an abbreviated version appeared in the October 6, 2008, issue of *The Nation*.

"The War Planned Years Before 9/11 by Cheney and Co.," in chapter 7, originally appeared as "The Widening Crusade" in the Village Voice (October 15–21, 2003) © 2009, Village Voice Media. Reprinted with the permission of the *Village Voice*.

"A Reporter's Itch to Return to the Action—and the Madness," in chapter 7, originally appeared as "The Itch: Why A Reporter Is Drawn to War," in the *Village Voice* (March 25, 2003) © 2009, Village Voice Media. Reprinted with the permission of the *Village Voice*.

For additional articles on war by Sydney Schanberg, please visit the website for this book at http://www.beyondthekillingfields.com.

Library of Congress Cataloging-in-Publication Data
Schanberg, Sydney H. (Sydney Hillel), 1934–
  Beyond the killing fields: war writings / Sydney Schanberg compiled and edited by Robert Miraldi.
    p. cm.
  Includes index.
  ISBN 978-1-59797-505-6 (alk. paper)
  1. War—Press coverage—United States—History—20th century—Sources. 2. Schanberg, Sydney H. (Sydney Hillel), 1934– I. Miraldi, Robert. II. Title.
  PN4888.W37S33 2010
  070.4'4935502—dc22

                                                              2009044858

Printed in the United States of America on recycled paper.

Potomac Books, Inc.
22841 Quicksilver Drive
Dulles, Virginia 20166

First Edition

10 9 8 7 6 5 4 3 2 1

To Pran and Jane—who made it happen

CONTENTS

PREFACE

HOW I CAME TO KNOW WAR AND WHY THIS BOOK

I knew nothing about war when I came out of college, or even after two years as an army draftee, stationed in Germany. It was that no-shooting era—the Cold War with Russia. Then I offered my services to *The New York Times*, where they hired me as a clerk at $49.50 a week, running errands and copy for the editorial writers on the tenth floor.

Ten years later, in 1969—after having covered the police beat, city government, and state government—I was awarded a foreign assignment as the bureau chief in New Delhi, responsible for South Asia (India, Pakistan, Afghanistan, Nepal, Sri Lanka, etc.). War didn't seem imminent in my new surroundings either. That didn't last very long.

In April 1970 President Richard Nixon, on Henry Kissinger's advice, ordered a major military "incursion" into Cambodia, a small, weak country that had been trying to stay neutral. The American push engulfed Cambodia in the Vietnam War. Extra correspondents were needed at this time to bolster the Saigon bureau and I was one of those sent in.

Later that year, back in South Asia, Pakistani elections gave rise to an autonomy movement in East Pakistan, and in March 1971, the Pakistani army was sent in to crush it. India got involved on behalf of the freedom movement and in December, war was declared and I covered it alongside the Indian advance. The Pakistanis surrendered within two weeks.

My life, essentially, had turned into a war assignment. In 1972, I was sent again to Vietnam when the Communists launched an offensive that lasted about six months.

I also kept returning regularly to Cambodia for long periods. The country was sinking steadily, and I stayed to report the final days as it fell to the genocidal Khmer Rouge guerrillas supported by China.

Why put together a collection of old war stories? What useful purpose does it serve? My answer is simple. To me, now a septuagenarian, it seems that our planet—and maybe Washington in particular—has become almost comfortable with regular wars. President Eisenhower's warning to America to beware of "the military-industrial complex" has been brushed aside.

We Americans are notoriously deficient about taking lessons from our own history. So perhaps this book will remind people what war is really like. Slaughter is no less bestial now than it has been through recorded history.

Armed with this knowledge, the next time a politician says we must invade and destroy evildoers who are being well contained by other means, maybe we'll think twice.

And, then, maybe we won't.

SYDNEY SCHANBERG
NEW PALTZ, NEW YORK
SEPTEMBER 2009

ACKNOWLEDGMENTS

No book gets created by one person alone. This one wouldn't have come into being if not for two good friends—Robert Miraldi, journalism professor and author, and his wife, investigative reporter Mary Beth Pfeiffer—who came to me with the idea, urged me to take it on, and offered to help. Rob agreed to be the overall editor. Mary Beth, among other things, did the archaeology, plowing through boxfuls of my work in search of the wheat.

Other helpers, who did research and detail work, were Dave Savercool, Kelsey Van Norman, Emily Atkin, and Jesse Ordansky. Jeanmarie Evelly handled a special research assignment.

Our agent, Robert Wilson, worked tirelessly in the hunt for a publisher in poor economic times. Our editor at Potomac Books, Hilary Claggett, guided us well throughout.

My thoughts, though, ranged into the past, fixing on people who had shaped my path to becoming a reporter—all the way back to Helen Bachose, my high school Latin teacher, and Robert Murphy, the debate coach. And to John Ligon, my army drill sergeant, out of Harlem and the Korean War.

I also owe a great deal to my editors at *The New York Times*, *Newsday*, and the *Village Voice* (the late Sheldon Binn, Tony Marro, and Don Forst), who gave me the freedom to operate independently. I must especially thank Jim Greenfield, Gerry Gold, Allan Siegal, and others on *The Times*'s foreign desk for how they looked after me and my copy during the 1970s, when I was covering wars. I also am indebted to the omnipresent Arthur Gelb for proposing and assigning me to write "The Death and Life of Dith Pran" when Pran escaped to freedom in 1979.

Finally, thanks will never be enough for all the foreign aides who guide correspondents overseas—translating, explaining, and saving us from harm with their sharper sense of imminent danger and their bravery. We couldn't do our jobs without them. Yet seldom are they acknowledged by the news organizations that benefit from their work. I salute the men who made my work better: P. J. Anthony, Kasturi Rangan, Barun Roy, Chan Vo, Koy Sarun, Put Sophan, Mean Leang, Junnosuke Ofusa—and, of course, Dith Pran.

CHAPTER ONE

CHAPTER ONE

Cambodia, an Unnecessary War

THE BIG PICTURE

Author's Note: This is an essay from Crimes of War: What the Public Should Know, *ed. Roy Gutman and David Rieff (New York: W. W. Norton, 1999), a study of the evils of war in modern times. All the remaining articles in this chapter are from* The New York Times.

For the last three decades, without surcease, Cambodia has been consumed by war, genocide, slave labor, forced marches, starvation, disease, and now civil conflict. It is to Asia what the Holocaust was to Europe.

Roughly the size of Missouri, bordered by Thailand, Laos, and Vietnam, Cambodia had a population of perhaps 7 to 8 million in 1975 when the maniacal Khmer Rouge guerrillas swept into Phnom Penh and began the "purification" campaign that was the centerpiece of their extremist agrarian revolution. Four years later, in 1979, the Khmer Rouge were pushed back into the jungle, leaving behind their legacy: 1.5 to 2 million Cambodians dead in what would become known to the world as "the Killing Fields." Twenty percent of the population erased. In America that would be 50 to 60 million people.

Some scholars say that technically what happened in Cambodia cannot be called a genocide because, for the most part, it was Khmers killing other Khmers, not someone trying to destroy a different "national, racial, ethnical or religious group"—which is how international law defines genocide.

To make such semantic or legalistic distinctions, however, is sometimes to forsake common sense—after all, the Khmer Rouge set out to erase an entire culture, a major foundation stone of which was Cambodia's religion, Theravada

Buddhism. And this may help explain why, over the years, the law has proved so poor a guide to the reality of human slaughter. For, whether you call the mass killing in Cambodia a genocide or simply a crime against humanity, it was the same by either name. It was a visitation of evil.

One might thus reasonably pick Cambodia as a paradigm for the law's weakness in dealing with such crimes. International law, after all, depends for its legitimacy on the willingness of the world's Nation-States to obey and enforce it. In Cambodia's case most Nation-States expressed shock and horror—and did nothing. Even after the Vietnamese Army pushed the Khmer Rouge out of power in 1979, ended the genocide, were welcomed as liberators, and installed a pro-Hanoi government in Phnom Penh, Western nations saw to it that Cambodia's seat at the United Nations continued to be occupied for several years by those very same Khmer Rouge. Washington and its allies, while denouncing the Khmer Rouge crimes, were still slaves to Cold War ideology; they decided it was better to keep them in the UN seat than to have it go to a government in the orbit of Vietnam and its mentor, the Soviet Union. Realpolitik, not the law, was the governing force.

For the human record, let us examine exactly what the Khmer Rouge did to the Cambodian population. Their first act, within hours of military victory, was to kidnap it, herding everyone out of cities and towns into work camps deep in the countryside. All villages that touched on roads were similarly emptied. Cambodia, in fact, was transformed into one giant forced-labor camp under the fist of Angka, "the organization on high." That was the mild part.

The Khmer Rouge had actively sealed off the country. The world could not look in. The horror could begin. Led by Pol Pot, their Paris-educated, Maoist-influenced "Brother Number One," the new rulers proceeded to completely shatter the three underpinnings of Cambodian society—the family, the Buddhist religion, and the village. In grueling migrations, people were marched to sites as far as possible from their home villages. Children were separated from parents and placed in youth groups, where they were indoctrinated to inform on their parents and other adults for any infractions of Angka's crushing rules. Marriage was forbidden except when arranged by Angka. The schools were shuttered, currency abolished, factories abandoned. Newspapers ceased to exist. Radio sets were taken away.

Buddhist temples were razed or closed. Of the sixty thousand Buddhist monks only three thousand were found alive after the Khmer Rouge reign; the rest had either been massacred or succumbed to hard labor, disease, or torture. The Chams, a Muslim minority, were also targets for elimination.

Religion, however, was but a starting point. Simply put, the Khmer Rouge marked for potential extinction all Cambodians they deemed not "borisot" (pure)—meaning all those with an education, those raised in population centers, those "tainted" by anything foreign (including knowledge of a foreign language), even those who wore glasses. Anyone, that is, suspected of not being in step with their pathological agrarian master plan. All suspect Cambodians were labeled "new people" and kept apart from the "pure" populations. In some instances, the "new people" were given special identifying neckerchiefs—reminiscent of the yellow Star of David—so they could always be picked out of a crowd, as they often were when taken away for execution.

The Khmer Rouge had a pet slogan: "To spare you is no profit; to destroy you, no loss." With this incantation, at least 1.5 million Cambodians were erased.

I was in Phnom Penh when the Khmer Rouge marched in victorious on April 17, 1975, their faces cold, a deadness in their eyes. They ordered the city evacuated. Everyone was to head for the countryside to join the glorious revolution. They killed those who argued against leaving. Two million frightened people started walking out of the capital. The guerrilla soldiers even ordered the wounded out of the overflowing hospitals, where the casualties had been so heavy in the final few days of the war that the floors were slick with blood. There was no time for anything but emergency surgery. When the doctors ran out of surgical gloves, they simply dipped their hands in bowls of antiseptic and moved on to the next operating table. Somewhere between five thousand and ten thousand wounded were in the city's hospitals when the order to evacuate came. Most couldn't walk so their relatives wheeled them out of the buildings on their beds, with plasma and serum bags attached, and began pushing them along the boulevards out of the city toward the "revolution."

Foreigners were allowed to take refuge in the French embassy compound. I watched many Cambodian friends being herded out of Phnom Penh. Most of them I never saw again. All of us felt like betrayers, like people who were protected and didn't do enough to save our friends. We felt shame. We still do.

Two weeks later, the Khmer Rouge expelled us from the country, shipping us out on two truck convoys to the border with Thailand. With this act, Cambodia was sealed. The world could not look in. The killing could begin.

But the story of Cambodia's misery did not start with the Khmer Rouge. It began in March 1970, when a pro-Western junta headed by Gen. Lon Nol, with Washington's blessing, deposed Prince Norodom Sihanouk, who was out of the country. Sihanouk, a neutralist, had kept Cambodia out of the Vietnam War by making concessions to appease both sides. He allowed the Americans to secretly bomb Viet Cong sanctuaries inside Cambodia while he allowed the Vietnamese Communists to use Cambodia's port city, Kompong Som (also called Sihanoukville) to ship in supplies for those sanctuaries.

With Sihanouk gone, the Lon Nol group in effect declared war on Hanoi, and President Richard Nixon, pleased to have partisans—not neutralists—in Phnom Penh, ordered American troops to push into Cambodia from Vietnam for a six-week assault on the Communist sanctuaries. However, not having real confidence in Lon Nol, the president didn't inform him of the invasion on his sovereign territory until after it had begun and after Nixon had informed the American public on national television.

This was probably the moment that marked Cambodia's transformation into a pawn of the Cold War, with the Chinese backing the Khmer Rouge, the Soviets backing Hanoi, and the Americans backing the Lon Nol regime—all of them turning the entire country into a surrogate Cold War battlefield. The great irony in this turn of events is that the Khmer Rouge were no serious threat in 1970, being a motley collection of ineffectual guerrilla bands totaling at most three thousand to five thousand men, who could never have grown into the murderous force of seventy thousand to 100,000 that swept into Phnom Penh five years later without the American intervention and the subsequent expansion of Chinese and Russian aid to the Communist side. The enlarged war gave the Khmer Rouge status and recruitment power. It also gave them tutelage and advisory help from Hanoi's forces (at least for the first two years before deep rifts drove the two apart).

This five-year war was marked by barbarism by all sides. Cambodian warriors have a battlefield custom, going back centuries, of cutting the livers from the bodies of their vanquished foes, then cooking them in a stew and eating them. The belief is that this imparts strength and also provides talismanic protection against being killed by the enemy. In this and countless other ways, the international conventions that say respect must be shown to the fallen enemy were universally disregarded.

Early in the war, in a town south of Phnom Penh, Lon Nol troops had killed two Viet Cong and recovered their badly charred bodies, which they hung upside-down in the town square to swing gruesomely in the wind—thereby sending a message to all who might consider aiding the foe. Henry Kamm, my *New York Times* colleague, tried to tell the Lon Nol commander that treating the bodies in this manner violated the Geneva Conventions. The commander found this amusing. He left the bodies twisting.

With the Vietnamese Communist units moving deeper into Cambodia, the Lon Nol government began whipping up anti-Vietnamese fervor. This visited fear and worse upon the 200,000-strong ethnic Vietnamese community in the country who, though they were citizens of Cambodia and had lived there for generations, soon became the targets of a public frenzy. Massacres began occurring. Many of the Vietnamese lived along the rivers, earning their living as fishermen; their bodies were soon floating down the Mekong by the dozens. One government general, Sosthene Fernandez, a Cambodian of Filipino ancestry who later rose to become chief of the armed forces, began using ethnic Vietnamese civilians as protective shields for his advancing troops, marching them in front into the waiting guns of the Viet Cong. This, too, is against international law. Fernandez disagreed. "It is a new form of psychological warfare," he said.

Saigon raised bitter protests against these pogroms, and Cambodia's Vietnamese population was finally interned in protective custody in schools and other public buildings. Many were eventually moved under guard to South Vietnam as a temporary measure until emotions cooled.

As the war progressed, the country—at least the part held by the Lon Nol government—progressively shrank. The energized Khmer Rouge kept grabbing more and more territory until the area under government control, aside from the capital, was reduced to a handful of transport corridors and several province towns. The Phnom Penh airport and the Mekong River were its lone links to the outside world. To preserve these lines of supply, the Americans bombed Khmer Rouge and Viet Cong targets in the countryside on a daily basis. Since most of the raids were by giant, eight-engine B-52s, each carrying about twenty-five tons of bombs and thus laying down huge carpets of destruction, the bombing was anything but surgical, and frequently hit civilian villages. The result was thousands of refugees fleeing into Phnom Penh and the province towns. The capital swelled from a population of 600,000 at the start of the war to 2 million at its end in 1975. The American embassy in Phnom Penh—and Henry Kissinger's team in Washington—insisted that the refugees were fleeing only one thing: attacks by the brutal Khmer Rouge. But in fact they were fleeing both the Khmer Rouge and the American bombs. I visited refugee camps regularly and consistently heard both accounts. Some peasants didn't flee at all; the Khmer Rouge used their anger about the bombing to recruit them as soldiers and porters.

The bombing raids illustrate what is pretty much an axiom in all wars: i.e., that so-called "conventional" weapons not forbidden by international law can produce the same horrific results as banned weapons.

In Cambodia, the B-52s usually flew in formations of three, with each of the mammoth planes carrying twenty-five to thirty tons of bombs, making the total load of a formation seventy-five to ninety tons. B-52s drop their bombs to form a grid, or "box," of destruction on the ground; the grid (an average one might be one kilometer wide and two kilometers long) can be altered to fit the size and shape of the troop concentration. Soldiers who manage to survive these massive explosions (which sometimes throw bodies and dirt as much as one hundred feet in the air) are often rendered unfit for further duty, having been put in permanent shock or made deaf or simply frightened to the bone of every sharp sound or movement. Such raids were what destroyed the retreating Iraqi troops on the road to Basra at the end of that war in 1991—the road that became known as the "Highway of Death."

In 1973, an accidental B-52 bombing of Neak Luong, a government-held Mekong River town, killed and wounded some four hundred Cambodians, most of them civilians. The American embassy apologized and gave monetary gifts to victims' families on a sliding scale—a few hundred dollars for the loss of a limb, more for multiple limbs, and still more for a death. When civilians die in wars, the military calls it unintentional, even though everyone knows civilian deaths are inevitable, especially when the weapons spray their lethality over large spaces. The phrase used by the Pentagon for civilian deaths is "collateral damage"—just as napalm was called "soft ordnance"—the idea being to give war a softer, sanitized sound for the lay public.

Napalm, incidentally, was dropped by B-52s in the Vietnam and Cambodian wars, in the form of CBUs—Cluster Bomb Units. (Other planes dropped napalm in different containers and forms.) A CBU is a large bomb, weighing five hundred pounds or more, that carries hundreds of smaller projectiles. A typical CBU is rigged to open in the manner of a clamshell a short distance above the ground, releasing its hail of explosive bomblets on the enemy troops beneath it. One variety was the CBU-3; its bomblets carried napalm, which set fire to the troops or robbed the air of oxygen, thus asphyxiating them. Another version carried special darts, which ripped through flesh or pinned the victims to trees or the ground. Sometimes it is hard for the layman to discern any great difference between these weapons and, for instance, the chemical arms banned by international law and custom. Both have a terror component. We have been told that the napalm and darts have since been taken out of the American CBU inventory—because of their bad image—but other varieties of CBUs are still used, as in the 1991 Gulf war with Iraq.

Actually, napalm is still being used as a firebomb, although the Pentagon refuses to call it by that name, saying the chemical formula has been altered. The new bomb is called the MK-47, replacing the MK-44. The only result of the chemical change has been to make the incendiary charge even fiercer.

And what about plain old rockets? Should all of them be banned, since they are frequently used as instruments of terror against civilians? The Khmer Rouge sent rockets shrieking into Phnom Penh throughout that five-year war. These were not precisely aimed munitions by any definition. They were crudely produced Chinese projectiles with a fan-shaped tail that whistled as it cut through the air overhead; you knew when it began its downward plummet because the whistling suddenly stopped. These rockets were launched from the city's environs, set off from hand-fashioned wooden platforms; there was no aiming at specific military targets—the effort was simply to get them to land somewhere, anywhere, in the refugee-packed city. And land they did—on markets, in schoolrooms, in backyards—spewing jagged metal and sliced limbs. The purpose was to demoralize the civilian population, and it worked.

An artillery piece can also be used as a weapon of terror against civilians. One afternoon in the summer of 1974, the Khmer Rouge trained a captured American-made 105 mm howitzer on Phnom Penh and fanned its muzzle across the city's southern edge. At first, as the shells fell in this half-moon arc, they exploded without result, but then the arc came to a colony of houses called Psar Deum Kor, and the death began. Fires started by the shells broke out and the houses were quickly in flames, whipped by high winds. Within a half hour, nearly two hundred people were dead and another two hundred wounded, virtually all civilians. The bodies were carted off on police pickup trucks. No military target was anywhere in the vicinity.

In the end—whether in Cambodia or any other killing field—there is nothing new either about the barbarity of people destroying people or, unfortunately, about its seeming inevitability in every age. One unchanging lesson is that war or genocide or crimes against humanity are states of violence that, where they exist, remove all breath from such notions as the law and civilized behavior.

Is it hopeless, then, to try to strengthen both the international law and its enforcement? No, never hopeless, not if you believe in the possibility of improvement, no matter how slight. Journalists are by blood and tradition committed to the belief, or at least to the tenet, of trying to keep bad things from getting any worse than they already are. Thus, this anthology.

WAITING FOR PEACE TO FALL FROM HEAVEN
November 2, 1972

PHNOM PENH—"We are the poor people who are waiting for the peace to fall from the heavens," the receptionist at a Western embassy in Phnom Penh says wistfully to a visitor. His remark is virtually a national litany. From President Lon Nol to the lowliest pedicab driver, Cambodians wait—helplessly, wishfully, at the mercy of nations and forces beyond their control—for the accord they hope will bring peace to their lush and beautiful country after two and a half years of a war they never wanted.

Cabinet Ministers tell you that the North Vietnamese and Vietcong troops will withdraw and the Cambodian Government will then settle its differences with the local guerrillas, the Khmer Rouge, "and everything will be the same again," but few foreign observers here think it will be that simple.

In the nine-point Indochina peace agreement unveiled two weeks ago, only one point deals with Cambodia and Laos. It says nothing about a cease-fire in these two countries, nothing about international supervision. It says only that all "foreign" troops shall withdraw from Cambodia and Laos. But since Hanoi has never admitted that its troops are present in these countries, most observers here see no reason to expect that the North Vietnamese will consider this provision binding.

"The Government thinks the North Vietnamese will just fade away," said one skeptical Cambodian. "This is the same naïveté they showed in 1970 when they issued their ultimatum to the North Vietnamese to get out. Now I suppose they will issue another ultimatum."

Marshal Lon Nol issued the first ultimatum to the Communists shortly after March 18, 1970, the day he and his coterie deposed Prince Norodom Sihanouk, who is now in exile in Peking. The putschists did not like the corruption in the Sihanouk Government; they also did not like Prince Sihanouk's permissive attitude in allowing the North Vietnamese border sanctuaries in Cambodia from which they could launch operations into South Vietnam.

The Communists responded to the 1970 ultimatum by thrusting west out of their sanctuaries and attacking points throughout the country. American troops thereupon crossed over from South Vietnam in an attempt to destroy the sanctuaries and wipe out that elusive enemy headquarters that the Pentagon had made famous as "COSVN."

Now, two and a half years later, the sanctuaries and supply routes are more extensive and developed than ever, COSVN is still alive and well, and the North Vietnamese and their Cambodian allies control at least two-thirds of Cambodia's territory—some estimates put it as high as 80 percent or more. The Government holds only the major towns and population centers—about 60 percent of Cambodia's 7 million people.

American aid to Cambodia has soared to about $300 million a year. With aid has come a degree of corruption in Government and business that has produced deep malaise among students and intellectuals and a fairly large if suppressed political opposition.

Even if the North Vietnamese troops were to leave Cambodia, the Government would still be faced with its own Cambodian insurgents, whom the North Vietnamese have built into a well-armed and aggressive guerrilla force. The Government is making frantic efforts to persuade the Khmer Rouge to come over to its side, but the available reports do not indicate much success.

Curiously, the Cambodians are not angry at the Americans for helping to drag them into full-scale war. They only pray the Americans will now bail them out. They know they will agree to any peace pact the Americans arrange for them, because they have no other choice.

"We have a vocation for compromise," said one Cambodian official. "It's another word for helplessness."

WORST ACCIDENTAL BOMBING OF THE INDOCHINA WAR
August 9, 1973

NEAK LUONG, Cambodia—The destruction in this town from the accidental bombing on Monday is extensive.

Big chunks of the center of town have been demolished, including two-story concrete buildings reinforced with steel. Clusters of wood and thatch huts where soldiers lived with their families have been erased, so that the compounds where they once stood look like empty fields strewn with rubbish.

On Monday evening the United States Embassy described the damage as "minimal."

"I saw one stick of bombs through the town, but it was no great disaster," said Col. David H. E. Opfer, the air attaché at the embassy, who briefed the press. "The destruction was minimal."

[A United States Embassy spokeswoman in Phnom Penh said Wednesday that American aircraft, in their third bombing error in three days, hit a village on the Phnom Penh–Saigon highway, Reuters reported. In Washington, the Pentagon denied the report.]

The nearly 400 casualties from Monday's bombing, which the Americans say was carried out by a lone B-52 with a 20-ton-plus load, make it the worst accidental bombing of the Indochina war. Official figures show 137 killed and 268 wounded, most of them soldiers and their families. The Americans originally put total casualties at around 150 but have since acknowledged their error.

However, the toll could be somewhat higher because the count does not include minor wounds. Moreover, some townspeople say they believe a few bodies remain in the wreckage. The smell of decaying flesh is still prevalent in parts of town.

The atmosphere in Neak Luong, on the east bank of the Mekong River 38 miles southeast of Phnom Penh, is silent and sad—and bewildered at being bombed by an ally. Everyone has lost either relatives or friends; in some cases entire large families were wiped out.

Yesterday afternoon a soldier could be seen sobbing uncontrollably on the riverbank. "All my family is dead!" he cried, beating his hand on the wooden bench where he had collapsed. "All my family is dead! Take my picture, take my picture! Let the Americans see me!"

His name is Keo Chan, and his wife and 10 of his children were killed. All he has left is the youngest—an 8-month-old son. The 48-year-old soldier escaped death because he was on sentry duty a few miles away when the bombs fell.

The bombs went right down the middle of the town from north to south as it lay sleeping shortly after 4:30 a.m. Over 30 craters can be seen on a line nearly a mile long, and people reported others in jungle areas outside the town that this correspondent could not reach.

Some witnesses said the bombs exploded above the ground, indicating that they might have been antipersonnel devices.

A large part of the market area in the center of town is smashed flat, and many of the two-story concrete shops and apartment buildings on either side are shattered and uninhabitable, with walls and roofs reduced to rubble. Other buildings still usable have large holes.

A third of the hospital is demolished, with the rest badly damaged and unusable until major repairs are made. Several patients were wounded and some are believed killed. A bomb fell on the northeast corner of the hospital, blowing some walls down and scattering concrete, beds and cabinets.

At his press briefing Colonel Opfer, who visited Neak Luong within a few hours of the bombing, said that there was "a little bit of damage to the northeast corner of the hospital" and talked about some "structural cracks" in a wall.

The bombs also hit a compound for marines which had a large field full of flimsy shacks in the back. The shacks were leveled and the main building, a two-story concrete structure, was turned into a stark shell, with only some walls left standing, and those badly cracked and tilted. The shacks, of thatch and wood and corrugated metal, where the marines lived with their families, is a rubbish heap crisscrossed with fallen coconut trees.

Ammunition also exploded in this compound and many people died. A woman's scalp sways on a clump of tall grass. A bloody pillow here, a shred of a sarong caught on barbed wire there. A large bloodstain on the brown earth. A pair of infant's rubber sandals among some unexploded artillery shells.

Colonel Opfer referred to the soldiers' shacks as "hootches," suggesting that not much of value had been destroyed. The attaché said further that the bombing "took place in what is essentially a small village." Actually, by Cambodian standards it is a big town; about 10,000 people live in and around Neak Luong, half of them in the town proper.

Asked the reaction of the people when he walked through Neak Luong, Colonel Opfer said, "They were sad, but they understand that this is war and that in war these things happen."

"I do not understand why it happened," said Chea Salan, a 21-year-old soldier who lost relatives and army buddies. "Before, every time we saw the planes coming we were happy because we knew the planes came to help us. Now I have lost heart."

Another soldier asked, "Did the government capture the pilot yet?"

"Why did this happen to us?" said Keo Sakhoun Tha, also a soldier. "I want world opinion to judge what happened here." He added, almost as an afterthought, "I am frightened at night now when the planes come."

"At first, after the bombing, I thought it must be a North Vietnamese plane," still another soldier commented. "I did not believe it could be an American plane. Now I believe it."

Though several soldiers and residents said they were angry, their tone carried no anger and little anti-American reaction was discernable. Rather the people were confused, hurt and bewildered that such a disaster should befall them, and especially that it could be caused by an ally.

"I am simply desolated," said a naval ensign, Phiboun Doutch, "but we must continue the struggle against the enemy."

Local people, in their confusion over the bombing, continually stressed that there had been no enemy activity in the vicinity.

The bombs struck a fuel and ammunition dump. Trees for acres around are stripped of leaves and charred, with sheets of tin from soldiers' huts hanging from some of the high branches. A magic necklace, specially blessed by a Buddhist priest to ward off harm and misfortune, lay broken.

There is one unexploded bomb buried in the main street near the central market. The people are jittery about it. "When are you Americans going to take it away?" a man called to a visitor.

THE CHILDREN ARE STARVING—TO DEATH
February 26, 1975

PHNOM PENH, Cambodia—Five years of war, with the resultant shortages and astronomical prices, have finally produced serious malnutrition in this once-bountiful country—and children are beginning to die in numbers. Scenes like the following are ordinary today:

A 3-month-old infant, his body wasted by severe malnutrition, lies in a bamboo basket. An oxygen tube is in his nose and an intravenous feeding tube in his arm, which is shrunken into a twig-like thing. Abandoned in a poor section of Phnom Penh, he was found by a pitying old woman who named him Lach Sao and took him to the nearest medical facility, the Chinese Hospital. But when the hospital learned she could not pay, it stopped all treatment and discharged the infant. The bewildered woman then carried him to a center of World Vision, an international relief agency here—and despite the oxygen and the intravenous feeding it is much too late. He dies the same day.

In a World Vision clinic, Ah Srey, a 2-month-old girl, grossly dehydrated from starvation, has just been brought in by her grandmother. Ten days before they were caught in the maelstrom of a battle a few miles from Phnom Penh. In the panic, the family became separated and the grandmother found herself alone with the child. For 10 days they have been surviving on handouts and scraps of garbage. The child had been malnourished before. Now she is a skeletal horror little more than bulging eyes and a protruding rib cage. Every few seconds she produces a wail that racks her body. In three hours she is dead.

On the table next to Ah Srey is an older child—19 months—who is dying right now. His name is Nuth Saroeun. From his mouth comes a steady whimper and rattle. His father was killed by a rocket three months ago. His 25-year-old mother, also suffering from malnutrition (she has beri-beri and her feet are going numb), stands at his side sobbing. A doctor tries to force a tube down the child's throat to get out the mucus that is blocking his breathing. Suddenly the child utters a tiny cry that sounds like "Mak" (Mother) and then his head slumps and he is gone.

Waves of mothers carrying gravely ill children—swollen children, children with stick-like concentration-camp bodies, children with parchment skin hanging in flaccid folds, coughing children, weeping children, silent children too weak to respond anymore, press forward every day against the doors of the relief agency clinics, desperate to get in. But there are not enough doctors or nurses or medicine or food for them all, so for every 500 who come, only 200 or so can be treated—only the most serious cases.

"How do you think I feel," said a Western doctor, "having to turn away 300 from our clinic every morning?"

Sometimes mothers burst into tears in the clinics simply out of relief that they have been allowed in with their children.

But even those who can get in must surmount more obstacles. Most of the children should be immediately hospitalized, but the hospitals here are full of war wounded and there is almost no room for malnourished children. The only beds are the ones that become available when other children die in the few special children's centers here.

Americans have stepped up an emergency airlift of supplies from Thailand because the insurgents have blockaded Cambodia's main supply line, the Mekong River, but until now the cargo these planes have brought is all military aid, mostly ammunition. There has been no food.

Yesterday the United States administration announced that beginning this week the airlift would begin bringing rice to Phnom Penh—but this is only to replenish stocks and maintain the status quo. The astronomical price of rice will not change, and the many Cambodians who are hungry now will continue to be hungry.

There are no accurate survey figures yet, but everyone involved in the Cambodian relief effort here believes that at minimum, from the firsthand evidence, tens of thousands of children are now dangerously malnourished and that at least dozens are dying daily—most of them in and around this capital city, bursting with refugees.

Yet it is not the official refugees—those living in camps or otherwise being fed by the relief agencies with U.S. food and funds—who are suffering most. It is instead the marginal people everywhere—those who are refugees but not registered as such, those who are trying to scrape by without a humiliating dole, underpaid civil servants, office workers, rickshaw peddlers and even soldiers.

In short, it is the general population that has been driven—over five years of having to eat less and less because they lack money—to a point of critical nutritional weakness.

"They're on the brink," says Dr. Penelope J. Key, World Vision's medical director. "A year ago we were seeing only a few malnourished children, and these were all under 3. The numbers are large, and some of the children are 10 and 11."

Agencies like World Vision, Care, Catholic Relief Services and the Red Cross are helping—mostly with American aid—feed and provide medical care and shelter for 400,000 people in Cambodia these days. But it is nowhere near enough: At least every other person in this country of seven million is a refugee from the war.

No sight is more common here than an oxcart caravan of villagers raising clouds of yellow dust as they flee the latest fighting. Many people have been uprooted three and four times. Even new refugee settlements erected by the relief agencies are sometimes burned down by the Communist-led insurgents, and the displaced must move on again.

Cambodia before the war was a country so rich in her food produce that even the very poor were never hungry. Everyone had a piece of land and there were always bananas and other fruit growing wild and a river or stream nearby where fish could be easily caught.

Now it is a country of landless nomads with empty stomachs—human flotsam living amid damp and filth in the flimsiest of shanties, thatch shacks and sidewalk lean-tos. The countryside is charred wasteland that either belongs to the Cambodian insurgents or is insecure, so the population huddles in the cities and towns, doing marginal work that never pays enough to feed a family adequately. Growing numbers of children and adults are taking to begging.

Under the Phnom Penh Government's distribution system each person is allowed 275 grams of rice at Government-controlled prices. The World Health Organization says a bare minimum daily diet is 450 grams. This means that those

Cambodians—maybe hundreds of thousands of them—who cannot afford to buy any more rice at the black market price are simply going hungry.

In early 1970, just before the war began, rice was 6 riels a kilogram on the open market. Now it is 350.

Even when people can put together enough to buy rice, they have no money left for the supplements to balance their diet—fish, beef, vegetables and fruit.

In such conditions adults usually become weak, but children begin to fail. The children have all the classic forms of malnutrition—kwashiorkor, marasmus, beri-beri and the vitamin deficiencies that lead to blindness—but they are succumbing also in their debilitated state to pneumonia, tuberculosis, dysentery and a host of other diseases. Virtually no child arrives at a clinic with only malnutrition.

"Kids are dying who shouldn't die," said Robert Beck, a World Vision doctor. "They die in our arms. It's hard to believe. There's no excuse for it."

Humanitarian relief for Cambodia has always been given a much lower priority by the White House than military aid. Ironically, the families of foot soldiers are among the worst sufferers here. They travel with their husbands and fathers and they are often shifted to a new battlefront suddenly without food. The pay is sometimes late. Many of the children showing up at malnutrition clinics in Phnom Penh are children of soldiers—a demoralizing truth for a government that is depending on its army for survival.

Although children are starving, the authorities here say that despite the latest insurgent offensive and the Mekong blockade, food supplies here right now are "adequate" for the next month or more.

"Up to now," said a Western diplomat, "the Cambodians have shown a tremendous ability to survive their physical hardship. But their strength has been sapped. And maybe now they've reached their limit and are beginning to topple."

KISSINGER, IN SECRET, BLOCKS PEACE TALKS
March 9, 1975

PHNOM PENH, Cambodia—Ambassador John Gunther Dean was rebuffed last year when he proposed to Secretary of State Kissinger that an attempt be made to establish contact with a key Cambodian insurgent leader to feel out the possibility of peace negotiations, according to sources in the United States Embassy here.

The sources said that Mr. Dean, who was new in Phnom Penh at the time but had already begun pushing for peace initiatives, recommended contact with Khieu Samphan, perhaps the leading figure in the insurgent movement. He is a

deputy premier and defense minister in the insurgents' Government and commander-in-chief of the rebel armed forces.

The United States Embassy would not comment on the matter. [In Egypt, Mr.
Kissinger's aides said he still felt it was hopeless to negotiate when the rebels had
the upper hand militarily.]

As the Dean move was disclosed, it was learned that the Cambodian command yesterday dismissed the commanding generals of two key units and
replaced them with younger men in a move apparently inspired by American officials to inject new life into the faltering defenses of Phnom Penh.

At the time of Mr. Dean's proposal last April, Mr. Samphan was touring Eastern Europe and Africa to rally support for his cause. Mr. Dean, according to the
embassy sources, felt this was a perfect opportunity for contact. The Ambassador
was quoted by those familiar with the episode as having said, "Every straw should
be grasped at."

Mr. Kissinger rejected the proposal, the sources said, on the ground that the
fighting was going poorly at the time and the United States would have been in a
position of negotiating from weakness. Longtime observers note, however, that
the situation has never been favorable for the Phnom Penh Government since the
war began in 1970.

The State Department did not mention the Dean proposal when it announced three days ago that Washington had made numerous attempts at negotiations with the insurgents but had been rebuffed.

The announcement was made at a news conference by Philip C. Habib, Assistant Secretary of State for East Asian and Pacific Affairs, who listed seven efforts
since 1973.

Mr. Habib was questioned by newsmen as to the seriousness of these efforts.
He insisted they had been sincere and he rejected suggestions, made in recent
news dispatches, that Mr. Kissinger was not enthusiastic about negotiations.

Mr. Kissinger's critics have said that he lacks interest in peace talks because
Cambodia is a small, inconsequential country, it is a losing situation for the United States and he does not want to be identified with defeats. It is also said that
he does not want to expend the limited leverage he has on Peking in obtaining
a Cambodian settlement that will be unsatisfactory for Washington in any case.

The Dean episode sheds light on the apparent gap between the embassy here
and public statements in Washington.

President Ford and Mr. Kissinger, in an effort to persuade Congress to grant
more military aid, have been saying that without the aid the Phnom Penh Gov-

ernment will fall within weeks but that with the aid there is a chance of convincing the insurgents of the wisdom of a compromise settlement.

The embassy, according to sources inside it, believes that there is no possibility of a compromise and that the best that can be hoped for is little more than a negotiated surrender.

This embassy assessment, based on conditions that have deteriorated since the insurgents began their offensive two months ago, is shared by virtually the entire diplomatic community.

At the moment, this city of two million people is being kept alive solely by an American airlift because other supply routes have been cut by the insurgents. Even the airlift has been disrupted by enemy shelling of the airport.

Ambassador Dean, who is 49 years old, played a large part in arranging the coalition peace settlement in Laos, and when he arrived here he made the same efforts to lay the groundwork for a possible compromise in Cambodia. But according to those familiar with his thinking, he has concluded that the same elements simply do not exist and the best that can be arranged is an orderly turnover of power to the Cambodian insurgents.

Author's Note: On the morning after "the Kissinger story" appeared on page 1 of The Times, *I got an unusual phone call from the American embassy. The ambassador, John Gunther Dean—author of the cables pressing Kissinger, in vain, to seek peace talks—wanted to see me right away. I guessed that Kissinger had been lashing Dean through the night with vitriolic cables, as was his practice when unpleasant truths were revealed about his doings (though Dean was not one of the sources for the story).*

I entered his office to find Dean lying prone on his sofa with a damp cloth on his forehead. "Look what you've done to me. I've been up all night, getting flogged from Washington," he blurted out, in pain. "I have no skin left. Do you realize what I've been through?"

"I can imagine," I said. "And I'm sorry they're beating you up." So it went for many awkward minutes. He was hurting. And I felt bad, but not about the story. It was true and it was important. I said all this in our meeting. He never questioned a word in the story.

As I left, I said to him, "This will sound odd to you today, but maybe someday you'll thank me for writing the story. Because you did the right thing."

Several years later, when Dean was working for UNICEF helping Cambodia recover, he phoned me out of the blue and invited me to lunch in New York. We no

sooner sat down at our table than he said, "Do you remember what you said to me
that morning in Phnom Penh?"

"Yes, I do," I said.

"Well," he said, "I want to thank you now for that story."

A reporter doesn't have that happen to him very often.

CORRUPTION OOZES FROM EVERY CORNER
March 16, 1975

PHNOM PENH—When the insurgent offensive broke out around Phnom Penh in the early hours of New Year's Day, the Cambodian President, Marshal Lon Nol, a superstitious mystic who has been partly crippled since a stroke four years ago, was taking a holiday at the beach resort of Kompong Som on the Gulf of Siam about 140 miles from the capital.

The Government Radio the following morning did not report that all hell had broken loose on fronts near the capital. It said only that the Marshal had been well enough to walk five yards in the surf at Kompong Som.

The Lon Nol regime, which came to power when the Marshal and some cohorts overthrew Prince Norodom Sihanouk five years ago, has been universally described as feckless, incompetent and deeply corrupt. There is no lack of evidence for these opinions.

As Ford Administration officials talk emotionally in Washington of the shame the United States will suffer if it abandons its besieged Cambodian allies, a Filipino band croons romantic ballads to satisfied well-dressed diners on the patio of one of Phnom Penh's expensive restaurants.

The band's electric guitars have full power and the colored lights that decorate the restaurant burn brightly. The reason the electricity is on—while much of the rest of Phnom Penh is thrown into darkness by the wartime fuel shortage—is that the restaurant has a generator chugging steadily in the street outside and there is plenty of fuel to run it. The generator is an Army Signals Corps machine installed in the back of an army jeep. The restaurant is owned by a Cambodian general.

To explain how a general who earns a base pay of about $20 a month can buy a posh restaurant is to explain where much of the hundreds of millions of dollars in American aid to Cambodia has gone.

Many Cambodians have grown enormously rich on this war—but it has not been the masses of refugees, villagers and urban workers, who have been reduced to such abject poverty by astronomical inflation and corrupt practices that their children, after five years of sliding downhill on thinner and thinner diets, are now dying of malnutrition.

A general who a few days ago was given a new and important command, in what was described as part of a reform shake-up to improve the army's fighting ability, used to demand and get big bribes from restaurant owners, in full view of the patrons, in return for letting the restaurant stay open past the evening curfew hour.

Indeed, corruption has become one of the hallmarks of this Government. You can buy almost anything here now: a draft exemption, a school graduation certificate, a visa to leave the country, or an automatic rifle that started out in Cambodia as American military aid.

Even the enemy, the Communist-led Cambodian insurgents, have taken advantage of this free market system. Some of the artillery shells now falling on Phnom Penh's airport have apparently been purchased from corrupt Cambodian commanders. Last year, for example, in the space of one month, five truckloads of 105-millimeter artillery rounds simply "vanished" on their way to a Government military base.

At one point about two years ago, American aid money was paying the salaries of as many as 100,000 nonexistent Cambodian soldiers, "phantoms" added to the payrolls by unscrupulous unit commanders who then pocketed the pay. This graft amounted to $2 million or more a month.

Austerity edicts have been announced periodically by the Lon Nol Government, under prodding by the Americans, only to be completely ignored. Imports of luxury goods were forbidden, but wines and cheeses and new Porsches kept coming in. The Exchange Support Fund, a $35-million-a-year fund consisting largely of American money that was meant to help the Cambodian Government pay for crucial foreign goods needed for the war effort, was used to buy such things as imported beer and cigarette lighters.

For a long time now, neither the Americans nor the Government have bothered to deny the corruption here. They simply say, weakly, that they are trying their best to combat it. In the meantime, Americans pay $500 a month in rent for villas that were built by generals and other high officials since the war began, presumably with corruption money generated by American aid.

The Sihanouk regime that preceded this one was also heavily laden with corruption, but diplomats with long service here point out that there is an enormous difference between the Prince's decadence in peacetime, when life was easy and languid in Cambodia, and the present corruption, when millions are suffering and some are being killed by arms sold to the enemy.

Contrasts between the elite and the poor are sharp in any country and have always been particularly vivid in Asia. But in Cambodia today, they are grotesque. While Cabinet ministers ride to and from their air-conditioned villas in chauffeured Mercedes, hungry begrimed refugees, crushed by food prices that have risen more than 1,000 percent since the war began, hunker beside their sidewalk lean-tos stirring the garbage in the gutter in search of a scrap of something salvageable.

The wounded fill the hospitals wall-to-wall. When soldier-amputees recover and emerge, they begin their new lives as beggars along with the thousands of other war cripples and malnourished children who now swarm along Phnom Penh's boulevards.

War widows stand weeping outside government offices because they cannot cut through the bureaucracy. That is, they don't have the bribe money necessary to get the pensions due them. At the same time, some army commanders personally collect and keep the death benefits of soldiers killed in their units. This money—one year's salary—is supposed to go to the family of the dead soldier.

But the commander produces fake relatives, paying them a small amount for the masquerade while keeping the bulk of the money for himself.

"They don't deserve to win this war," a Western diplomat here said the other day. "The Communists may be no better and I've no love for them, but this side has treated its people so badly and so corruptly that it has forfeited all right to govern them."

REPORTERS MAY BE WEARY BUT THE PEOPLE'S LOT IS DEADLY
March–April 1975, Times Talk

Author's Note: Times Talk *is an in-house newsletter published several times a year and distributed inside The New York Times Company.*

PHNOM PENH, March 21—There is usually a sense of excitement in covering a war—the excitement of any good story. But if there ever was any excitement covering the war in Cambodia, it's gone now.

Everyone is achingly weary here. The Cambodians. The foreign diplomats. Even us manic reporters, who are supposed to be able to turn on for any headline holocaust.

The reporters are weary because the electric power is off most of the time now, and without air-conditioning you have to work in your underwear or sarong or towel with sweat inching down your back, and at night you have to work by candlelight or by the light of a battery-powered lamp that runs out of juice every time on your third take, and you can't sleep much because you have to leave the windows open and burn anti-mosquito incense and be startled awake when rockets crash down nearby at 2:30 A.M. and again at 5:30, and then it's morning and the hotel's out of orange juice for breakfast and without electricity and there's no toast. And after that the dozen daily cables from the foreign desk arrive with new ideas. Joy.

But every time I start feeling sorry for myself I think of why the Cambodians are weary. It's because they're in a hospital having a mangled arm or leg amputated, and when they emerge they will join the army of maimed beggars here—on crutches, in wheelchairs and sometimes pulling themselves like insects across the sidewalks. It's because they are foot soldiers forced to fight without rest and without even boots to protect their feet in the jungles while their corrupt commanding generals return to Phnom Penh from the front every night to dine in fancy restaurants, sleep in their air-conditioned villas and partake of other sybaritic pleasures. And it's because they haven't had enough to eat for five years and now the adults are very weak and the children are slipping into starvation and dying by the dozens.

I go to the clinics when I'm up to it and I literally watch infants dying, and I have to go outside and turn my back because I don't want the Cambodians to see that I've lost control of my face. I think every time of my own two little girls and how well they are and how doomed these children are—and I don't have any control anymore.

Times Talk pieces are supposed to be about reporters' experiences and all the odd and amusing things that happen to them—but I'm going to tell you about Cambodian experiences instead. I know it's depressing but maybe I think everybody ought to be as depressed as I am.

In Neak Luong, a river town about 40 miles southeast of Phnom Penh that is encircled and being bombarded to death, the shells are falling so heavily that no one can come out of the bunkers to cremate the dead according to Buddhist tradition. The bodies just lie where they fall, or get stacked in piles, if someone's brave enough to slip out for a few minutes to gather and pile them.

I talked to a woman in the hospital yesterday with shrapnel in the back of her head, who came out of Neak Luong on a helicopter, and she said there were so many gravely wounded in the town for whom there was no room on the few available choppers that some were asking to be killed quickly rather than be allowed to lie there and die slowly in pain.

The other day, a few miles north of Phnom Penh a shelling attack killed several people in a marketplace. One was a four-year-old boy whose mother had gone to the next town and left him with his grandmother. The grandmother sat keening over the broken body. She was in hysterics. Her husband came along and, though shattered and weeping himself, tried to calm her. He asked where the mother, their daughter was. The grandmother said she was due back soon. The grandfather began to look for her and ask questions of people nearby. He grew worried. Finally, shaking, he slowly began to examine the bodies of the other shelling victims wrapped in straw mats in a row alongside his grandson. The third mat he turned back revealed his daughter.

Sometimes shells and rockets fall on the airport. A week ago, in one of these barrages, shrapnel sheared off the foot of a man sitting on the back of a truck on the tarmac. Another Cambodian jumped out of his car parked nearby and ran to help him. The chicken he had in his car for supper leapt out too and went skittering down the tarmac. Chickens are a prize here, for they are extremely costly, so an airport guard gave chase. He caught the chicken and his face lit up. Then a rocket fell at his feet and blew him and the chicken to nothingness.

This morning our stringer, Dith Pran, was just leaving his house for work when a rocket crashed into the house of a neighbor. A child, a little 6-year-old girl, was severely wounded. Her stomach was hanging out. Pran raced her to the hospital in his car, with her mother screaming and sobbing all the way. The child did not survive.

My mind keeps coming back to the children. They simply don't go to school anymore. At least only the children of the elite go to school. The rest—to survive—beg and steal and crouch alongside sidewalk restaurants, waiting for a tiny morsel to be left on someone's plate, whereupon they leap up and snatch it and push it in their mouths quickly before another child can snatch it away from them. They still smile sometimes, the famous Cambodian smile. All children smile. But then, while they are smiling, rockets fall on their shacks, and those who are not killed or maimed run shrieking in terror in all directions, and with some children it is days before the frightened look fades from their eyes and they stop whimpering and can talk normally again.

There are a million and a half people who have fled to Phnom Penh who just want to go back to their villages. But almost none of their villages exist anymore—

they were long ago reduced to rubble and ash in the fighting. But these refugees want to go back and rebuild and start planting their rice fields again. That's all they want. They don't talk politics and they don't think ideology. They have seen both sides—the Cambodian insurgents who sometimes burned their villages and the Phnom Penh Government whose corruption keeps rice from their tables and makes them sick with hunger—and they just want to go back to their villages.

One out of every seven Cambodians has been killed or wounded in the war—that would work out to 30 million Americans if this were happening in the United States. Half the population of seven million have been turned into refugees—that would be 100 million in America.

A few weeks ago I was driving on a dirt road and some refugees escaping from a battle up the road were coming toward me. They were carrying their wretched sacks of belongings on their heads, under their arms, over their bent shoulders. Dust swirled around them and the bright sun played tricks with it, flashing designs in the motes. Suddenly, for a few brief moments, the people looked to me as if they had holes in them, like Swiss cheese. People living and walking, but with holes in them. People who were not all there. People whom you could see through in places. Maybe the holes were in my mind or in my weariness or maybe I was being poetic or melodramatic, but to me they had holes in them. And then I shook my head to clear it, and there were no holes, and Dith Pran asked me what was the matter and I told him and he did not think it was peculiar.

Only the poor get drafted here. The rich buy their way out. You could look through Army ranks for days and not find a man from a well-to-do family. Sometimes when the Government is trying to round up more of the poor for cannon fodder, the rickshaw drivers and other abject souls like them take to hiding places all over town, staying out of sight and off the streets until the roundup is over.

But I always come back to the children. There are a lot of children in the Army—10, 11, 12 years old. Nearly all are volunteers, which seems curious. Sometimes they join to be with their fathers. But mostly they join because they can get paid and fed. It's better, these little boys feel, than begging in some foul gutter in Phnom Penh.

Of course, some of them end up begging anyway—after they get wounded and wind up on crutches or simply with stumps slithering along the sidewalks.

"Aut" is a Cambodian word that means "there is no" or "there are no." It is used with increasing frequency these days.

"Aut plung" means "there is not electric power." Sometimes in hospitals, it's "aut medicine." At the front, it's "aut boots." In the countryside, it's "aut houses." In some homes it's "aut food."

Out of this misery there has arisen in the press corps a gallows-humor line which says that if this war goes on much longer, it's going to be "aut Cambodia."

CAPITAL DEFENSES BEGIN TO CRUMBLE
April 11, 1975

PHNOM PENH, Cambodia—The wary and thinly stretched army defending this encircled city fell back at several points today, leaving large gaps in its defense.

Government commanders were making frantic but poorly coordinated efforts to plug the holes, which put the insurgents less than three miles from the airport, Phnom Penh's last link with the outside world.

The Communist-led Cambodian insurgents have been shelling the airport daily with artillery and rockets. But now they are close enough to fire their even more accurate mortars. This morning the American airlift that keeps this Government alive was interrupted briefly by a barrage that killed and wounded several Cambodian cargo handlers.

As yet, no large concentrations of insurgent troops have poured through the defense gaps directly north of the airport, but as one pessimistic military source put it tonight, "The stage is set."

Other developments added to the feeling that the process of deterioration may be accelerating:

Under increasing pressure, more Government units abandoned their positions on the banks of the Mekong River opposite the city, with many soldiers trying to swim to safety. Shells from those shores, less than two miles from Phnom Penh, began to fall on the capital.

Government casualties were running at least 50 percent higher than at any time in the last week. Nearly 300 wounded were brought to the main military hospital in a steady stream of ambulances. Many seemed exhausted, tattered and even malnourished.

The American Embassy, on instructions from Washington, strongly urged the press corps of about 45 foreign newsmen to thin its ranks immediately because the embassy "cannot guarantee their departure on U.S. Government–provided transportation, at the last moment if it should become necessary."

Ambassador John Gunther Dean made the appeal to the newsmen, sometimes emotionally, and some reporters, including the Voice of America man, who as a Government employee is the only one the embassy can order out, began leaving on embassy flights to Thailand.

One of the Cambodian Government's few official acts was to warn foreign newsmen that those who reported "tendentious news," such as that some Government officials support the idea of an orderly surrender, "will no longer be tolerated" and would be expelled from the country.

With United States military aid to Cambodia about to run out and with Congress expected to refuse any more, there were growing indications that the American Embassy, which has already evacuated most of its staff, including Cambodians, may be preparing to be able to pull out in a week or less. It is the only foreign mission left here.

In the last few days the embassy evacuated most of the American civilian pilots who have been working for private domestic airlines here, flying aging DC-3's between Phnom Penh and the isolated provincial towns. The departure of the pilots makes these enclaves even more isolated and vulnerable to enemy pressure.

Meanwhile, Government leaders continued private discussions on ways of meeting the crisis. Most informed observers here believe they have but one realistic option—to negotiate some kind of a surrender to the insurgents.

This morning, about 200 crippled soldiers massed at the Veterans Ministry to protest that their pensions had not been paid. Getting no satisfaction, they broke up some desks and grabbed two sacks of rice and spilled them in the street. Hungry refugees living in nearby shanties rushed forward to scoop up the rice and stuff it in their clothes and pockets.

But not all Cambodians were hungry or troubled or wounded. A lieutenant colonel whose troops are in disarray on a highway southwest of the city enjoyed a long and expensive lunch with his family near the pool of the Hotel Le Phnom. Asked about an episode in which Government artillery batteries mistakenly fired on their own troops in his area last night, the colonel called the mistake "regrettable." But he quickly added that such things happen all the time in war.

The mistaken firing killed at least 20 men and panicked Government troops into a sizable retreat along a substantial front. Reports from the field indicated that the Government had retaken all or most of the yielded ground today, but at heavy cost.

There were conflicting reports about the case of the mistaken shelling. One said that the insurgents, using field radios, had duped the Government artillery crews into firing on their own positions. But another said it was a case of Government confusion.

The biggest setback, however, was the gaping hole that the insurgents punched in the Government's thin defenses north of the airport, which sits five miles west of Phnom Penh. The insurgents first overran the village of Samrong Tiev, less than three miles from the airport, and later seized a village nearly a mile closer, Ang Ta Kov, where an unseasoned unit of military policemen was said to have broken and run.

At nightfall, despite hectic Government efforts to re-establish its defense line, gaping holes remained and the insurgents controlled Samrong Tiev. There were no late reports about who controlled the other village. If the insurgents continue to hold it, they will be able to fire virtually every heavy weapon they have against the airport with accuracy and in quantity.

If the break in the defense line, perhaps a mile wide, is not repaired quickly, not only could the airport be shut down, but the entire line could collapse, which would lead to the fall of the city.

There were few signs that the Cambodian command was marshaling its resources in a coordinated fashion. At several command posts, unit commanders seemed to be more occupied with recriminations over who was responsible for what failure than with pulling their troops together to hold the line.

"The situation is more and more critical," said one brigade commander. "The units on my flanks are getting worse every day. If they collapse, I will not be able to hold my position."

Villagers showed no confidence in the Government troops. A mile east of the breach, at one of the biggest refugee settlements in the Phnom Penh area, many of the 10,000 people there were hitching up their bullock carts and pulling out.

MARINE HELICOPTERS EVACUATE U.S. EMBASSY
April 13, 1975

PHNOM PENH, Cambodia—The American Embassy pulled out of Cambodia today in a sudden morning evacuation in which fully armed marines who flew in to provide security were shelled by the insurgents as they prepared to board the last helicopters.

None of the marines were hurt; they simply crouched and paid little attention to the four or five shells that landed behind them, two within 50 yards of their line.

But crowds of curious Cambodian children had gathered to watch the evacuation and one teenaged boy was killed by shrapnel and another wounded in the back. An American corpsman rushed over to bandage his wound before departing on a helicopter, and the boy was later removed to a local hospital.

The helicopter evacuation took place from a soccer field in the southeastern section of Phnom Penh, a few hundred yards from the embassy and even closer to the residence of Ambassador John Gunther Dean.

Mr. Dean, who remained calm throughout the operation unlike some embassy officials who at times lost their temper and their poise, boarded one of the green CH-53 marine helicopters at 10:15 A.M. Under his right arm he carried the furled American flag that had been lowered from the embassy flagpole minutes before, and in his left hand he carried a gray suitcase.

The armed helicopters that flew in the few hundred marines presumably came from the aircraft carrier Okinawa, which has been standing by in the Gulf of Siam since February. The marines wore full battle dress. Armed with everything from knives to machine guns to antitank weapons, they surrounded the embassy. One marine stood poised on the roof with his automatic rifle etched against the sky where helicopters were circling as was an American spotter plane.

The embassy's swinging gates were bolted shut. So was the door on the pedestrian entrance, behind which stood marine guards and embassy officials to answer knocks and allow authorized persons to pass through.

After spending the day denying rumors that evacuation was imminent, embassy officials—who apparently got the word from Washington—began sounding the alert shortly after dawn today. Newsmen and other Americans and foreigners for whom the embassy accepted responsibility were awakened at 7 A.M. or earlier by loud knocks on their hotel room doors and told to report immediately to the embassy for evacuation.

Confusion and loud arguments developed later over luggage, because the embassy ordered everyone for space reasons to leave everything behind except one small handbag that could be held on the lap. Tape recorders, suitcases full of clothing, radios and other personal belongings were left helter-skelter in embassy corridors. They were immediately looted by Cambodian employees.

Other looting also began immediately at some homes of embassy officials. They were entered and ransacked, particularly by military policemen assigned to guard them, as soon as the officials had left.

At the landing zone, just as the last helicopter took off at 11:30 A.M. a swarm of Cambodians rushed forward and emptied a nearby American pickup truck of knapsacks, shovels, smoke grenades and other equipment the marines had jettisoned.

Yet there was no discernible anger toward the Americans in the small crowds of Cambodians who gathered to watch their departure, or any expressions of betrayal or abandonment. However, some tearful Cambodian families who had heard of the evacuation did try unsuccessfully to press their way into the embassy compound to get on one of the helicopters.

At about 9:15 A.M., as Cambodian officials linked to the Americans were hurrying into the compound with their families, there was a knock on one embassy door. The marine guard opened it a crack. A note was passed in. It read, in English, "Will you please bring me and my family out of the country?" But the man was a stranger not connected to the embassy. "Give it back," said an American colonel, "give it back." The note was passed back through the crack in the door. No one inside ever saw the face of the man who made the appeal.

One of the assistant military attachés, learning that an American newsman had decided not to leave, asked him to reconsider. When the newsman said his decision was final, the major said, "Don't you want something for protection?" and offered the reporter his rifle. The reporter declined, but even as the truck carrying the major to the helicopters was going out the gate the major was still offering the rifle.

Nearly everyone in the embassy compound was armed today. Even a refugee official was carrying a pistol. As it turned out, there was nothing to fear from panicky or angry Cambodians and much of the heavy security seemed overdone—until the shells began to fall around the landing zone.

It happened toward 11 o'clock, after the civilians had been evacuated and only the marines who had surrounded and guarded the soccer field remained to be flown out. The first shell exploded as the marines were boarding the two helicopters.

The Cambodians scattered, but the marines remained cool. "Man," said one marine, smiling, "What have they got me here for? Are they trying to get me killed?"

He wasn't even looking in the direction of the blast.

The second shell landed a few minutes later, hitting several Cambodians.

The insurgents, who were firing from positions only a couple of miles away, on the eastern banks of the Mekong River opposite the city, were clearly shooting at the marines and clearly had the range.

The shells seemed to be either mortar or rounds from 75-mm. cannon. A few fell around the landing zone before the last helicopter took off with the last marines less than three and a half hours after they had arrived. In all, about 300 people were evacuated. They were flown to the carrier Okinawa in the Gulf of Siam.

A handful of Americans, opting against evacuation, stayed behind. They included a few journalists and photographers and at least one United Nations official. A few European journalists also stayed, as did some officials, doctors and nurses of the International Committee of the Red Cross.

FEAR FOR SCHANBERG AND DITH PRAN, WHO STAYED BEHIND
April–May 1975, Times Talk

Author's Note: Times Talk *is an in-house newsletter published several times a year and distributed inside The New York Times Company.*

At 7:44 A.M. on Saturday, April 12, the teletype that links Phnom Penh, Cambodia, with the 43rd Street communications center broke into chattering speech. It tapped out a message from Sydney Schanberg to Foreign Editor James Greenfield:

> I HAVE MADE JUDGEMENT TO STAY. I WOULD APPRECIATE YOUR SUPPORTING THAT JUDGEMENT RATHER THAN SENDING ME ALARMIST CABLES WHICH WILL ONLY MAKE A DIFFICULT SITUA-TION MORE DIFFICULT. DITH PRAN [*The Times* Cambodian correspondent] IS WITH ME. HE HAS ALSO DECIDED TO STAY ON HIS OWN JUDGEMENT. WE EVACUATED HIS WIFE AND FOUR CHILDREN . . . I NEED YOUR SUPPORT NOT A CONFRONTATION. I MADE MY JUDGEMENT SANELY AND I WILL DO MY BEST FOR THE PAPER. I WILL FILE WHATEVER AND WHENEVER I CAN . . . PLEASE GIVE ME YOUR SUPPORT AND PLEASE CALL JANICE [his wife in Singapore] AND TELL HER I AM WELL AND WILL PROBABLY SEE HER SOON AND WOULD BRING HER HERE EXCEPT IT'S UNCOMFORTABLE WITHOUT AIR-CONDITIONING.

So began an episode that was to bring *The Times* one of its most important stories in years. Schanberg's risky decision paid off with what *Time Magazine* called "a remarkable retrospective on the Communist takeover that filled more than two pages in *The Times* and supplied the first really close look at Cambodia's extraordinary peasant revolution."

KHMER ROUGE CLOSE IN
April 15, 1975

PHNOM PENH, Cambodia—The Communist insurgents drove to within three miles of the western edge of the city yesterday. To the north, one report said, the insurgents raised their flags over factories less than five miles from the edge of the city, along Route 5.

Despite heavy bombing by the Government air force, the Communists pushed to less than a mile from the airport, which was closed to civilian traffic.

This correspondent, driving through the market of Pochentong town, two miles from the western edge of Phnom Penh, saw three soldiers in insurgent dress—black cotton shirt and trousers, a red-checked neck scarf, with ammunition bandoliers across their chests. They carried Chinese AK-47 rifles. They were just looking around and the few civilians in the vicinity did not appear frightened.

At 4 P.M. a battle was reported to be going on 500 yards from the Pochentong market. Cambodian reporters returning from the scene said the fighting was heavy.

This correspondent and others driving along the road to the airport watched as single-engine bombers tried to stop the insurgent advance only a half mile or so north of the road.

The planes dived low, trying to drop their bombs exactly on target. The explosion and black clouds of smoke were a backdrop for a steady stream of refugees flowing out of side roads and jamming the main road into the city.

While the battle was raging, one pilot turned against the Government, veering his fighter-bomber toward the city and dropping two 250-pound bombs on command headquarters in the city center before flying off, presumably to land in insurgent territory.

The bombs fell on a military transport office inside the compound, killing at least seven persons and wounding many. Six ambulances were seen driving to and from the scene. No high-ranking commanders were reported hurt. The pilot was later identified as Lieut. Khiev Yos Savath.

It was difficult to get a coherent picture of the overall situation. About the only thing that could be said definitely by late afternoon yesterday was that the insurgents had not entered the city in force.

The seriousness of the situation was suggested by jeeps carrying officers into and out of command headquarters, the radio antenna that the International Red Cross hurriedly set up on the roof of the Hotel Le Phnom to communicate with Geneva, and the crowd of Frenchmen and Cambodians who gathered at the French Embassy for sanctuary.

The insurgents' objective seemed to be to cut off the city from the airport, which is the last supply link with the outside world, and then to move on the city proper.

As darkness descended, the battlefields fell surprisingly quiet. The insurgents were still close to the city's edges but the noises of fighting, as heard from the center of the capital, subsided. It was as if both sides were resting for the next round.

The Government imposed a 24-hour curfew starting at noon, and, in radio broadcasts, appealed to the city's two million people to remain calm.

Telegraph and telephone communications to the outside world were still open, but one of the transmission stations at Kambol, west of the city, went dead, after it had come under attack and its staff had fled. When the curfew began, people were still walking and riding in apparent calm along the boulevards in contrast to the scenes of flight on the airport roadways a few miles west of the city.

Not only were villagers and refugees marching on the city in a caravan of fear, but a number of soldiers were also leaving their posts and fleeing with them, fully armed, carrying everything from their rifles to radios.

Most refugees said they had not seen the insurgents and had fled as the shelling and bombing came closer. There were unconfirmed reports that insurgent infiltrators, some in uniform, had actually entered the city.

The Minister of Information, Thong Lim Huong, called a French newsman to his office to tell him that the military situation had improved. The Minister said there was more harassment than in preceding days. Mr. Huong, who is sleeping in his office these days, also said there had been no insurgent infiltration into the city.

The attack seemed to be coming mainly from the west and northwest. Military planes were still flying, and two internal domestic planes coming from some province capitals were seen landing in the midst of the battle. But the gates of the airport were locked and barricaded with barbed wire.

Only a few soldiers could be seen inside, and the immediate perimeter of the airport seemed poorly defended. Apparently, all available troops had been rushed to the front lines to the north.

The armed forces commander, Lieut. Gen. Saksut Sakhan, was in the headquarters at the time of the bombing.

He came on the radio two hours later to report the bombing and identify the perpetrators. Until then the radio had been broadcasting patriotic music and messages as well as programs in honor of the three-day Cambodian New Year, which began today.

The broadcast was the first acknowledgment of anything unusual. General Saksut Sakhan, who heads the military junta formed three days ago when the

Americans withdrew, mentioned only the headquarters bombing and said nothing about how close the insurgents were to the city.

He said that he and the other leaders of the country were "continuing to direct the Government until there is peace." General Saksut Sakhan said the Americans "are continuing to aid us even though they have temporarily withdrawn their embassy."

He said the Americans could not land supplies because the airport was being shelled, but said United States planes would drop ammunition, fuel and food by parachute on Phnom Penh and isolated province capitals such as Prey Veng, Takeo and Kampot. No airdrops have been observed over Phnom Penh.

General Saksut Sakhan said, "We are also asking other countries and humanitarian organizations to help us with food supplies."

He concluded his brief speech by saying the 24-hour curfew was being imposed at noon, which was five minutes after he finished speaking.

The normal curfew was from 9 P.M. to 5 A.M., but three days ago it was moved back to 7 P.M.

There was no panic as the curfew began but the number of worried faces increased as the news of the close fighting on the western outskirts began to filter into town.

When communications lines went down because of the attack on the Kambol transmission station, the four telephone operators handling international calls at the Post Office sat knitting peacefully before their silent switchboard. When an American came in to try to make a call, one of the operators looked up from her needles and said, "If you are leaving the country and you ask me to come with you, I will come right now with all my family."

Government clerks with strained looks huddled in corridors nervously discussing the news. Efforts by foreigners to cheer them up were useless. The Cambodians are known for their charming smiles, but there were no such faces here today.

Yet it was the refugees streaming down the road from the airport who were really in distress. Some came from new refugee settlements and have spent the entire war fleeing from one battle or another.

"Some of my children are lost," Men Seung told newsmen who had stopped to talk with him. "I lost them as we ran. We got separated."

His wife and six of their children were gathered around the 44-year-old peasant. Four children were missing.

"I have nowhere to go," he said. "I have fled so many times."

The refugees came down the road in a hurry but not in a stampede. It was a crowd scene, but not a mob scene. Cambodians have grown accustomed to such hardships.

They came on bullock carts and bicycles with pigs, chickens, mattresses, pots and pans and bundles of firewood. There were monks and children and soldiers. One soldier was pushing his family along in a two-wheeled handcart.

One girl, riding on top of her family's belongings on a bullock cart, put her fingers in her ears to keep out the thunder of the nearby bombing.

It is difficult to tell whether the Government has a chance of holding the city. If the insurgents cut the roads between the city and the airport, they would cut off the Government from its main ammunition supplies, which are stored beyond the airport.

One unconfirmed report, passed on by a Cambodian journalist who said he got it from Government soldiers, said the insurgents at the Pochentong market had told soldiers they found there, "Don't worry. We will not harm Cambodians. We have come to kill all the Americans."

It is unknown exactly how many Americans are left in the city, but only six are known to this correspondent, almost all of them newsmen or freelance photographers.

Other foreigners include 15 officials of the International Red Cross, six United Nations officials, about a dozen Western European journalists and about 150 French citizens.

Except for the French, nearly all the foreigners are staying at the Hotel Le Phnom. The Red Cross representatives are asking their Geneva headquarters to try to get approval from Prince Norodom Sihanouk in Peking to declare the hotel a protected neutral zone. Prince Sihanouk is the nominal leader of the insurgents.

The Red Cross contingent includes a Scottish medical team that was still performing surgery as the insurgents approached. The surgeon, Dr. Michael Daley, and the anesthetist, Dr. Murray Carmichael, at Preah Keth Mealea Hospital treated some of the wounded from the bombing of the military headquarters.

"I will keep on operating to the end," the bearded Dr. Daley said, as he scrubbed his hands for his next case, a soldier lying on a blood-soaked stretcher on the tiled floor of the operating room.

It is uncertain how long communications to the outside world will last. With the transmission station at Kambol abandoned, this dispatch is being written inside the Post Office in downtown Phnom Penh and is being sent out on an emergency transmitter that telegraph employees said had never been used before.

The new military Government, in the midst of all its troubles, was sending out cablegrams to its embassies, informing them of the formation of the junta and telling them of the steps it had taken "to mobilize all the energies of the nation and to adopt draconian martial law measures to assure order and security."

The cablegrams ended by saying:

"We are counting on all of you to convince the country to which you are accredited of the justness of our struggle and our cause, which seeks only to achieve peace through negotiations and reconciliation between Khmers."

Author's Note: Following this dispatch, the desk in New York added a brief news story: The Defense Department said today that 17 airdrops of supplies had been made over Cambodia since Saturday, but none of them in the Phnom Penh area.

A spokesman added that the airdrops were carried out by C-130 transports based in Thailand and belonging to the Bird Air Company, a private concern. The spokesman declined to give the location of the airdrops.

CITY SCENES TURN SURREAL
April 15, 1975

PHNOM PENH, Cambodia—This capital was full of strange scenes today—the inevitable contrasts between the confusion and fear at the front and the blissful oblivion of those a few miles away.

With insurgents only three miles down the road, a driver leaned on the fender of his Land Rover, a mirror in one hand and tweezers in the other, pulling stray hairs from his chin.

Government employees laughed and joked as they went through their regular morning marching exercises on the grassy mall outside their building—part of a national preparedness program.

An elderly French woman, a teacher who is a legendary figure at the Hotel Le Phnom, sat in her regular chair at poolside this morning, wearing a white dress as always, with a white shawl over her shoulders.

She was waiting for the Cambodian children for whom she is now the governess and tutor. The only difference was that she was the only person at the pool, the other foreign and Cambodian habitués having been distracted by events. The children also did not come, but the teacher sat there unperturbed, her face a mask of calm.

Later a grimacing beggar entered the hotel lobby and began to assail all the foreigners in sight in a loud, whining voice. He rattled everyone's already frayed nerves so badly that they paid him handsomely just to go away. He probably got more in that five minutes than he normally does in a month.

At the front desk, the receptionists were listening to the radio spew forth patriotic speeches and assurances that the armed forces would defend the capital against all assaults. As they listened they were making out bills for guests who wanted to be ready to depart at a moment's notice—if departure was possible.

The Government radio station was a source of odd and incongruous programs. Occasionally the New Year's music and folk theater would be interrupted by a reminder of the need to obey the law in these difficult times.

At one point an announcer reported that the Government had denied all the rumors about Battambang, a province capital under attack about 180 miles northwest of Phnom Penh. The announcer did not say what the rumors were; he simply said that they were untrue and that all the people in Battambang, Cambodia's second largest city, "are unified in their determination to continue the struggle."

The rumors, which have been making the rounds for a couple of days, were that Battambang had surrendered to the Communist-led insurgents. The Battambang story was only one of many rumors that coursed through the capital today. One said that a squad of workers was cleaning up the former royal palace in preparation for the return of Prince Norodom Sihanouk. Another said that officers at the high command's headquarters who were ordered to the front had refused to go. Still another said that some Government units had stopped fighting and were making their own accommodations with the advancing insurgents.

The insurgents' successes and the absence of American support elicited a message from an American to the Cambodian military leaders. It read, "I apologize for my country's total lack of consideration for the Khmer people who fight so courageously for their freedom. My shame is deep." It was from Lieut. Col. Mark Berent, a former assistant air attaché at the embassy here, who is retired and living in Metairie, La.

REPORTER'S NOTEBOOK: THE DAY BEFORE THE CITY FALLS
April 17, 1975

PHNOM PENH, Cambodia—Last night, with this city facing imminent capture by the insurgents who surround it, the National Bank of Cambodia sent a cablegram to the Irving Trust Company in New York, asking the American bank, where it presumably has dollar credits, to confirm that it was carrying out an earlier order to pay $1 million to Marshal Lon Nol. The earlier order was sent by letter on April

1, the day that the marshal, Cambodia's former President, went into exile under American prodding.

Perhaps the marshal was worried that if Phnom Penh fell to the insurgents before the transaction was confirmed, he would never get the money.

How did the marshal come by the money? It was always rumored here that he was deeply corrupt and had used American aid to build large bank accounts abroad. But no one could ever pin it down. Maybe Irving Trust can shed some light now.

In any case, it was only one of the many peculiar things that have happened here in the last few days as the insurgents closed in. Here are a few of them.

✦

It is possible that people in the outside world imagine us hunkered down in bunkers, praying as shells fall all around us. Sometimes, near a front line, things do get hairy, and even in Phnom Penh, as this is being written, the sounds of shelling are fierce just outside the southern gates of the city. But there have always been oases. Two nights ago, near the hotel's pool, I dined on a lovely vegetable soup and *petit poussin*, accompanied by a jigger of a friend's specially saved 21-year-old Chivas Regal. And after that some brandy.

✦

I started this piece at 1:30 A.M. on April 16. I had to stop working in order to go to the transmission center where I tried to get things revived. Our line had been down since late yesterday afternoon and I was getting desperate, knowing I would soon miss the first edition with my story. I spent all night watching bewildered mechanics turn dials on an ancient Chinese transmitter they could not fathom. It had been pressed into service because the insurgents had overrun the main transmission center at Kambol. Anyway it is 7 A.M. now.

✦

As the capital's defense perimeter shrinks, so do the Government's daily military briefings. The briefing notice on Tuesday morning said nothing about the insurgents driving to the city's edge. It said only, "Our troops have counterattacked against the Khmer Rouge north of Pochentong [airport] and Boeong Prayap. The Khmer Rouge have set fire to houses at Tuol Sampou west of Prek Phnou."

✦

A cable arrived this morning at the Ministry of Agriculture, apparently from a Cambodian on a trip to the United States sponsored by the American Government. The cable read, "I go back May 9 but if Cambodia becomes Communist would you want me to go back or not? U.S. Government feed me if stay. Reply back telegram if possible."

✦

On Monday evening, at La Taverne restaurant across from the cable office, the barman was in an ebullient mood even though the place was empty because of the curfew—except for two newsmen who had come across for a drink. It was a few hours after a defecting Government pilot had bombed the headquarters of the high command in the center of the city, killing and wounding many people, but missing all the top brass.

"They bombed the military headquarters," the barman said, laughing giddily. "You find that amusing?" one of the newsmen asked, drawing him out. "Yes," he replied, chortling again, "It's very amusing indeed."

✦

Along the road leading to the airport yesterday, less than a mile from the fighting, several soldiers were collapsed on the grass. "We fought all night," one of them said. "We are tired now." They were taking slugs of palm toddy from a bottle and several were already drunk. "We must rest," said one holding up the bottle and taking another swig.

✦

A bit down the road stood a woman with a foot-treadle sewing machine, apparently her most prized possession. Though the road beyond her was absolutely deserted and eerie, and the sky was filled with helicopter gunships strafing insurgent positions, she seemed unworried. "Where are you going?" she was asked. "I'm moving to a relative's house a mile closer to the capital," she said. Five minutes later, her husband arrived calmly with a handcart, they loaded the sewing machine aboard, and they strolled leisurely down the highway toward the city.

✦

Ever since the American Embassy was evacuated by helicopter Saturday, taking out most Americans and a number of foreigners and Cambodians who wanted to go, the American television networks and news agencies have been trying to land a plane in Phnom Penh to pick up their Cambodian employees who were left behind. So nearly every day they have circled over the center of the city for an hour or so in a C-46, talking to a journalist with a field radio at the Hotel Le Phnom, trying to find out if it is safe to land at the airport. So far it has not been. In fact it is now impossible. So they are talking about taking a helicopter instead.

The Cambodian hotel employees are fascinated as a Westerner crouches by the pool shouting into the radio's hand microphone at a shiny silver bird wheeling above. The bird answers and the voice comes out of the radio. "It's just like the movies," a Cambodian says. "They all use that funny language."

"Sunday calling charter, over. Sunday calling charter," says the man on the ground.

"That's a Roger," says the bird. "Can you read me?" says the ground man. "Affirmative," replies the bird. A German television man films it all for posterity.

✦

The insurgent radio today was saying that its troops were "penetrating deep" into the city. At the moment this was still an exaggeration. The capital remained strangely calm. The Government is broadcasting its usual zestful marching songs and other patriotic music. In the parks, teenagers play Cambodian New Year's games that resemble tag and beanbag. The three-day Cambodian New Year ended today. Because of the crisis, it was not an official holiday this year and Government officials had to report to work.

The curfew was also tightened and violators were arrested by the military police. But things are always flexible in Cambodia, even in the middle of a siege, so the people arrested did not seem too upset as they milled on the sidewalk, waiting for a truck to come and take them to central police headquarters. They knew that a little bribe would have them out in no time.

✦

The curfew keeps changing, almost by the hour. This morning, in the space of three hours, Phnom Penh radio announced two changes. As this was being written, which is ten minutes past noon, the curfew is noon. "Until further notice."

✦

The curfew has fouled up lots of things. People never know when they can come out and shop for food. The Hotel Le Phnom's shopping activities have also been curtailed. Yesterday morning at breakfast, the hotel had no eggs or bread. Sometimes it runs out of ice. It has not had orange juice for nearly two months. Langoustine stopped appearing with the fall of the Mekong River town of Neak Luong about two weeks ago, because that is where the large river shrimp came from.

✦

Food has become a preoccupation among the denizens of the hotel, perhaps to distract themselves from the lethal events going on around the city. The other night, a Belgian United Nations official came to the hotel restaurant with a can of mussels, savoring the idea of having them with French-fried potatoes. When the waiter told him there were no potatoes, he was crestfallen and left without eating.

✦

More on food. One night a guest was complaining about how many things were no longer available at the hotel restaurant—especially ice for his Pepsi-Cola. A Frenchwoman sitting at a table behind him listened to his hour and a half of protest with sympathy. Finally, she said with a heartfelt sigh, "C'est la guerre."

THE FINAL HOURS
April 17, 1975

Author's Note: This story, and the "Reporter's Notebook" that accompanied it on April 17, 1975, describe the chaos just before the surrender. They were the last dispatches I would be able to file for three weeks. The Khmer Rouge immediately blacked out communications and quarantined all foreigners under guard for that period.

PHNOM PENH, Cambodia—The Cambodian military Government asked yesterday for an immediate cease-fire from the Cambodian insurgents, who were attacking Phnom Penh from all sides. The Government said it would turn over power to them.

Several hours later, reports from Peking said that Prince Norodom Sihanouk, the nominal leader of the insurgents who is in exile there, had rejected the cease-fire proposal as unacceptable.

The Phnom Penh Government's proposal, which might be described as conditional surrender, had called for a complete transfer of power to the insurgent side under the supervision of the United Nations and representatives of the International Committee of the Red Cross who are now in Phnom Penh.

A second major point among the five in the proposal was a demand for assurances that there would be no reprisals against persons or organizations for their activities during the five-year war.

The cease-fire proposal, which was transmitted through the Red Cross delegation here, came as this suffering city of more than two million, relatively calm until now, began to show signs of collapse.

Throughout the day, the Communist-led insurgents had pressed closer and closer on all sides, inflicting enormous casualties and sending scores of thousands of refugees pouring frightened into the city from the near outskirts. Exhausted soldiers who had had enough joined the refugees. Many of the refugees came into the very center of this cosmopolitan city with bullock carts and squealing pigs looking for a place to rest and a bit to eat.

In the hospitals there were wounded two and three to a bed, floors slippery with blood and children's shrieks of pain that tore any visitor's heart out.

Insurgent shells began landing last night at regular intervals in the northern part of the city. The airport, west of the city, was said to be falling.

Fear was spreading. French residents of Phnom Penh started putting up French flags on their gates and walls to identify their nationality, since France has recognized the insurgent government.

Premier Long Boret, speaking in a telephone interview before the Sihanouk rejection had been reported, cited the United States decision to evacuate its embassy last Saturday and end its material support as the key factor in his Government's decision to ask for a cease-fire.

"We feel completely abandoned," he said in a voice whose weariness was discernible even over the telephone.

The 42-year-old Premier said the decision was made at about 11 A.M. yesterday at a meeting of the seven-member military-dominated Supreme Committee, which has been running the country since the Americans left last Saturday.

He said the decision was unanimous. Asked if there were any dissenting voices anywhere in the Government, such as some of the generals, he said, "No, we are realistic."

Mr. Long Boret, who with other Cambodian leaders has been marked for execution by the insurgents, said the military situation had become impossible, and added, "We have no more material means." As he spoke, rockets were exploding only about 200 yards from the telegraph office from which this correspondent was telephoning.

The Premier said that after the morning meeting, held at the headquarters of the military high command, the proposal was taken to the head of the Red Cross delegation here, André Pasquier, who was asked as a neutral intermediary to pass it to Prince Sihanouk. The Prince, the former Cambodian chief of state, was ousted by the Phnom Penh Government in 1970.

Mr. Long Boret, who declared "our first objective is to end the suffering of the people," said Mr. Pasquier informed him later that he had transmitted the message to Red Cross headquarters in Geneva at 3 P.M. Cambodian time (4 A.M. New York time) and that Geneva had quickly passed it to Prince Sihanouk in Peking.

Mr. Pasquier sent the message over his shortwave radio from the Hotel Le Phnom, which was today turned into a Red Cross–protected neutral zone for the treatment of the sick and the wounded. Huge Red Cross flags were hung around the building and atop it.

As dusk came, refugees and soldiers who had fled the fighting fronts wandered forlornly through the darkening streets looking for shelter and food. The setting sun was clouded by billows of black smoke from fires all around the city.

Last night, reports from refugees indicated that the airport, five miles to the west, was falling and might have already gone. It had been the government's last supply link with the outside world.

Insurgents were said to be inside the airfield. Government T-28 fighter-bombers were reported dropping napalm on them to try to halt their advance, apparently to little effect. The control tower was said to be in insurgent hands. Retreating Government troops were reported trying to pull together a defense line south of the airport.

Beyond the airport, the Government ammunition dumps, where everything including bombs is stored, are now cut off from the city. One of them may have fallen to the insurgents yesterday.

On the south, northwest and west, the insurgents were at the capital's edges. In the north, refugees who reached Phnom Penh said the rebels were only a little more than a mile from the city limits and advancing steadily down Route 5.

It was on this front that perhaps the greatest Government casualties were suffered today. Many were civilians caught in crossfire or hit by blindly fired insurgent rockets as they ran from the fighting.

Another battle raged along the city's southern border, centering on the United Nations Bridge, which spans the Bassac River. Though newsmen could not get very close, the fighting seemed to be intense only a few hundred yards to the east of the bridge in a neighborhood called Chbar Ampou.

On Tuesday night, much of that neighborhood burned down as fierce fighting swirled in and around it. Hundreds of houses were reported destroyed in the blaze, which lit the sky.

Government reinforcements were being rushed to the bridge area yesterday. These soldiers looked somber as their trucks raced through the streets of the capital in the morning.

Insurgent shells, some of them deadly accurate 105-mm. rounds, were exploding sporadically in the southern districts of Phnom Penh.

A curfew was in effect from noon yesterday "until further notice."

Nowhere was there the slightest sign of hope for the Phnom Penh Government. The main military hospital, which normally gets an average of about 200 wounded a day, had received more than 500 by 6 P.M. yesterday and the ambulances were still coming in every five minutes.

Inside the emergency reception center, a converted basketball court, people were bleeding, moaning, whimpering and dying.

A 12-year-old boy died of head wounds on a bed. Someone covered most of his body with a blue scarf. Then a soldier came in carrying his wife, bleeding from the head. There were no empty beds, so he pushed the dead boy to one side and placed his wife there as well.

Rivulets of blood flowed across the floor. A 13-year-old girl named Chan Ny, whose body was torn by shrapnel, lay on the floor yelling, "Help me! Help me! The pain is awful."

Many in this hospital were wounded children whose parents had been killed alongside them. The chief doctor tried, by questioning the children, to find out where the bodies had fallen so he could have the parents cremated.

Behind the receiving center are the operating rooms, where surgery must be quick. An 80-year-old woman whose right leg had just been amputated lay groaning on a wheeled bed outside the operating room. Her leg lay in a cardboard box a few feet away with a lot of other amputated limbs.

Author's Note: After leaving the hospital, we went to the public cable office, where I typed and filed through the night—until the line to the outside world went dead around 5:00 a.m. As the sun came up, we drove cautiously around the city. The Khmer Rouge, in their black-pajama garb, were pouring in from all sides. We were taken prisoner and put before a firing squad. But Pran—with great bravery and cunning and nonstop pleading—saved us.

CAMBODIAN REDS HERD MILLIONS INTO THE COUNTRYSIDE

Author's Note: This and the following three stories were published as a package, starting on page 1 of The New York Times, *on May 9, 1975—after the Khmer Rouge victors released into Thailand the hundreds of foreigners they had interned for three weeks inside the French Embassy compound following the fall of Phnom Penh.*

May 9, 1975

BANGKOK, Thailand—The victorious Cambodian Communists, who marched into Phnom Penh on April 17 and ended five years of war in Cambodia, are carrying out a peasant revolution that has thrown the entire country into upheaval.

Perhaps as many as three or four million people, most of them on foot, have been forced out of the cities and sent on a mammoth and grueling exodus into areas deep in the countryside where, the Communists say, they will have to become peasants and till the soil.

No one has been excluded—even the very old, the very young, the sick and the wounded have been forced out onto the roads—and some will clearly not be strong enough to survive.

The old economy of the cities has been abandoned, and for the moment money means nothing and cannot be spent. Barter has replaced it.

All shops have either been looted by Communist soldiers for such things as watches and transistor radios, or their goods have been taken away in an organized manner to be stored as communal property.

Even the roads that radiate out of the capital and that carried the nation's commerce have been virtually abandoned, and the population living along the roads, as well as that in all cities and towns that remained under the control of the American-backed Government, has been pushed into the interior. Apparently the areas into which the evacuees are being herded are at least 65 miles from Phnom Penh.

In sum, the new rulers—before their overwhelming victory they were known as the Khmer Rouge—appear to be remaking Cambodian society in the peasant image, casting aside everything that belonged to the old system, which was generally dominated by the cities and towns and by the elite and merchants who lived there.

Foreigners and foreign aid are not wanted—at least not for now. It is even unclear how much influence the Chinese and North Vietnamese will have despite their considerable aid to the Cambodian insurgents against the Government of Marshal Lon Nol. The new authorities seem determined to do things themselves in their own way. Despite the propaganda terminology and other trappings, such as Mao caps and Ho Chi Minh rubber-tire sandals, which remind one of Peking and Hanoi, the Communists seem fiercely independent and very Cambodian.

Judging from their present actions, it seems possible that they may largely isolate their country of perhaps seven million people from the rest of the world for a considerable time—at least until the period of upheaval is over, the agrarian revolution takes concrete shape and they are ready to show their accomplishments to foreigners.

Some of the party officials in Phnom Penh also talked about changing the capital to a more traditional and rural town like Siem Reap in the northwest.

For those foreigners, including this correspondent, who stayed behind to observe the takeover, the events were an astonishing spectacle.

In Phnom Penh two million people suddenly moved out of the city en masse in stunned silence—walking, bicycling, pushing cars that had run out of fuel, covering the roads like a human carpet, bent under sacks of belongings hastily thrown together when the heavily armed peasant soldiers came and told them to leave immediately, everyone dispirited and frightened by the unknown that awaited them and many plainly terrified because they were soft city people and were sure the trip would kill them.

Hospitals jammed with wounded were emptied, right down to the last patient. They went—limping, crawling, on crutches, carried on relatives' backs, wheeled on their hospital beds.

The Communists have few doctors and meager medical supplies, so many of these patients had little chance of surviving. On April 17, the day this happened, Phnom Penh's biggest hospital had over 2,000 patients and there were several thousand more in other hospitals; many of the wounded were dying for lack of care.

A once-throbbing city became an echo chamber of silent streets lined with abandoned cars and gaping, empty shops. Streetlights burned eerily for a population that was no longer there.

The end of the old and the start of the new began early in the morning of the 17th. At the cable office the line went dead for mechanical reasons at 6 A.M. On the previous day, amid heavy fighting, the Communist-led forces had taken the airport a few miles west of the city, and during the night they had pressed to the capital's edges, throwing in rockets and shells at will.

Thousands of new refugees and fleeing soldiers were filling the heart of the capital, wandering aimlessly, looking for shelter, as they awaited the city's imminent collapse.

Everyone—Cambodians and foreigners alike—thought this had to be Phnom Penh's most miserable hour after long days of fear and privation as the Communist forces drew closer. They looked ahead with hopeful relief to the collapse of the city, for they felt that when the Communists came and the war finally ended, at least the suffering would largely be over. All of us were wrong.

That view of the future of Cambodia—as a possibly flexible place even under Communism, where changes would not be extreme and ordinary folk would be left alone—turned out to be a myth.

American officials had described the Communists as indecisive and often ill-coordinated, but they turned out to be firm, determined, well-trained, tough and disciplined.

The Americans had also said that the rebel army was badly riddled by casualties, forced to fill its ranks by hastily impressing young recruits from the countryside and throwing them into the front lines with only a few days' training. The thousands of troops we saw both in the countryside and in Phnom Penh, while they included women soldiers and boy militia, some of whom seemed no more than 10 years old, looked healthy, well organized, heavily armed and well trained.

Another prediction made by the Americans was that the Communists would carry out a bloodbath once they took over—massacring as many as 20,000 high officials and intellectuals. There have been unconfirmed reports of executions of senior military and civilian officials, and no one who witnessed the takeover doubts that top people of the old regime will be or have been punished and perhaps killed or that a large number of people will die of the hardships on the march into the countryside. But none of this will apparently bear any resemblance to the mass executions that had been predicted by Westerners.

[In a news conference Tuesday President Ford reiterated reports—he termed them "hard intelligence"—that 80 to 90 Cambodian officials and their wives had been executed.]

On the first day, as the sun was rising, a short swing by automobile to the northern edge of the city showed soldiers and refugees pouring in. The northern defense line had obviously collapsed.

By the time I reached the Hotel Le Phnom and climbed the two flights of stairs to my room, the retreat could be clearly seen from my window and small-arms fire could be heard in the city. At 6:30 A.M. I wrote in my notebook, "The city is falling."

Over the next couple of hours there were periodic exchanges of fire as the Communists encountered pockets of resistance. But most Government soldiers were busy preparing to surrender and welcome the Communists, as were civilians. White flags suddenly sprouted from housetops and from armored personnel carriers, which resemble tanks.

Some soldiers were taking the clips out of their rifles, others were changing into civilian clothes. Some Government office workers were hastily donning the black pajama-like clothes worn by Indochinese Communists.

Shortly before 9 A.M. the first rebel troops approached the hotel, coming from the north down Monivong Boulevard. A crowd of soldiers and civilians, including newsmen, churned forth to greet them—cheering and applauding and embracing and linking arms to form a phalanx as they came along.

The next few hours saw quite a bit of this celebrating, though shooting continued here and there, some of it only a few hundred yards from the hotel. Civilians and Buddhist monks and troops on both sides rode around town—in jeeps, atop personnel carriers and in cars—shouting happily.

Most civilians stayed nervously indoors, however, not yet sure what was going on or who was who. What was the fighting inside the city all about they wondered; was it between diehard Government troops and Communists or between rival Communist factions fighting over the spoils? Or was it mostly exuberance?

Some of these questions, including the nature of the factionalism, have still not been answered satisfactorily, but on that first day such mysteries quickly became academic, for within a few hours, the mood changed.

The cheerful and pleasant troops we first encountered—we came to call them the soft troops, and we learned later that they were discredited and disarmed, with their leader declared a traitor; they may not even have been authentic—were swiftly displaced by battle-hardened soldiers.

While some of these were occasionally friendly, or at least not hostile, they were also all business. Dripping with arms like overladen fruit trees—grenades, pistols, rifles, rockets—they immediately began clearing the city of civilians.

Using loudspeakers, or simply shouting and brandishing weapons, they swept through the streets, ordering people out of their houses. At first we thought the order applied only to the rich in villas, but we quickly saw that it was for everyone as the streets became logged with a sorrowful exodus.

Cars stalled or their tires went flat, and they were abandoned. People lost their sandals in the jostling and pushing, so they lay as a reminder of the throng that had passed.

In the days to follow, during the foreign colony's confinement in the French Embassy compound, we heard reports on international news broadcasts that the Communists had evacuated the city by telling people the United States was about to bomb it. However, all the departed civilians I talked with said they had been given no reason except that the city had to be reorganized. They were told they had to go far from Phnom Penh.

In almost every situation we encountered during the more than two weeks we were under Communist control, there was a sense of split vision—whether to look at events through Western eyes or through what we thought might be Cambodian revolutionary eyes.

Was this just cold brutality, a cruel and sadistic imposition of the law of the jungle, in which only the fittest will survive? Or is it possible that, seen through the eyes of the peasant soldiers and revolutionaries, the forced evacuation of the cities is a harsh necessity? Perhaps they are convinced that there is no way to build a new society for the benefit of the ordinary man, hitherto exploited, without literally starting from the beginning; in such an unbending view people who represent the old ways and those considered weak or unfit would be expendable and would be weeded out. Or was the policy both cruel and ideological?

A foreign doctor offered this explanation for the expulsion of the sick and wounded from the hospital: "They could not cope with all the patients—they do not have the doctors—so they apparently decided to throw them all out and blame any deaths on the old regime. That way they could start from scratch medically."

Some Western observers considered that the exodus approached genocide. One of them, watching from his refuge in the French Embassy compound, said, "They are crazy! This is pure and simple genocide. They will kill more people this way than if there had been hand-to-hand fighting in the city."

Another foreign doctor, who had been forced at gunpoint to abandon a seriously wounded patient in mid-operation, added in a dark voice, "They have not got a humanitarian thought in their heads!"

Whatever the Communists' purpose, the exodus did not grow heavy until dusk, and even then onlookers were slow to realize that the people were being forcibly evacuated.

For my own part, I had a problem that preoccupied me that afternoon: I, with others, was held captive and threatened with execution.

After our release, we went to the Information Ministry, because we had heard about a broadcast directing high officials of the old regime to report there. When we arrived, about 50 prisoners were standing outside the building, among them Lon Non, the younger brother of President Lon Nol, who went into exile on April 1, and Brig. Gen. Chim Chhuon, who was close to the former President. Other generals and cabinet ministers were also there—very nervous but trying to appear untroubled.

Premier Long Boret, who the day before had made an offer of surrender with certain conditions only to have it immediately rejected, arrived at the ministry an hour later. He is one of the seven "traitors" the Communists had marked for execution. The others had fled except for Lieut. Gen. Sisowath Sirik Matak, a former Premier, who some days later was removed from the French Embassy, where he had taken refuge.

Mr. Long Boret's eyes were puffy and red, almost down to slits. He had probably been up all night and perhaps he had been weeping. His wife and two children were also still in the country; later they sought refuge at the French Embassy, only to be rejected as persons who might "compromise" the rest of the refugees.

Mr. Long Boret, who had talked volubly and articulately on the telephone the night before, had difficulty speaking coherently. He could only mumble yes, no and thank you, so conversation was impossible.

There is still no hard information on what has happened to him. Most people who have talked with the Communists believe it a certainty that he will be executed, if indeed the execution has not already taken place.

One of the Communist leaders at the Information Ministry that day—probably a general, though his uniform bore no markings and he declined to give his name—talked soothingly to the 50 prisoners. He assured them that there were only seven traitors and that other officials of the old regime would be dealt with equitably. "There will be no reprisals," he said. Their strained faces suggested that they would like to believe him but did not.

As he talked, a squad crouched in combat-ready positions around him, almost as if it was guarding him against harm. The officer, who appeared no more than age 35, agreed to chat with foreign newsmen. His tone was polite and sometimes he smiled, but everything he said suggested that we, as foreigners, meant nothing to him and that our interests were alien to his.

Asked about the fate of the 20 or so foreign journalists missing in Cambodia since the early days of the war, he said he had heard nothing. Asked if we would be permitted to file from the cable office, he smiled sympathetically and said, "We will resolve all problems in their proper order."

Clearly an educated man, he almost certainly speaks French, the language of the nation that ruled Cambodia for nearly a century until the nineteen-fifties, but he gave no hint of this colonial vestige, speaking only in Khmer through an interpreter.

In the middle of the conversation he volunteered quite unexpectedly, "We would like you to give our thanks to the American people who have helped us and supported us from the beginning, and to all people of the world who love peace and justice. Please give this message to the world."

Noting that Congress had halted aid to the Phnom Penh Government, he said, "The purpose was to stop the war," but he quickly added, "Our struggle would not have stopped even if they had given more aid."

Attempts to find out more about who he was and about political and military organization led only to imprecision. The officer said, "I represent the armed forces. There are many divisions. I am one of the many."

Asked if there were factions, he said there was only one political organization and one government. Some top political and governmental leaders are not far from the city, he added, but they let the military enter first "to organize things."

Most military units, he said, are called "rumdos," which means "liberation forces." Neither this commander nor any of the soldiers we talked with ever called themselves Communists or Khmer Rouge (Red Cambodians). They always said they were liberation troops or nationalist troops and called one another brother or the Khmer equivalent of comrade.

The nomenclature at least is confusing, for Western intelligence had described the Khmer Rumdos as a faction loyal to Prince Norodom Sihanouk that was being downgraded by Hanoi-trained Cambodians and losing power.

The Communists named the Cambodian leader, who was deposed by Marshal Lon Nol in 1970 and has been living in exile in Peking, as their figurehead chief of state, but none of the soldiers we talked with brought up his name.

One overall impression emerged from our talk with the commander at the Information Ministry: The military will be largely in charge of the early stages of the upheaval, carrying out the evacuation, organizing the new agrarian program, searching for hidden arms and resisters, repairing damaged bridges.

The politicians—or so it seemed from all the evidence during our stay—have for the moment taken a rear seat. No significant political or administrative apparatus was yet visible; it did not seem to be a government yet, but an army.

The radio announced April 28 that a special national congress attended by over 300 delegates was held in Phnom Penh from April 25 to 27. It was said to have been chaired by the Deputy Premier and military commander Khieu Samphan, who has emerged—at least in public announcements—as the top leader. Despite that meeting the military still seemed to be running things as we emerged from Cambodia on Saturday.

One apparent reason is that politicians and bureaucrats are not equipped to do the dirty work and arduous tasks of the early phases of reorganization. Another is that the military, as indicated in conversations with Khmer-speaking foreigners they trusted somewhat, seemed worried that politicians or soft-living outsiders in their movement might steal the victory and dilute it. There could be severe power struggles ahead.

After leaving the prisoners and the military commander at the ministry, we headed for the Hotel Le Phnom, where another surprise was waiting. The day before, the Red Cross turned the hotel into a protected international zone and draped it with huge Red Cross flags. But the Communists were not interested.

At 4:55 P.M. troops waving guns and rockets had forced their way into the grounds and ordered the hotel emptied within 30 minutes. By the time we arrived 25 minutes had elapsed. The fastest packing job in history ensued. I even had time to "liberate" a typewriter someone had abandoned since the troops had "liberated" mine earlier.

We were the last ones out, running. The Red Cross had abandoned several vehicles in the yard after removing the keys, so several of us threw our gear on the back of a Red Cross Honda pickup truck and started pushing it up the boulevard toward the French Embassy.

Several days before, word was passed to those foreigners who stayed behind when the Americans pulled out on April 12 that, as a last resort, one could take refuge at the embassy. France had recognized the new Government, and it was thought that the new Cambodian leaders would respect the embassy compound as a sanctuary.

As we plodded up the road, big fires were burning on the city's outskirts, sending smoke clouds into the evening sky like a giant funeral wreath encircling the capital.

The embassy was only several hundred yards away, but what was happening on the road made it seem much farther. All around us people were fleeing, for there was no refuge for them. And coming into the city from the other direction was a fresh battalion marching in single file. They looked curiously at us; we looked nervously at them.

In the 13 days of confinement that followed, until our evacuation by military truck to the Thai border, we had only a peephole onto what was going on outside but there were still many things that could be seen and many clues to the revolution that was going on.

We could hear shooting, sometimes nearby but mostly in other parts of the city. Often it sounded like shooting in the air, but at other times it seemed like small battles. As on the day of the city's fall, we were never able to piece together a satisfactory explanation of the shooting, which died down after about a week.

We could see smoke from the huge fires from time to time, and there were reports from foreigners who trickled into the embassy that certain quarters were badly burned and that the water-purification plant was heavily damaged.

The foreigners who for various reasons came in later carried stories, some of them eyewitness accounts, of such things as civilian bodies along the roads leading out of the city—people who had apparently died of illness or exhaustion on the march. But each witness got only a glimpse, and no reliable estimate of the toll was possible.

Reports from roads to the south and southeast of Phnom Penh said the Communists were breaking up families by dividing the refugees by sex and age. Such practices were not reported from other roads on which the refugees flooded out of the capital.

Reports also told of executions, but none were eyewitness accounts. One such report said high military officers were executed at a rubber plantation a couple of miles north of the city.

In the French Embassy compound foreign doctors and relief agency officials were pessimistic about the survival chances of many of the refugees. "There's no food in the countryside at this time of year," an international official said. "What will they eat from now until the rice harvest in November?"

The new Communist officials in conversations with United Nations and other foreign representatives during our confinement and in statements since have rejected the idea of foreign aid, "whether it is military, political, economic, social, diplomatic, or whether it takes on a so-called humanitarian form." Some foreign observers wondered whether this included China, for they speculated that the Communists would at least need seed to plant for the next harvest.

Whether the looting we observed before we entered the French compound continued is difficult to say. In any case, it is essential to understand who the Communist soldiers are to understand the behavior of some of them in disciplinary matters, particularly looting.

They are peasant boys, pure and simple—darker skinned than their city brethren, with gold in their front teeth. To them the city is a curiosity, an oddity, a carnival, where you visit but do not live. The city means next to nothing in their scheme of things.

When they looted jewelry shops, they kept only one watch for themselves and gave the rest to their colleagues or passersby. Transistor radios, cameras and cars held the same toy-like fascination—something to play with, as children might, but not essential.

From my airline bag on the day I was seized and threatened with execution they took only some cigarettes, a pair of boxer underwear shorts and a handkerchief. They passed up a blue shirt and $9,000 in cash in a money belt.

The looting did not really contradict the Communist image of rigid discipline, for commanders apparently gave no orders against the sacking of shops, feeling, perhaps, that this was the least due their men after five years of jungle fighting.

Often they would climb into abandoned cars and find that they would not run, so they would bang on them with their rifles like frustrated children, or they would simply toot the horns for hours on end or keep turning the headlights on and off until the batteries died.

One night at the French Embassy, I chose to sleep on the grass outside; I was suddenly awakened by what sounded like a platoon trying to smash down the front gates with a battering ram that had bright lights and a loud claxon. It was only a bunch of soldiers playing with and smashing up the cars that had been left outside the gates.

Though these country soldiers broke into villas all over the city and took the curious things they wanted—one walked past the embassy beaming proudly in a crimson-colored wool overcoat that hung down to his Ho Chi Minh sandals— they never stayed in the villas. With big, soft beds empty, they slept in the court- yards or the streets.

Almost without exception, foot soldiers I talked with, when asked what they wanted to do, replied that they only wanted to go home.

OUR BRUSH WITH DEATH
May 9, 1975

BANGKOK, Thailand—Some of the foreigners who stayed behind after the Ameri- can evacuation of Phnom Penh learned quickly and at first hand that the Com- munist-led forces were not the happy-go-lucky troops we had seen in the initial stage of the Communist takeover.

I had my first experience with the tough Khmer Rouge troops early in the afternoon of the first day of the takeover.

With Dith Pran, a local employee of *The New York Times*, Jon Swain of the *Sunday Times* of London, Alan Rockoff, a freelance American photographer, and our driver, Sarun, we had gone to look at conditions in the largest civilian hospi- tal, Preah Keth Mealea. Doctors and surgeons, out of fear, had failed to come to work and the wounded were bleeding to death in the corridors.

As we emerged from the operating block at 1 P.M. and started driving to- ward the front gate, we were confronted by a band of heavily armed troops just then coming into the grounds. They put guns to our heads and, shouting angrily, threatened us with execution. They took everything—cameras, radio, money, typewriters, the car—and ordered us into an armored personnel carrier, slamming the hatch and rear door shut. We thought we were finished.

But Mr. Dith Pran saved our lives, first by getting into the personnel carrier with us and then by talking soothingly to our captors for two and a half hours and finally convincing them that we were not their enemy but merely foreign newsmen covering their victory.

We are still not clear why they were so angry, but we believe it might have been because they were entering the hospital at that time to remove the patients and were startled to find us, for they wanted no foreign witnesses.

At one point they asked if any of us were Americans, and we said no, speaking French all the time and letting Mr. Dith Pran translate into Khmer. But if they had looked into the bags they had confiscated, which they did not, they would have found my passport and Mr. Rockoff's.

We spent a very frightened half hour sweating in the baking personnel carrier, during a journey on which two more prisoners were picked up—Cambodians in civilian clothes who were high military officers and who were, if that is possible, even more frightened than we.

Then followed two hours in the open under guard at the northern edge of town, while Mr. Dith Pran pulled off his miracle negotiation with our captors as we watched giddy soldiers passing with truckloads of looted cloth, wine, liquor, cigarettes and soft drinks, scattering some of the booty to soldiers along the roadside.

We were finally released at 3:30 P.M., but the two Cambodian military men were held. One was praying softly.

GRIEF AND ANIMOSITY IN THE FRENCH EMBASSY COMPOUND
May 9, 1975

BANGKOK, Thailand—For the 800 foreigners, including this correspondent, who spent two weeks in the French Embassy in Phnom Penh after the Communists took over, the time seemed like a chaotically compressed generation of life.

A baby was born, another died. A dozen marriages were performed—all marriages of convenience to enable Cambodians to get French passports so that they could escape the country and its peasant revolution.

There were days of deep sorrow. Cambodians without foreign papers had to go on the trek into the countryside. Friends were torn apart. Families broke up as Cambodian husbands were separated from their European wives. On those days sobbing could be heard in every corner of the compound.

And there were days when hopes rose, days when the rumors said that evacuation was imminent.

Heroes and knaves emerged—more of the latter that the former. There was no running water and the food was limited, and out of this grew tensions and rivalries between groups. Between French officials living well in the embassy and French civilians living in the driveways and gardens outside. Between the outside French and the French staff of Calmette Hospital, who were also living fairly well. And between the non-French foreigners, including the favorite targets—Americans and journalists—and everyone else.

There was more selfishness than sharing. A minor example: put a pack of cigarettes on a table for 10 seconds and turn around, and it would be gone.

The first convoy of foreigners who had taken refuge in the embassy for 13 days, including this correspondent, arrived in Thailand Saturday after three and a half days on the road. Hundreds of other refugees remained in the embassy even longer and arrived in Thailand today.

To describe what life was like in the compound is to describe sheer incongruity. A French doctor walked the hospital's pet sheep around the gardens. (The hospital's pet gibbon was taken by the Communists and led around the street outside in a pink dress.) Some of the Frenchmen in the compound fed their dogs better than other people were able to feed their children.

Our group of foreigners lived in the building that used to be the ambassador's residence, one of three buildings on the grounds; the others are a chancellery and a large cultural center. Eighteen of us, using sofa cushions and pillows as mattresses and linen tablecloths for blankets, slept on the floor of a large living room—surrounded by humming air conditioners, an elegant upright piano, a crystal chandelier and some of the embassy's best silver, except for the silver teapots, which were used to boil water over wood fires outside.

For a few days it might have been fun—a curious experience to dine on when you got home. But as time wore on, nerves frayed more and more and hardly an hour went by without an argument somewhere in the compound, usually over something petty.

The water supply ended a few days after our arrival, after which we had to rely on water tapped from our air-conditioners and that delivered periodically in barrels by the new Government. There was never enough for bathing, and the odor of unwashed people was ripe.

With food limited and with no running water, sanitation deteriorated and there were scores of cases of diarrhea—the evidence of which filled every walkway and garden in the compound.

The compound was difficult at times, but never as difficult as was suggested by the radio news reports we kept listening to, which said our situation was "more and more precarious." Sometimes when we were hearing those bulletins we were swilling scotch and smoking long cigars.

Though some people managed not to fare too badly, for most of those in the compound the situation was far more than a series of annoyances; there was nothing funny about it.

There was nothing funny for Ms. Nha, an Air France employee who sat sobbing under a tree on the morning of April 19. Her mother and father were missing, and in two days she would be forced to take her young son and go into the countryside herself.

"I was an optimist," she said as the tears coursed down her cheeks. "Not only me. All Cambodians here thought that when Khmer Rouge came it would be all welcomes and cheering and bravo and the war would be over and we would become normal again. Now we are stunned, stunned."

There was nothing funny for Mrs. Praet, a Belgian whose Cambodian husband was being forced to leave her and join the march. As she wept into her handkerchief he embraced her gently. "Courage, *ma cherie*. Courage, *ma cherie*," he whispered. She could not control herself and her small body shook with her weeping as their two little girls looked on, uncomprehending.

Some Cambodian women, realizing that their infants could not survive the long trek, tearfully gave theirs to French families for foster care or adoption.

"My first baby, my only baby!" a mother in shock shrieked. "Save him! Save him! You can do it."

It was raining as the Cambodians left. The hospital's sheep, tethered to a truck, was bleating mournfully; no one paid any attention.

At one time, about 1,300 people were living in the attractively landscaped compound which is 200 yards by 250 yards or so. Then the Communists ordered out all Cambodians without foreign passports or papers, which forced about 500 people to take to the road.

Family or not, we all lost someone close to us, and when the Cambodians trudged through the gate we foreigners stood in the front yard, weeping unashamedly.

The forced evacuation was part of an apparent campaign to make it clear to Jean Dyrac, the consul and senior French official at the embassy, and to everyone else in the compound that the new Government, not foreigners, was in charge—and under its own rules.

The first thing the Communists did was declare that they did not recognize the compound as an embassy, simply as a regroupment center for foreigners under their control. This shattered the possibility of asylum for high officials of the ousted regime who had sought sanctuary. On the afternoon of April 20, in a gloomy drizzle, Lieut. Gen. [Sisowath] Sirik Matak, who was among those marked for execution, and a few other leading figures were taken away in the back of a sanitation truck.

Throughout our stay the Communists continued their campaign of proving their primacy—refusing to let a French plane land with food and medical supplies, refusing to allow us to be evacuated in comfort by air instead of by rutted road in the back of military trucks, and, finally, shutting down the embassy radio transmitter, our only contact with the outside world.

At the same time they did not physically harass or abuse us—the only time our baggage was searched was by Thai customs officials when we crossed the border—and they did eventually provide us with food and water. The food was usually live pigs, which we had to butcher.

Though the new rulers were obviously trying to inflict a certain amount of discomfort—they kept emphasizing that they had told us in radio broadcasts to get out of the city before the final assault and that by staying we had deliberately gone against their wishes but there was another way to look at it. From their point of view we were being fed and housed much better than their foot soldiers were and should not complain.

But complain we did—about the food, about each other, about the fact that embassy officials were dining on chicken and white wine while we were eating plain rice and washing it down with heavily chlorinated water.

Among the embassy denizens, even in the midst of the tears and heartache, a search for the appearance of normalcy went on.

A French woman picked orange-colored blossoms from a bush and twined them in her laughing child's hair.

Gosta Streijffert, a former Swedish Army officer from a patrician family who is a Red Cross official, sat erect in a straight-backed chair he had carried outside and read a British news magazine with his monocle fixed.

At a table nearby a United Nations official and a Scottish Red Cross medical team played bridge and drank whiskey; someone carped loudly about the way his partner conducted the bidding.

In the midst of all of this an American airplane mechanic who did not leave Cambodia on the day the United States Embassy staff was evacuated because he was too drunk, had an epileptic seizure. The Red Cross doctors carried him on the run to the building where the hospital staff was quartered with their equipment.

The American recovered slowly. His case interrupted the staff's dinner—steak. We were envious, and they seemed embarrassed and angry when journalists made notes about their full larder.

Why was there not more sharing, more of a community spirit? What made us into such acquisitive, self-protective beings?

Why did all the Asians live outside, in the heat and rain, while many of the Caucasians, like my group, lived inside, with air-conditioning? We explained it by saying the living arrangements were up to the embassy, but this was clearly not an answer. Was our behavior and our segregation a verdict on our way of life?

Amid the generally disappointing behavior of the Westerners there were exceptions—people who rose above the squabbling and managed to hold things together.

There was François Bizot, a Frenchman who worked for many years in the countryside restoring ancient temples and ruins. He lost his Cambodian wife and mother-in-law, who were forced on the march. Yet his relationship with the Communists was strong and they trusted him, for he had met some in his work in the interior and he speaks Khmer fluently.

It was Mr. Bizot who, in the early days of our confinement, was allowed to scout for food and water. And it was he who successfully argued the cases of some Asians whose papers were not in perfect order. A number of people who were in the compound probably owe their futures to him.

There were others who performed constructive roles, among them Douglas A. Sapper 3d, an American with a Special Forces background who was involved in a private airline company.

Sapper, as everyone calls him, organized our group's kitchen and food rationing to make sure supplies would last. His ranger training—and his colorful language, none of which can be reproduced here—kept us eating regularly and kept pilferers out of the larder.

These special people notwithstanding, the general level of behavior remained disappointing throughout our stay. We held constant group meetings and made endless lists of who was supposed to perform what chores, and we were constantly going through the movements of organizing, but we never really got organized.

Lassitude and depression set in as the days dragged on. People lay dozing on their makeshift beds throughout the day, waiting only for the next feeding. One journalist slipped into a torpor in which he had energy only to lift his aerosol insecticide can and spray away flies.

Occasionally, however, there was an occurrence dramatic enough to break this morphic aura—such as the sighting of a Chinese plane on April 24 coming in for a landing at the airport, possibly carrying high Cambodian and Chinese officials from Peking.

There was also the unexpected arrival the day before of the seven Russians who had been holding out at the Soviet Embassy. They had been desperately trying to make friendly contact with the new Cambodian leaders to counterbalance Chinese influence.

But it was the Chinese and not the Russians who had been supplying the Khmer Rouge with arms. The Cambodian Communists rebuffed the Soviet overtures, fired a rocket through the second floor of their embassy, looted the building and ordered the Russians to the French compound.

This phase came to an end for us in the early hours on April 30 when—after an evening of sipping champagne "borrowed" from embassy stocks and singing determinedly hardy traveling songs such as "It's a Long Way to Tipperary"—we were awakened as scheduled, after a few hours' sleep, and told to board the trucks.

As we stepped into the pleasantly cool air with our sacks and suitcases, we could see in the night sky the lights of many planes coming from the direction of South Vietnam and heading west. Saigon was falling, and South Vietnamese pilots, carrying their families and other refugees, were making their own evacuation journey to Thailand.

EVACUATION CONVOY TO FREEDOM IN THAILAND
May 9, 1975

BANGKOK, Thailand—The evacuation journey by truck to Thailand from Phnom Penh, where hundreds of foreigners had been confined in the French Embassy compound for nearly two weeks, gave a brief but revealing glimpse into the covert spy system and communally organized countryside of the Cambodian Communists—a glimpse that as far as is known no Westerners ever had before.

We traveled on some of the well-defended dirt roads that had been built by hand and used as clandestine supply routes during the five years of the war that ended with the seizure of the Cambodian capital on April 17.

None of these roads show on maps of Cambodia, yet some were only half a mile or so from the main highways.

On the 250-mile trip we saw reservoirs, dikes, bridges—all built with hand tools. No machines or earth-moving equipment were visible.

We also saw boy militia units on patrol everywhere and male-female work crews repairing roads.

For those in the truck convoy the trip was arduous. It was especially difficult for the very young and the very old, and some fell ill. On our second day out, as we stopped in Kompong Chhnang for the night, a 9-month-old retarded child died in the bedlam of the governor's residence where we spent the night. French doctors who accompanied us said they knew before we started that the child could never survive such a trip. But the parents had no alternative—they could either take the child with them and pray for a miracle or leave him behind in Phnom Penh to die.

For the strong and healthy, the trip was tolerable. During rest stops we were able to forage for coconuts, mangoes and other fruit. And at every stop there were a few abandoned houses with big clay urns filled with rainwater, which we poured over our steaming heads.

The petty squabbling between various groups that often dominated our lives in the French Embassy compound followed us on the journey to the border. A group of Soviet diplomats refused to share their food with anyone. They even complained that they were not getting their proper convoy ration of rice.

At one point, in pique, the Russians threatened to expose stowaways on our truck. We in turn advised them that if they persisted with their threats we would write a long story about their behavior, which, we suggested, would not go down very well in Moscow. They eased up a bit after that and offered us some vodka and tinned meat.

The French and the Vietnamese with French passports also continued to act like badly behaved zoo denizens whenever the Communists brought us food.

If the Communists were looking for reasons to expel us as unfit and unsuited to live in a simple Asian society, we gave them ample demonstration on this journey.

The trip from the French Embassy began early on April 30 in virtually the same welter of chaos in which we had entered the embassy as refugees 13 days earlier.

In the darkness before dawn there was utter confusion in the embassy yard as more than 500 of us clambered into the 26 Soviet, Chinese and American-made military trucks for the journey.

There were supposed to be exactly 20 persons to each truck. But in the darkness and confusion some stowaways managed to sneak aboard. Five were on our truck—three Asian wives of Westerners whose papers were incomplete but who were fiercely determined to get out, a child of one of these women, and a German television correspondent.

The German sat upright, but the other stowaways slipped under our legs and we covered them with towels, bush hats and other oddments. Somehow, the officials who checked the convoy never noticed them.

At 6 A.M., with the sun just coming up, the convoy moved out. As it did, we saw a fresh battalion of troops marching single file into the city from the north.

Then the scenes changed and we met new images. The streetlights burned, casting their artificial ray along the boulevards of a deserted city. Abandoned cars and assorted trash marked the trail of the departed population.

Every shop had been broken open and looted. Not a single civilian was visible—only the many soldiers camping in the shops and on the sidewalks.

We suddenly turned right—that is, west—down the road to the airport, and this was puzzling because we were supposed to be heading north and northwest toward Thailand.

We did not know it yet, but this was to be the detour that kept us from seeing that early stretch of Route 5 north of Phnom Penh that had been clogged with refugees forced out of Phnom Penh and may now be dotted with bodies.

Our convoy started southwest out of the capital down Route 4, then cut north along a rutted secondary road until we picked up Route 5 near Kompong Chhnang.

From there to the border, along Route 5, we encountered a wasteland of broken bridges, abandoned fields and forcibly evacuated highway towns.

The trip was a grueling one—with our trucks often lost or broken down for long hours either in the blistering sun or torrential downpours.

Some of these areas we passed through had been badly bombed by the United States Air Force in the early years of the war. Fields were gouged with bomb craters the size of swimming pools. But our American group and other Westerners encountered almost no hostility from the local people.

While some sections we passed through were battered, others showed that they had been developed and organized over a long period of time and that they had remained untouched sanctuaries throughout the war.

The whole trip—with us jammed in the back of the bone-jarring military trucks—took more than three days. It was Saturday morning, after riding and bouncing all night, before we arrive at Poipet, the border town on the Cambodian side. Formalities took about an hour, but the Communist officials never searched our baggage or film or anything else we imagined they might be interested in.

Finally, at 11:20 A.M. I crossed over the rickety frontier bridge into Thailand. The first person to greet me was Chhay Born Lay, a Cambodian reporter for The Associated Press who left his country with his family on a press-evacuation flight.

As we walked forward to embrace each other, the back of my right hand caught on a roll of barbed wire marking the border and the scratch began to bleed. Lay instantly bent his head, grabbed the hand and began sucking the blood from the cut. I tried to pull my hand away, but he held tight.

This is what it is like to have a Cambodian friend. We both had left many Cambodian friends behind. We were both crying.

CHAPTER TWO

The Killing Fields

THE DEATH AND LIFE OF DITH PRAN
January 20, 1980, The New York Times Magazine

I began the search for my friend Dith Pran in April 1975. Unable to protect him when the Khmer Rouge troops ordered Cambodians to evacuate their cities, I had watched him disappear into the interior of Cambodia, which was to become a death camp for millions. Dith Pran had saved my life the day of the occupation, and the shadow of my failure to keep him safe—to do what he had done for me—was to follow me for four and a half years.

Then, on October 3, 1979, Dith Pran crossed the border to Thailand and freedom. This is a story of war and friendship, of the anguish of a ruined country, and of one man's will to live.

In July 1975—a few months after Pran and I had been forced apart on April 20—an American diplomat who had known Pran wrote me a consoling letter. The diplomat, who had served in Phnom Penh, knew the odds of anyone emerging safely from a country that was being transformed into a society of terror and purges and "killing fields." But he wrote, "Pran, I believe, is a survivor—in the Darwinian sense—and I think it only a matter of time before he seizes an available opportunity to slip across the border."

Pran is indeed a survivor. When he slipped across the border into Thailand, he was very thin, his teeth were rotting, and his hands shook from malnutrition—but he had not succumbed.

Pran's strength is returning and he wants the story told of what has happened, and is still happening, to his people. He wants to talk about the unthinkable statistic that Cambodia has become: an estimated two million or more people, out of a population of seven million in 1975, have been massacred or have died of starvation or disease.

✦

I met Pran for the first time in 1972, two years after the war between the Khmer Rouge and the American-supported Lon Nol government had begun. I went to Cambodia that year after several months of helping cover a major offensive by Hanoi in South Vietnam for *The New York Times*. For some time, Pran had worked with Craig Whitney, our Saigon bureau chief, as his assistant on his occasional trips to Phnom Penh. When my plane touched down at Pochentong Airport on that September day, Pran had received my cable and was there to meet me.

His notebook was full of the things that had been happening since *The Times'* last visit. A spacious suite with balcony was waiting for me at the Hotel Le Phnom, my press card and cable-filing permission had already been arranged for, and he had a list of valuable suggestions about what I should see and whom I should talk to. I felt immediately easy with him.

It is difficult to describe how a friendship grows, for it often grows from seemingly contradictory roots—mutual needs, overlapping dependencies, intense shared experiences, and even the inequality of status, with one serving the other.

Our bond grew in all these ways. Other reporters and television crews also vied for Pran's services, but more and more he politely turned them down and worked only for me. By the middle of 1973, his value to the paper now apparent, the foreign desk, at my urging, took Pran on as an official stringer with a monthly retainer. This took him completely out of circulation for other journalists, some of whom expressed their disappointment openly.

Pran and I realized early on that our ideas about the war were much the same. We both cared little about local or international politics or about military strategy. I had been drawn to the story by my perception of Cambodia as a nation pushed into the war by other powers, not in control of its destiny, being used callously as battle fodder, its agonies largely ignored as the world focused its attention on neighboring Vietnam. But what propelled both of us was the human impact—the ten-year-old orphans in uniforms, carrying rifles almost as tall as themselves; the amputees lying traumatized in filthy, overcrowded hospitals; the skeletal infants rasping and spitting as they died while you watched in the all-too-few malnutrition clinics; and the sleepless, unpaid soldiers taking heavy fire at the front lines, depending on the "magic" amulets they wore around their necks while their generals took siestas after long lunches several miles behind the fighting. And then, always, the refugees. While White House policy-makers were recommending only a few million dollars for relief aid, as compared with somewhere around one billion dollars in military aid, on the ground that there was really no major refugee problem in Cambodia, Pran was taking me to the jammed and underfed refugee camps and to the dirt roads not far from Phnom Penh where villagers were streaming away from the fighting, leaving their homes and rice fields behind.

We were not always depressed by the war, however, because the opposite side of depression is exhilaration—the highs of staying alive and of getting big stories. And he and I covered many big stories. Like the time in 1973 when an American B-52 bomber, through an error by the crew in activating its computerized homing system, dropped twenty or more tons of bombs on the heavily populated Mekong town of Neak Luong, thirty-eight miles southeast of Phnom Penh. About 150 people were killed and more than 250 wounded. The mortified American Embassy played down the destruction ("I saw one stick of bombs through the town," said the air attaché, "but it was no great disaster.") and then tried to keep reporters from getting there. They succeeded the first day, barring us from helicopters and river patrol boats, but on the second, Pran, his competitiveness boiling as keenly as mine, managed, through bribes and cajoling, to sneak us aboard a patrol boat. We brought back the first full story of the tragedy.

But first we were put under house arrest for one night by the military in Neak Luong—we always believed the orders came from the Americans. We spent the night in a house with some of the survivors. They stayed up all night, listening for the sound of airplanes, in dread that another "friendly" plane would rain death on them again.

On our way back up the river, on another patrol boat, the crew was less interested in getting us back to Phnom Penh in time to file before the cable office shut down for the night than in scouring the riverbanks for Communist machine-gun and rocket nests. Every time they thought they spotted something—be it driftwood or the real thing—they turned the craft toward the shore and opened up with their .50-caliber machine gun.

We were going to be too late if this continued, so Pran told them—on my frantic instructions—that he would double the bribes if only they would ignore their military targets and move at full speed to Phnom Penh. They understood our motives not at all—I'm sure they regarded me as deranged—but their official salary was a pittance, and they did as they were asked.

Days and nights spent like this were what drew Pran and me together.

✦

I pause here to say that this chronicle, of all the stories I have written as a journalist, has become the hardest for me to pull out of my insides. To describe a relationship such as Pran's and mine demands candor and frankness about self, not romantic memories. I feel exposed and vulnerable. I also wonder nervously what he will think when he reads this. As I write, there is a tension pain under my right shoulder blade, the same pain I felt in April 1975, in the final days before the fall of Phnom Penh, after the American Embassy had been evacuated. We ran chaotically around the city and its perimeter every day, trying to piece together what was happening and how close the Communists were. Our nights were spent at the cable office—I typed while Pran urged the Teletype operators to keep going and push the copy out. Our two drivers, Hea and Sarun, were there, too, bringing me wet washcloths and glasses of weak tea to keep me awake. The city's power was off and there was no air-conditioning. When I would begin to slump, Sarun would bring me back by rubbing my shoulders and pulling on my ears, a traditional Cambodian massage.

Among the papers strewn about me now is a picture of Sarun, shirtless and sweating, pulling on my ears. It is not easy for me to look at that picture. Sarun is dead now, killed in 1977 when the Khmer Rouge, for some unknown reason, decided to execute all the men in his village. Sarun's wife later met Pran in Siem Reap Province and told him that Sarun had cried out horribly, pleading for mercy as they dragged him off, his hands bound tightly behind him.

My mind searches for happier times. I remember our visit to Battambang in 1974, when, over a tasty fish dinner, Pran and I smoked pot, he for the first time, and then went gamboling through the unlighted streets of the town, astonishing soldiers at checkpoints as we bayed at the moon. I remember the time in late 1973 when frayed, and needing a breather, we flew to the seaport resort of Kompong Som and played on the beaches for three days. I can see Pran in the water, giggling as he groped among the rocks, looking for the sweet crabs that lived in abundance there.

But as I wander mentally over the landscape of those war years, starker memories swarm, disjointed, out of sequence, clamoring for precedence.

In 1973, Thomas O. Enders, an arrogant protégé of Secretary of State Henry A. Kissinger, became acting ambassador in Phnom Penh, taking over from Emory Swank, who had refused to supervise the heavy American bombing and who was relegated by Kissinger to a State Department dustbin because he no longer had any stomach for this futile war. Enders, who made no secret of the low regard in which he held the Cambodians for their inability to defeat the Communist army, had no such reservations. According to participants, he ran the morning bombing meetings at the embassy, where targets were chosen for the daily carpet bombing by the giant B-52s, with spirit and relish.

Enders also became known around Phnom Penh for remarks that some listeners considered openly callous and racist. He would ask, rhetorically, at cocktail parties, diplomatic dinners, and press briefings why Cambodians did not seem to care as much about human life as we Westerners. If they did care, he posited, they would rise up in anger over the terrorist rocket attacks that were killing innocent victims daily in the capital, and march out into the countryside to smite the Communist army.

Pran had heard about Enders's remarks, but we had not discussed them. Finally, fed up, I asked Pran one day what he would reply to Enders if the diplomat asked him, "Do Khmers care less about the death of their loved ones than other people do?"

Pran lowered his head for several minutes. Then softly he said, "It's not true. You have seen for yourself the suffering. The only difference, maybe, is that with Cambodians the grief leaves the face quickly, but it goes inside and stays there for a long time."

In 1975, the Khmer Rouge rockets began falling on the neighborhood where Pran lived with his wife and children. One morning he was late coming to work. He explained that just as he was leaving the house, a rocket crashed into the house of a neighbor. A six-year-old girl was severely wounded. Her stomach was hanging out. Pran raced her to the hospital in his car, her mother screaming all the way. The child did not survive.

Another visit to Neak Luong, in 1975, is also part of the mosaic. By this time, the strategic river port is surrounded by the Khmer Rouge, who are bombarding it with rockets and mortars. Thirty thousand refugees are trapped there. Food is short. The gravely wounded are so numerous and the medivac helicopters so few that some of the victims are asking to be killed quickly rather than be allowed to lie there and die slowly in pain. Pran and I flew in by helicopter on January 14; the meadow where we land is filled with dead and dying. Every fifteen minutes or so, another shell screams down and another half-dozen or so are killed or wounded. Inside the tiny military infirmary, an eleven-year-old boy has just expired on the blood-slicked floor. In the bedlam, no one has time to cover him or even to close his staring eyes.

When we arrive back in Phnom Penh, I am frantic to get my film to Saigon, where it can be radiophotoed to New York. There's only one more flight today, an American Embassy plane, leaving in half an hour. While I run to the airline terminal building to call the embassy for permission to send film on the plane, I send Pran to the tarmac with the film, in case the plane comes early, so he can try to wheedle it aboard. When I return, having got permission, Pran has disappeared. None of the Americans on the tarmac—military men in civilian clothes responsible for supervising the delivery of United States military supplies to Phnom Penh—will tell me what has happened to him. With five minutes to go before takeoff, I spot Pran waving at me from behind a warehouse a couple hundred yards away. I recover the film from him, just manage to get it on the plane, and then walk back to ask him what in the world happened.

He tells me that an American colonel ordered him off the airport, citing security reasons. Washington contends that it has no advisers here and that the Cambodians are running their own war, yet an American officer orders a Cambodian off a Cambodian airport.

"The Americans are king here now," Pran says dejectedly. "It's his land, not mine anymore."

I ask the embassy for an explanation and for an apology to Pran. We get neither.

Our lives proceeded in this fashion—from one intense experience to another, an unnatural existence by the standards of normal life, but perfectly natural when living inside a continuous crisis. We broke our tension—we had to, for psychic survival, to push away the bloody images—with good food, laughter that was often too loud, and occasionally an evening of carousing and smoking pot, which was plentiful and cheap in the central market. (Pran abstained after his howling at the stars in Battambang.)

My trips to Cambodia from Singapore, where I was based, became more frequent and my stays longer. I was becoming part of the war, and it was placing bad strains on my wife, Janice, and my two young daughters, Jessica and Rebecca, and on my relationships with each of them.

Once, returning to Singapore after a three-month tour in Cambodia, I noticed that Jessica, then only five, was very shy and distant with me. I tried to draw her out, asking if there was something wrong. "No, Daddy," she said uncomfortably, having difficulty finding the words without offending me, "I love you. But I keep losing you. Just when I'm getting to know you again, I lose you."

But I kept going back to Phnom Penh; my obsession with the story was filling my life. Pran, too, was hooked, for some of my reasons but also for some very personal ones of his own. He had no background in journalism when the war began, but as his skills improved and his interest in the craft grew, he began to see in journalism a way to reveal his people's plight.

Born on September 27, 1942, Pran was raised in a middle-class family with three brothers and two sisters in the township of Siem Reap, in the northwestern part of the country, near the famed Angkor temples. His father was a senior public-works official, who supervised the building of roads in the area. Pran went through high school there, learning French in the classroom and English on his own at home. After high school, in 1960, he got a job as an interpreter in Khmer, the Cambodian language, for the United States Military Assistance Group then in Cambodia. When Cambodia broke relations with Washington in 1965, charging that American troops had launched attacks from South Vietnam on Cambodian border villages, the Americans left and Pran got a job as an interpreter for the British film crew that was producing *Lord Jim*.

After that, he became a receptionist at Cambodia's best-known tourist hotel, Auberge Royale des Temples, situated just opposite the main entrance to the Angkor complex. Tourism ended with the beginning of the war in 1970, and Pran went to Phnom Penh with his wife, Ser Moeun, and their children to find work as a guide and interpreter for foreign journalists.

As the war dragged on and conditions deteriorated, I drove Pran very hard. I was driven, so I drove him. As always, I pushed him to go a little faster, get a little more done, interview a few more people. When, for example, the cable line out of Phnom Penh would go down, as it did frequently, I would send him over to the cable office to try to coax and bribe the operators into doing something special for us to get it working again. I would raise my voice every time some obstacle arose that could impede my getting a story out, telling him to get the problem resolved, even when I knew that in a country whose communications system was as primitive as Cambodia's, there was often little he could do.

He almost never complained or demurred. He says he never got angry at me, although I'm convinced there were times when he dearly wanted to bounce a chair off my head. He insists he accepted my relentless behavior as merely an attempt to teach him how to succeed as a journalist. "I never got angry," he says, "because I understand your heart. I also understand that you are a man who wants everything to succeed."

Pran was a survivor even then. He also tended to give me heroic qualities, to make me bigger than life—as I am perhaps doing to him now.

There was one day, however, when he did eventually reveal his annoyance. We had interviewed the prime minister, In Tam. Pran's translation of his remarks, which were in Khmer, was literal, and I was looking for the subtleties that would reveal the prime minister's intent. Pran first gave one meaning and then a different one, and we began to have a royal argument. I demanded to know what Pran thought In Tam's meaning had really been; I wanted the whole truth. Finally he retaliated, "I can't tell you the whole truth—I can only tell you eighty percent," he snapped. "Twenty percent I have to keep for myself."

My persona came to have a wider audience. I was dubbed "Ankalimir" by other Cambodian assistants in the press corps and employees at the Hotel Le Phnom, who had become accustomed to my outbursts. Ankalimir, in Khmer legend, was an ogre who went around cutting off the fingers of people who annoyed him, until he got to his hundredth finger, which was his mother's. She was having none of this. She told him he'd been a bad man and it was time for him to reform. And he did. So dramatically did he change that he eventually was transformed into an enlightened disciple of Buddha's.

I was the man, my Cambodian friends explained, who made a lot of bad noises in the beginning but at bottom was a good person. I liked the ending and accepted the nickname as comradely, if critical, flattery.

On the day of the United States Embassy evacuation—April 12, 1975—all the Americans at the hotel, mostly newsmen, left the premises early in the morning. The employees thought all of us had left the city on Marine helicopters and, feeling abandoned with the Communists closing in on the city, became desolate. A few of us had decided to stay, however, and I was the first to walk back into the hotel at noontime. The receptionists and room boys came to life, jumping to their feet. "Ankalimir is still here," one shouted. Perhaps these gracious men took heart from my presence, as if I had some special information that we would all be safe when the Khmer Rouge came.

That evacuation day remains, paradoxically, both clear and muddled in my mind. What I do remember is Joe Lelyveld, then *The Times'* Hong Kong bureau chief, who had come in to help with the coverage in the final weeks, banging on my door at 7 that morning.

He tells me that this is it, the embassy is leaving, we have to be there with our bags by 8:30, the gates close at 9:30. My first thought, utterly irrational, is that I can't possibly pack in time. My next thought is an equally irrational wish that it's only a test run, because I don't really want to leave.

Eventually I have a lucid thought. I have to talk to Pran. We had worked until 3 in the morning and he's probably still sleeping. First, I speed to the embassy to convince myself it's the real thing. It is, so I race back to the hotel, send a messenger for Pran, and, as a contingency, I pack. I guess this means that I am not going to make a final decision until I can look into his face.

When he arrives, I tell him quickly about the evacuation and ask him if he wants to leave. Knowing this day was coming, we had discussed the options several times before and agreed that if we felt in no direct danger, we would stay. Though we have little time, his face is calm. He knows I want to stay, and he says he doesn't see any immediate risk and therefore no reason we should leave now. He says he wants to stay to cover the story. We reinforce each other's compulsions and desires. He is as obsessed as I am with seeing the story to the end.

But he adds that with rockets falling on his neighborhood, he wants to evacuate his wife and children. I had already taken the precaution of getting approval of a sympathetic senior embassy official, Robert Keeley, to accept any Cambodian friends I might bring to the embassy on the day of the evacuation. I sent Pran rushing home to collect his family in his aging green Renault, and I go to wait for them at the embassy, now surrounded and secured by Marines in full battle dress.

In the sky, the helicopters swarm like wasps, heading in and out of the landing zone nearby, taking evacuees to the aircraft carrier USS *Okinawa* in the Gulf of Siam, which will then head for Thailand. A steady stream of foreigners, Cambodians, and embassy officials arrive at the building and pass through a special metal door. Brown tags with their names on them are placed around their necks, and they are then moved to the flatbed trucks that will take them to the landing zone. Some have tears in their eyes, but most mask their feelings. Some Cambodians who try to get into the embassy have no authorization and are turned away. One distraught man slips a note in English through a crack in the metal door. It reads, "Will you please bring me and my family out of the country?" But the man has no connections at the embassy. "Give it back," growls a nervous American colonel, "give it back." The note is passed back through the slit. No one inside ever sees the face of the man making the appeal.

At 9:20—with only ten minutes to spare—Pran drives up with his family. As his wife and their four children are loaded onto the last truck, an Army military attaché who is going out on the same truck tries to persuade us to come with him. When he realizes our decision to stay is final, he holds out his automatic rifle and asks, "Don't you want something for protection?" I tell him that I am touched by his offer, but that I'm all thumbs and I'd probably blow off a toe if I tried to use it. He keeps holding out the rifle to me, even as the truck goes out the embassy's back gate.

At 11:13, the last helicopter takes off. The dust on the landing zone, a soccer field, settles. The skies are silent.

Very suddenly the city takes on a strange, new atmosphere—a feeling of emptiness, if that's possible in a refugee-crowded capital of two and a half million. The Americans were the last power base. Now, it's like having the city to ourselves; we're on our own for everything. We don't admit it to each other, but it's more than a little eerie. We begin to feel a heightened kinship with the Westerners who have stayed—more than seven hundred French colonials, a score of mostly French and Swedish journalists, and another score of international relief officials. There are also five other Americans, ranging from a freelance photographer to an alcoholic airline mechanic who has drunkenly slept through the evacuation calls.

✦

Much of what happened over the next five days—until the Khmer Rouge came—was reported at that time in *The New York Times*. Pran and I sped around the city and its perimeter every day in our two rented Mercedes-Benzes, trying to visit every front line, every hospital, every possible government official—to put together as clear a picture as possible of the increasingly chaotic situation. One thing was certain: the enemy circle around Phnom Penh was tightening.

These were long, frenetic, sweaty days. Our lives—and our options—had been reduced to necessities. We carried basic needs with us—typewriters and typing paper in the cars, survival kits (passport, money, change of shirt and underwear, camera, film, extra notebooks, soap, toothbrush) over our shoulders, Pran's in a knapsack, mine in a blue Pan Am bag.

Although I kept my room at the hotel, we rarely stopped there. We spent most of our nights at the cable office, filing stories—or trying to. The main transmission tower, in a suburb called Kambol, was eventually overrun, and the last remaining transmitter was an ancient Chinese-made contraption that kept overheating and going dead. We caught only a couple of hours of sleep each night, on straw mats on the cable office floor. There was little time to bathe or change clothes, but since we all smelled alike, no one took offense.

There was also little time to reflect on what might happen when the Khmer Rouge took the city. Our decision to stay was founded on our belief—perhaps, looking back, it was more a devout wish or hope—that when they won their victory, they would have what they wanted and would end the terrorism and brutal behavior we had written so often about. We all wanted to believe that, since both sides were Khmers, they would find a route to reconciliation. Most of the high officials in the government put their lives on this belief and stayed behind too. Those who were caught were executed.

✦

On April 14, the Khmer Rouge begin their final push, driving on the airport, one of the city's last lines of defense.

Inside the capital, there remains a strange disconnection from the reality that is such a short distance away. Some of the Frenchmen who have stayed behind, believing that as old residents and relics of the colonial past their lives will not be disrupted, are playing chess by the hotel pool. In a nearby street, a driver leans on the fender of his Land Rover, a mirror in one hand and tweezers in the other, pulling stray hairs from his chin. Government employees laugh and joke as they go through their regular morning marching exercises on the grass outside their buildings—part of a national preparedness program. For two days, the government news agency carries nothing on the evacuation of the Americans, but it has a long story on the death of the entertainer Josephine Baker. The government radio announces the appointment of a new Minister of State for Industry, Mines and Tourism. A delicious *petit poussin* is served in the hotel restaurant, but an American patron complains because the hotel has run out of ice and he objects to drinking his Pepsi warm.

This surrealism is to come to an end on the morning of April 17, a Thursday, when the new rulers march into the anxious city. On the night of April 16 it is clear that the collapse of Phnom Penh is only hours away. Enormous fires from the battles that ring the very edge of the city turn the night sky orange. The last government planes—single-engine propeller craft diving low over the treetops— futilely try to halt the Communist advance with their final bombs. Refugees by the thousands swarm into the heart of the capital, bringing their oxcarts, their meager belongings, and their frightened bedlam. Deserting government soldiers are among them.

Pran turns to me and says, "It's finished, it's finished." And as we look at each other, we see on each other's faces for the first time the nagging anxiety about what is going to happen to us.

We spend that final night filing stories from the cable office, as artillery shells crash down periodically a few hundred yards away. The line goes dead just before 6 a.m. on April 17; two of my pages still have not been sent. I am annoyed and complain edgily to the morning crew chief, badgering him to do something to get the line restored. Within a moment, I feel as foolish and contrite as it is possible for a man to feel. The telephone rings. It is a message for the crew chief.

One of his children has been killed and his wife critically wounded by an artillery shell that has fallen on his home in the southern section of Phnom Penh. As his colleagues offer words of solace, he holds his face under control, his lips pressed tightly together. He puts on his tie and his jacket and he leaves, without ever saying a word, for the hospital where his wife is dying.

We leave the cable office and take a short swing by car to the northern edge of the city. The sun is rising but it offers no comfort. Soldiers and refugees are trudging in from the northern defense line, which has collapsed. Fires are burning along the line of retreat.

By the time we reach the hotel, the retreat can be clearly seen from my third-floor balcony, and small-arms fire can be heard. Soldiers are stripping off their uniforms and changing into civilian clothes. At 6:30 a.m., I write in my notebook, "The city is falling."

Pran is listening to the government radio, which is playing martial music and gives no hint of the collapse. The day before, the prime minister, Long Boret, had sent a virtual surrender offer, via Red Cross radio, to the Khmer Rouge side; it asked only for assurances of no reprisals against people and organizations who had worked on the government side. Prince Norodom Sihanouk, as titular head of the Khmer Rouge, immediately rejected the offer from his exile in Peking. The government radio went off the air last night without mentioning the truce offer; it said only that the military situation "is boiling hotter and hotter" and quoted government leaders as "determined to fight to the last drop of our blood."

Now, as Pran glues his ears to the radio, I decide that, not having bathed in two days, I shall shower and change clothes. "If we're going to meet the new rulers of Phnom Penh today," I tell him jokingly, "I'd better look my best." He laughs amused at another irrational act by the man whose first thought on the day the Americans left was that he didn't have time to pack. I emerged from my shave and shower feeling halfway recycled. At 7:20 a.m., the Khmer Rouge break in on the radio to announce, "We are ready to welcome you."

It is the apprehensive population of Phnom Penh that does the welcoming—hanging white flags, fashioned from bed sheets, from windows and rooftops and on government gunboats on the Tonle Sap River and the Mekong. The crews of the armored personnel carriers in the streets outside the hotel stick bouquets of yellow allamanda flowers in their headlights.

The first units of Communist troops seem friendly and celebratory. They are wearing clean black pajama uniforms and look remarkably uncalloused and unscarred. It soon becomes clear that they are not the real Khmer Rouge—we never did learn who they were, maybe misguided students trying to share in the "revolution," maybe part of a desperate plot by the government to confuse and subvert the Khmer Rouge—but within hours they and their leader are disarmed and under arrest and the genuine Khmer Rouge take over and begin ruthlessly driving the people of the city into the countryside. Most of the soldiers are teenagers, which is startling. They are universally grim, robot-like, brutal. Weapons drip from them like fruit from trees—grenades, pistols, rifles, rockets.

During the first confused hours of the Communist victory, when it looks as if our belief in reconciliation is a possibility, Pran and I and Jon Swain of *The Sunday Times* of London, who has been traveling with us, decide to chance a walk to the cable office. The transmitter is still out of order, so we can send no copy, but a beaming Teletype operator chortles at us, "C'est la paix! C'est la paix!"

Outside, at 10:40 a.m., we have our first conversation with an insurgent soldier. He says he is twenty-five years old, has been five years in the "movement" and has had ten years of schooling. He is traveling on a bicycle and is wearing green government fatigues over his black pajamas. The government-unit patches have been torn off. He has a Mao cap and shower sandals, and around his neck he wears a cheap, small pair of field glasses. Like all the others we meet later, he refuses to give his name or rank. We guess he is an officer or sergeant.

Will the Khmer take revenge and kill a lot of people? I ask Pran to ask him in Khmer. "Those who have done corrupt things will definitely have to be punished," he says.

Pran tries to get him to relax and at one point does evoke a small smile from this man from another planet. It is one of the few smiles I will see on a Khmer Rouge face for the two weeks I am to be under their control. I offer him cigarettes and oranges. He refuses, saying that he is not allowed to accept gifts. I ask him if he can give gifts: what about his Mao cap, would he give it to me as a souvenir? He refuses coldly. The smile is gone. He pedals off.

After a breakfast of Pepsi-Cola at a restaurant whose French proprietor is glad for company but who has no other food, we walk back to the hotel and decide it is still safe to move around. So we drive to the biggest civilian hospital—Preah Keth Mealea—to get some idea of casualties. Al Rockoff, an American freelance photographer, has joined us. Only a handful of doctors have reported for duty. People are bleeding to death on the corridor floors. A Khmer Rouge soldier, caked with blood, is getting plasma from one of the few nurses who have showed up, but he is nevertheless dying of severe head and stomach wounds. All he can manage to whisper over and over is, "Water, water." A few yards away, hospital aides are trying to mop some of the blood off the floor. They mop carefully around three stiffening corpses.

We can stand to look at these scenes no longer, so we depart. But as we get into our car and start to leave the compound, some heavily armed Khmer Rouge soldiers charge in through the main gate. Shouting and angry, they wave us out of the car, put guns to our heads and stomachs, and order us to put our hands over our heads. I instinctively look at Pran for guidance. We have been in difficult situations before, but this is the first time I have ever seen raw fear on his face. He tells me, stammering, to do everything they say. I am shaking. I think we're going to be killed right there. But Pran, having somehow composed himself, starts pleading with them. His hands still over his head, he tries to convince them we are not their enemy, merely foreign newsmen covering their victory.

They take everything—our car, cameras, typewriters, radio, knapsacks—and push us into an armored personnel carrier, a kind of light tank that carries troops in its belly, which they have captured from the government army.

We all get in—three journalists and our driver, Sarun—except for Pran. We hear him continuing his entreaties in Khmer outside. We naturally think he is trying to get away, arguing against getting into this vehicle. Most of my thoughts are jumbled and incoherent, but I remember thinking, For God's sake, Pran, get inside. Maybe there's some chance this way, but if you go on arguing, they'll shoot you down in the street.

Finally, he climbs in, the rear door and top hatch are slammed shut, and the armored car starts to rumble forward. After a few minutes of chilled silence, Sarun turns to me and in French asks me if I know what Pran was doing outside the vehicle. I say no, since the talk was in Khmer. Sarun tells me that Pran, far from trying to get away, was doing the opposite—trying to talk his way into the armored car. The Khmer Rouge had told him to leave, they didn't want him, only the Americans and "the big people." He knew we had no chance without him, so he argued not to be separated from us, offering, in effect, to forfeit his own life on the chance that he might save ours.

As the armored car moves through the city, it becomes an oven. Sweat starts pouring off us as we stare at one another's frightened countenances. The vehicle suddenly stops. Two Cambodian men are pushed inside. They are dressed in civilian clothes, but Pran recognizes them as military men who have taken off their uniforms to try to escape detection. One of them, a burly man with a narrow mustache, wearing a T-shirt and jeans, reaches over and tries to shove his wallet into my back pocket. He explains in whispered French that he is an officer and must hide his identity. I tell him it is useless to hide anything on me because we were all in the same predicament. Pran takes the wallet and stuffs it under some burlap sacks we are sitting on. The officer's companion, a shorter, leaner man with a crew cut, dressed in a flowered shirt and brown trousers, has a small ivory Buddha on a gold chain around his neck. He puts the Buddha in his mouth and begins to pray—a Cambodian Buddhist ritual to summon good fortune against imminent danger. His behavior is contagious. I take from my pocket a yellow silk rose that my daughter Jessica had given me two weeks earlier when I had taken a five-day breather in Bangkok with my family, knowing the fall of Phnom Penh was near. I had cut off the wire stem and carried it in my pocket ever since, as my personal amulet. Sweat has turned it into a sodden and scruffy lump. I clutch it hard in my right fist for luck.

Looking across at Jon Swain, I see in his eyes what must also be in mine—a certainty that we are to be executed. Trying to preserve my dignity and to get that terrible look off his face, I hold out the rose and say, "Look, Jon, I've got Jessica's good-luck rose with me. Nothing can really happen to us." He forces a wan grimace; I know he thinks I am crazy.

Meanwhile, Pran is keeping up his pleading with the driver of the armored car, telling him that we are not soldiers or politicians or anything hostile to the Khmer Rouge. No one here is American, he insists, they are all French, they are only newsmen. Whatever meager words we exchange among ourselves are in French. Rockoff speaks no French, so we run our hands across our lips in a sealing motion to let him know he should keep his mouth shut.

Suddenly, after a forty-minute ride, the vehicle stops and the rear door clangs open. We are ordered to get out. As we move, crouching through the door, we see two Khmer Rouge soldiers, their rifles on their hips pointing directly at us. Behind them is a sandy riverbank that slopes down to the Tonle Sap River. Rockoff and I exchange the briefest of fear-struck glances. We are thinking the same thing—they're going to do it here and roll us down the bank into the river.

But we climb out, like zombies, and no shots are yet fired. Pran resumes his pleas, searching out a soldier who looks like an officer. For a solid hour he keeps this up—appealing, cajoling, begging for our lives. The officer sends a courier on a motorbike to some headquarters in the center of the city. We wait, still frozen but trying to hope, as Pran continues talking. Finally, the courier returns, more talk—and then, miraculously the rifles are lowered. We are permitted to have a drink of water. I look at Pran and he allows himself a cautious smile. He's done it, I think, he's pulled it off.

Strangely, in the surge of relief, my first thought is of my notebooks, which were in my airline bag, confiscated when we were seized. I feel more than a little silly to be thinking now of pieces of paper. But my sense of loss is overwhelming—the notebooks hold all my thoughts, everything I had observed, for the last several months.

We are still under guard, but everything has relaxed. They now let us move into the shade of a concrete approach to a bridge blown up by sappers early in the war. We watch jubilant Communist soldiers rolling by in trucks loaded with looted cloth, wine, liquor, cigarettes, and soft drinks. They scatter some of the booty to the soldiers at the bridge. We also watch civilian refugees leaving Phnom Penh in a steady stream—our first solid evidence that they are driving the city's entire population of more than two million into the countryside to join their "peasant revolution." As the refugees plod along, the soldiers take watches and radios from them.

Our captors offer us soft drinks. One of them toys with me. He holds out a bottle of orange soda, and when I reach for it, he pulls it back. Finally I say, "Thank you very much," in Khmer. Having made this point, that I am his subject, in his control, he hands me the bottle, grinning.

At 3:30 p.m. we are released. Suddenly a jeep drives up, and many of our belongings are in it—including the airline bag. Sheepishly, I ask Pran if he thinks he can get it back. He sees nothing unusual in the request and immediately begins bargaining. A few minutes later, a Khmer Rouge soldier, after haphazardly groping through its insides, hands me the bag. In it, with the notebooks, is a money belt holding nine thousand dollars and my American passport, which, if they had bothered to look at it, could have given me away. Our hired 1967 Mercedes-Benz and my camera, among other valuables, were kept as booty.

As we move off, I look back. The two men who shared the armored car with us are still under guard. The smaller man still has the Buddha in his mouth, having never stopped praying. There is no doubt in our minds that they are marked for execution.

Much later, I ask Pran about the extraordinary thing he had done, about why he had argued his way into that armored car when he could have run away. He explains in a quiet voice, "You don't speak Khmer, and I cannot let you go off and get killed without someone talking to them and trying to get them to understand. Even if I get killed, I have to first try to say something to them. Because you and I are together. I was very scared, yes, because in the beginning I thought they were going to kill us, but my heart said I had to try this. I understand you and know your heart well. You would do the same thing for me."

The rest of the day is an adrenaline blur, a lifetime crammed into a few hours. We see friends going off to certain death, families pleading with us to save them as we professed our helplessness, roads awash with people being swept out of the city like human flotsam. Some are the severely wounded from the hospitals, who are being pushed in their beds, serum bottles still attached to their bodies.

After our release, we head for the Information Ministry because earlier Khmer Rouge radio broadcasts have called on all high officials of the defeated government to report there. We find about fifty prisoners standing outside the building, guarded by wary Khmer Rouge troops. They also begin to guard us as we approach the men who appear to be their leaders and seek to interview them. Among the prisoners are cabinet ministers and generals, including Brigadier General Lon Non, younger brother of Marshal Lon Nol, who went into exile some weeks before. Lon Non, considered one of the most corrupt men in Cambodia, is smoking a pipe and trying to look untroubled. He says calmly to us, "I don't know what will happen to me."

A Khmer Rouge official, probably a general, though like all the others his uniform bears no markings of rank, addresses the group with a bullhorn, telling them that they will be dealt with fairly. He asks for their cooperation, saying, "There will be no reprisals." The prisoners' strained faces suggest they do not believe him. (Whether this entire group was killed is not known, but Lon Non's execution is confirmed a short time later.)

Three Cambodian women suddenly walk into this tense scene. They go straight to the leader and tell him they wish to offer their help. They are officials of the Cambodian Red Cross—middle-aged patrician ladies dedicated to good works. They do not seem to understand what is happening. The leader smiles and thanks them for coming. They depart as incongruously as they came.

The Khmer Rouge leader, who seems no older than thirty-five, then turns to talk to us and a few French newsmen who have joined our group. He is polite but says very little. Pran serves as interpreter. When we ask if we will be allowed to cable stories to our publications, he says, "We will resolve all problems in their proper order." He also volunteers "our thanks to the American people, who have helped us from the beginning."

He suggests to Pran that the foreign newsmen stay at the Information Ministry to be registered. Pran, sensing trouble, declines politely and motions discretely to us to leave. We slip away, smiling as broadly as we can.

Just then, the prime minister of the old government, Long Boret, arrives in a car driven by his wife. He is a courageous man who could have left with the

Americans but stayed behind to try to work out a peaceful transition of power. He has failed and he looks wretched. His eyes are puffed. He stares at the ground. He is one of the seven "traitors" specifically marked by the Khmer Rouge for execution, and he knows what faces him now. I want to get away, but I feel I must say something to him, and Pran understands. I take Long Boret's hands and tell him what a brave thing he has done for his country and that I admire him for it.

Pran takes his hands, too. I feel dehumanized at not being able to do anything but offer a few words. Long Boret tries to respond but cannot. Finally he mumbles, "Thank you." And we must leave him.

As we head back to the hotel on foot, a gray Mercedes approaches us and stops. The driver jumps out and comes toward me, haggard and stuttering, holding some pieces of paper. It is Ang Kheao, a gentle middle-aged man who used to teach at the university and sometimes did translations of documents for me. For the past week, I have had him monitoring government radio broadcasts. His large family is jammed into the car; like everyone else, they are leaving the city under the Khmer Rouge orders of evacuation. It is hard to believe, but in the midst of chaos, with his family in jeopardy, Ang Kheao has kept on working to complete his assignment.

I look at the papers he hands me—it is his translation of the final broadcast of the defeated government, transmitted around noontime. The government announcer had started reading a message saying that talks between the two sides had begun, when a Khmer Rouge official in the booth with him interrupted to say, harshly, "We did not come here to talk. We enter Phnom Penh not for negotiation, but as conquerors."

Ang Kheao and I say good bye as if in a ritual. I pay him for his services and offer him my meaningless wishes for good luck. He wishes me good health in return and drives off toward the northwest, up Highway 5. Another friend I shall probably never see again.

It is exactly 5:20 p.m. when we reach Hotel Le Phnom. It is deserted. Insurgent troops sit in a truck outside the gate, their rocket launchers trained ominously on the building. I run up to the only foreigner in sight, a Swedish Red Cross official standing on the front steps. "What's going on?" I ask. Peering at me through his monocle, he says calmly, "They gave us half an hour to empty the hotel. They gave no reason." "When did they give you that half hour?" I asked nervously. "Twenty-five minutes ago," he replies.

So the overflowing hotel, which the Red Cross had tried to turn into a protected international zone, is no longer a sanctuary, and we must fall back on the contingency plan that has been worked out among the foreigners remaining in Phnom Penh, which is to seek refuge in the French Embassy about a half-mile away.

I have five minutes to collect the loose clothes I left behind as dispensable. Jon Swain, his hotel key confiscated by the Khmer Rouge with his other belongings, will now need them. Also in my room—and more important—is a cupboard full of survival rations, collected judiciously for just such an event: canned meat, tins of fruit and juice, sardines. While I'm in the bedroom throwing the clothes into a suitcase, I yell at Rockoff to empty the cupboard. He packs up a few things—a can of Dinty Moore beef stew, a jar of Lipton's powdered iced tea and a tin of wafers—but he completely ignores everything else, including a fruitcake and a large jar of chunky peanut butter. In the days ahead, when we are often hungry, we rag him good-naturedly—but continually—about this lapse.

We are the last ones out of the building, running. The Red Cross has abandoned several vehicles in the hotel yard after removing the keys. We have too much to carry, so we throw our gear in the back of one of their Toyota vans, put it in neutral, and start pushing it up Monivong Boulevard toward the French Embassy. The broad avenue is awash with refugees bent under sacks of belongings, marching into the unknown, their eyes hurt with the knowledge that, being soft city people, the trek into the interior will certainly kill many of them.

In the tidal crush, people have lost shoes and sandals, and footwear litters the street. Cars with flat tires stand abandoned in the middle of the road. Clouds of smoke from the final battles wreathe the city. Coming from the north along Monivong is a fresh, heavily armed battalion, marching in single file. As we pass, we eye one another like people from different universes.

At the French Embassy, there is pandemonium. The gates are shut and locked to prevent the mob from surging in, but people by the dozens, including Cambodians, are coming in anyway—passing their children over the tall iron-spiked fence, then hurling their belongings over and finally climbing over themselves. We do the same.

Entering the compound, we are immediately segregated racially by the French officials. Westerners are allowed inside the embassy's four buildings. (About eight hundred eventually gather in the compound.) Cambodians and other Asians must camp on the grass outside. A French Embassy official with a guard dog bars me from taking Pran and our two drivers, Hea and Sarun, and their families inside our building, the Salle de Reception; we sneak them in after dark. At about 9 p.m., a report sweeps the compound that the Khmer Rouge are ordering all Cambodians out of the embassy and into the countryside. The five hundred Cambodians outside the embassy buildings sit up all night in anxiety, ready to run and hide, afraid to go to sleep. In a few days, this report will become a reality, and the Cambodians will indeed be pushed out.

Talks are begun between the Khmer Rouge and our side (embassy officials and representatives of the United Nations and other international agencies), but our basic requests—for delivery of food from the outside world, for an air evacuation of everyone in the compound—are curtly rejected. The Khmer Rouge make it clear that we and our requests are not merely unimportant but irrelevant. At one point they say that the "indispensable" evacuation of Phnom Penh "does not concern you." More disquieting, even though France has recognized their government, they reject the international convention that the embassy is foreign territory and therefore a place of asylum, inviolate and protected. They enter the compound at will, taking away people they consider "high enemies," including Sirik Matak, a Cambodian general and former prime minister. In a funereal drizzle he walks out the gate into Khmer Rouge custody. "I am not afraid," he says, as he is led to the back of a flatbed garbage truck, his back straight and his head high. "I am ready to account for my actions." He is executed soon after.

From our small window on their revolution—the embassy's front gate—we can see glimpses of their "peasant revolution." There is no doubt that the Khmer Rouge are turning Cambodian society upside down, remaking it in the image of some earlier agrarian time, casting aside everything that belongs to the old system, which has been dominated by the consumer society of the cities and towns. Some of the Khmer Rouge soldiers we talk to speak of destroying the colonial heritage and use phrases like "purification of the people" and "returning the country to the peasant."

"They haven't a humanitarian thought in their heads," says Murray Carmichael, a doctor on a Red Cross surgical team, as he describes the emptying of the hospitals where he worked. "They threw everyone out—paralytics, critical cases, people on plasma. Most will die. It was just horrible."

On the second day in the embassy—April 18—the French ask us to be ready to turn in our passports the next day so they can catalog who is in the compound. This means that what we feared is true: the Cambodians with us cannot be protected. I discuss the situation with the drivers, Hea and Sarun. They agree that their chances are better if they leave the embassy now on their own rather than later in a conspicuous group of hundreds of Cambodians. I give each of them a thousand dollars in hundred-dollar bills for potential bribe money. We have a hard time looking at each other as our parting nears. At 2:25 p.m., Hea and Sarun and their families, loaded with sacks of food and other needs, slip out a rear gate that a French guard quietly opens for them, and head north out of the city.

We have one last hope for Pran: Jon Swain happens to have a second British passport. It is in Swain's name, but we think we can doctor it and alter the name skillfully enough to give Pran a foreign identity. Al Rockoff sets to work with a pen, a razor blade and some glue. Swain has a hyphenated middle name, so by erasing "Jon" and "Swain" and the hyphen, Pran has a new name. But it's an upper-class English tongue twister—Ancketill Brewer—and Pran spends hours trying to learn how to pronounce it and make it his own. We substitute Pran's photo for Swain's, and the next day—April 19—we turn the passport in to the French with our own. A day later, the French come to Swain and tell him the ploy won't work; they say that the Khmer Rouge will spot the forgery as quickly as they did and that it could compromise the entire compound. They will kill him on the spot, the French say, and maybe us, too. They insist Pran has to leave.

I do not tell Pran right away. I want time to think about other possible subterfuges. I am also trying to get up the courage. My mind is blank. I talk to Swain and others and we can think of no way to hide him. Finally I tell him.

I ask him if he understands—we have tried everything we can think of but we are stymied. He says yes, he understands. But it is I who do not understand, who cannot cope with this terrible thing. He saved my life and now I cannot protect him. I hate myself.

It does not ease my conscience or my feeling of responsibility that on the morning Pran and I have this talk, members of the embassy staff are moving through the compound, telling all the Cambodians they must leave. "We'd like to help you," one French official says, "but there's no way. If you stay here, there will be trouble. You're better off out there. It's a good moment to leave now because later the Khmer Rouge will come into the embassy to search."

Pran packs his essential belongings in a small bag. He destroys any piece of identification that might link him to foreigners or make him anything but a simple member of the working class. All the other Cambodian journalists in the embassy—most of them freelance photographers—do the same, although a few do not jettison their cameras. Some have families with them.

We give them all our "private" food and cigarettes and Cambodian money. I also give Pran twenty-six hundred dollars for bribe money. At 10:15 a.m. on April 20, Pran and his group—twenty-one persons in all—gather at the embassy's front gate, their belongings in the back of a gasless Toyota wagon, which they will push up the road.

I put my arms around Pran and try to say something that will have meaning. But I am wordless and he is too.

I watch him pass through the gate and out of sight, and then I put my head against a building and start banging my fist on it.

Jon Swain comes over to comfort me. "There was nothing you could do," he says. "Nothing you could do. It will be all right, you'll see. He'll make his way to the border and escape. You know how resourceful he is."

In the months and years to come, that scene—Pran passing through the gate—becomes a recurring nightmare for me. I will awake, thinking of elaborate stratagems I might have used to keep him safe and with me. I am a survivor who often cannot cope with surviving.

The night of Pran's departure, Jean Dyrac, vice-consul and senior official in the embassy, comes to our quarters to brief us on his latest negotiations with the Khmer Rouge. He is a decent man who had suffered cruelties as a prisoner of war during World War II. He is now overwhelmed and drained by the demands on him, by the appeals to save lives, appeals he has been powerless to respond to. He talks small talk at us first—he has made no headway with the Communists—and then his feelings begin to show. He is suffering remorse and heartache over the expulsion of the Cambodians from the compound. "We are not policemen," he says, "but we had to turn them out. They could have been shot on the spot, and those believed responsible would be compromised." His eyes well up now and his voice falters, the words coming out so painfully soft we have to strain to hear. "It is a very sad thing to say. When we do such things, we are no longer men." Unable to continue, he walks swiftly from the room, looking at no one. I feel very close to Jean Dyrac at that moment.

The next day, April 21, the rest of the Cambodians in the embassy—there are several hundred left—are forced to leave. It is a time of mass grief. Cambodian husbands are separated from European wives. Wailing rends the compound.

Louisette Praet, a Belgian woman whose Cambodian husband, an engineer, is being taken from her, is crying softly into her handkerchief. He embraces her and whispers, "*Courage, ma Cherie. Courage.*" But she cannot control herself, and her small body shakes with her sobs as their two little daughters look on, uncomprehending.

Vong Sarin, a Cambodian friend who had held a senior job in the former government's communications system, is turning his seven-month-old boy over to a Frenchwoman to care for. He gives me some money to put in a bank for the boy. "Do you think they will punish people like me?" he asks. I cannot tell him what I really think. "I doubt it," I say. "You were not a soldier or a politician." He and I both know the truth is elsewhere, and his face remains fixed in gloom. His wife is hysterical at having to give up her child and about what awaits them. She grabs my arm and pleads, "My first baby, my only baby! We'll never see him again. Save us, save us! Get papers for us, sir. You can do it." It was a time of not being able to look into people's eyes.

Nine days later—April 30—the final evacuation of the embassy begins. The first of two truck convoys sets out at dawn for the border with Thailand, carrying about five hundred of the eight hundred foreigners in the compound. I am on it. We awake to pack at 2 a.m., and as I am leaving our building an hour later to walk to the trucks, I see in the foyer a huge vinyl suitcase that someone has discarded. It is large enough for Pran to have crawled into; I could have cut air holes in it for him. I stand frozen for a minute to breathe, looking at it, and then someone is calling me, telling me if I don't hurry, I'll miss the convoy. I move on woodenly.

+

Three and a half days later—after a monsoon-soaked journey whose metronome had swung crazily between petty fights among the evacuees over food and the awe and fear stirred in us by the sight of the grim Khmer Rouge work gangs, under guard, building roads and dikes with their hands—we arrived at the border. As I crossed the rickety frontier bridge, the first person to greet me was Chhay Born Lay, a Cambodian reporter for the Associated Press, who had left Phnom Penh on a press-evacuation flight on April 12, the day the American Embassy personnel pulled out. As Lay and I embraced, he asked me where Pran was. I was able to get out the words, "He couldn't come," before I started crying. Lay looked at me and understood everything and cried with me.

I went to Bangkok to write my long chronicle of the fall of Phnom Penh and our captivity for *The Times*. Then I returned to Singapore and my wife and children. I was supposed to be getting a new foreign assignment, and they were packed and ready to return to the United States for our home leave. But I was not yet prepared to face "normal" life again, and I took a long time getting myself together for the trip.

It was mid-July before we arrived in the States. My wife sensed my dropout mood and decided to stay in Los Angeles, where her family lives, until I made up my mind about what I wanted to do next. After a week there, I left for New

York to see my editors, stopping first in San Francisco to look after Pran's wife, Ser Moeun, and their four children. They had settled in that city, with its large Asian population, with the help of *The Times* and a refugee-relief agency it had enlisted. *The Times* and I were sharing her living expenses.

Since her evacuation from Phnom Penh in April, Ser Moeun, then thirty, had naturally been frightened and uncertain about her future; she was in a strange country and did not speak anything but Khmer. Through interpreters, I had tried to reassure her, by telephone and letter, but without Pran she remained disoriented. I had told her, in a letter, that "it might take some time before he can reach the border," but "I know he will be out before long." This rosy optimism had been a mistake, as I was to learn when I visited her in the cramped railroad flat that was the family's first quarters.

The children were excited to see me, but Ser Moeun was distraught and trying not to show it. We were sitting beside each other on a sofa when she broke down and ran into the bathroom. It was some time before she emerged, her eyes red, a damp washcloth in her hand. I begged her to tell me what was wrong—though certainly I knew. She hesitated a long time. Finally she said, her words falling on me like a verdict, "I thought when you come you bring Pran with you." And her tears began again. I then told her the whole story of our taking refuge at the embassy and why Pran and other Cambodians were not allowed to stay.

Over the next few days, I kept talking to Ser Moeun—to myself, really—about the need to be strong and to keep our faith alive, that his courage, intelligence, and determination would see him through. In the ensuing years, as we followed the reports of massacres and starvation brought out by escapees, both of us wavered in that faith many times. We had nothing else to go on; Cambodia was closed to the outside world in all normal senses—no mail, no telephone or cable system, no government an outsider could communicate with, and no possible legal entry.

I made up scenarios to help us believe: the reason Pran had not crossed into Thailand was that he reunited with his parents and they were too elderly and infirm to make the arduous escape attempt; or that Pran was simply being cautious and ingenious, as he had always been, and would make his move to the border only when he thought the odds of success were very good. The latter turned out to be the truth.

In New York, I finally said what I knew I had to—that I wanted a leave of absence to write a book about Cambodia. Everyone at *The Times* understood, and the answer was yes. I returned to my family in Los Angeles, feeling relieved, even buoyed at times. But I was unable to put Pran out of my mind, and every time I thought of him, I was blocked and the book would not come.

Instead, I wrote letters, searching for Pran or the tiniest glimmer of news of him, to everyone I could think of. To the government of Thailand, to the American embassies in Bangkok and Singapore, to private refugee and relief agencies working in Thailand near the border with Cambodia, to the International Red Cross, to the World Health Organization, to the United Nations' refugee organization, to journalists and other friends in Southeast Asia, and to intelligence officials and other sources operating near the border who I thought might help in some special and even extralegal way.

To some, I wrote many times, even though I knew that the odds of their being able to do anything to help Pran escape were hopeless. I had fifty prints made of each of two photographs of Pran and had them distributed along the Thai border with Cambodia. This filled my days and made me feel—sometimes—that I was doing something useful. In my mind, as long as I kept up this activity, Pran would not disappear, would not die.

One relief-official contact in Thailand who joined in the search for Pran wrote back about his own frustrations and those of other Westerners who had left Cambodian friends behind. "Everyone who came out of Cambodia," he said gloomily, "has gone through a period of almost psychotic depression at what has happened."

I used the telephone as I did the mails, making call after call to official and unofficial contacts. But for long periods of time, I did not want to see anyone face to face, not even my own family. I would closet myself in my corner of the house, and, when there were no more letters to write or calls to make, I would read every page of the local newspaper or watch television.

I could not bring myself even to visit Pran's family; I couldn't endure again Ser Moeun's "I thought when you come you bring Pran with you."

So I kept in touch with her by telephone and with letters. I also wrote persistently to the relief agency assigned to the family to discuss Ser Moeun's adjustment problems. She was and is a strong woman, but her anxiety about Pran was constant, and she, too, was not sleeping well. She had frequent dreams about Pran. Some were good; most were bad. She kept remembering an incident that had occurred just before the collapse of Phnom Penh. A picture of Pran had inexplicably fallen off the wall in their living room, smashing the glass in the frame; she had cried and cried because she interpreted this to mean he would be separated from her. Every time she recalled it, she wept again.

Ser Moeun and the children—and I—were shored up by two new friends, William and Trudy Drypolcher, he a real-estate entrepreneur who had been a reconnaissance platoon leader in Vietnam and she a business executive who had volunteered for refugee work during the collapse of Vietnam and Cambodia in 1975. They had, in effect, adopted Ser Moeun and her family in every respect but the legal one, guiding them through supermarkets, through the bus system, and through the thickets of American bureaucracy. They also became surrogate parents at report-card time, when the youngest, Titonel, showed up with top marks in everything but deportment—in which the imp regularly got "U's," for "Unsatisfactory." His teachers explained that he was a fine student but never stopped chattering in class.

Ser Moeun was learning English, but it was much more difficult for her than for the children, who were doing well in special classes. She had chosen San Francisco as their home because a small community of Cambodians had already settled there, and it was a wise decision. As the gateway for Oriental immigration into America, San Francisco has over generations built up a special system of social services for resettling people like her. Her adjustment, however, was complicated by her social worker, who believed Ser Moeun should get accustomed to living in Spartan conditions and being regarded as a member of the welfare class. The Drypolchers and I tried to convince the woman that Ser Moeun's financial support was substantial and guaranteed. But nothing we said or did made a dent in her perverse attitude.

One day, Ser Moeun's landlord—a friend of the social worker's—made a pass at her and told her that if she was "nice" to him, he would forget about the rent. Ser Moeun threw him out of the apartment. The social worker's response when Ser Moeun complained was to tell her that since she was a "refugee woman" she had to expect things like that. After a couple of years of this difficult relationship, Ser Moeun gained enough confidence, both in her English and in her ability to cope on her own, to resolve the problem, and she severed all ties with the social worker.

✦

In February 1976, ten months after the fall of Phnom Penh, our first concrete reason to hope arrived in the mail. A letter from a friend working with refugees in Thailand, Warren Hoffecker, reported that one of the refugees, a man who had gone to high school with Pran, brought out a report that Pran had been seen some months earlier in Siem Reap Province, driving an oxcart to pick up rice for people in his work camp. The man gave a lot of accurate details about

Pran; I was persuaded the sighting was reliable. Siem Reap was Pran's home province, and that was where he was heading when he left the French Embassy. I told Ser Moeun the good news but also cautioned her that it might still be a long time before Pran could make his way out.

Hoffecker, in his letter, said he faced the same burden—of telling Cambodian friends that their relatives inside might not be coming out for a long time. "Try to find some gentle way of getting her to accept the fact," he wrote, adding with sardonic sadness, "There must be a less agonizing way of making a living than attempting to explain that the era of American miracles is over and there is nothing you can do."

Hoffecker had some good contacts with members of an anti-Communist resistance group, which periodically sent armed patrols into Cambodia to gather information, harass the Khmer Rouge, and sometimes to extract people. I offered a reward if they could find Pran and bring him out. Warren made the arrangements. These guerrillas continued their forays, but they never located Pran. There was only one more reported sighting of this kind. A year later, in the spring of 1977, two of my sources independently reported that Pran had been seen in Kompong Thom, a province in central Cambodia, a long distance from Siem Reap. They also said the reports indicated that he had become active in some capacity in the resistance.

None of this made much sense—why would he move to the interior, away from the border? Why would he suddenly take up arms now, when he had no training as a soldier? But these sources had been reliable in the past, and I clutched at the news as at a life preserver. If he was still alive, two years after the Communist takeover, with at least hundreds of thousands of others dead by massacre and disease, then I had a chance to see him again.

When Pran escaped last October, I asked him about these reports. The first was correct: he had been driving an oxcart in Siem Reap in the latter half of 1975. The second was erroneous: he was never in Kompong Thom Province. But one of his brothers had been there, whose name was very similar—Dith Prun. When the Vietnamese army overran Cambodia early in 1979 and overthrew the Khmer Rouge, Pran finally learned what had happened to Prun, the oldest of his three brothers.

Prun had been a colonel in the Lon Nol army. He escaped to Kompong Thom with his wife and five children in 1975. For more than two years, until late 1977, he was able to conceal his military past, but then someone informed on him. The Khmer Rouge murdered the entire family. One report Pran received said that all seven were thrown alive to crocodiles.

✦

In the spring of 1976, I returned to work at *The Times* as assistant metropolitan editor. That same week, the Pulitzer Prizes for 1975 were announced, and I won it in the foreign reporting category for my coverage of Cambodia; I accepted it on behalf of Pran and myself.

My family joined me in New York the following year. Though pieces of the book were written, it was nowhere near finished. Regardless, I felt I had to come back to the real world.

I continued to write letters and make telephone calls in my search for Pran, but my job gave me little time now to get depressed.

Ser Moeun would call, troubled, from time to time. Newspaper reports of the mass killings in Cambodia would stir her doubts again, and she would ask me to tell her once again exactly what Pran had said when he left the French Embassy. "Was he going to try for the border? What did he say about me and the children?" What she was really asking me, but was afraid to put into words, was whether I thought Pran could still be alive. And I kept saying, as much for me as for her, that I knew he would eventually emerge safe. Early in 1978, one of her woman friends in the Cambodian community suggested to Ser Moeun that she ought to think about remarrying, at least for the children's sake. The woman mentioned a well-to-do Cambodian widower who was looking for a wife. Ser Moeun dismissed the notion out of hand. She was going to wait for Pran.

The miracle began to happen shortly after 9 a.m. on April 18, 1979. I was shaving and the phone rang. It was Andreas Freund of our Paris bureau. "I have good news for you, Sydney," he said. And then he told me that an East German correspondent based in Paris had been traveling through Cambodia in a group of Soviet-bloc journalists; while in Siem Reap he had met Pran and was carrying a message from him for me. The message had eight words, in English— the eight most exquisite words I have ever heard: "Dith Pran survivor, living in Siem Reap Angkor." I wanted to kiss Andreas through the phone; someday I'll do it in person.

I then called the East German, Gerhard Leo, who works for *Neues Deutschland*. Like a crazy man, I pumped him for every last detail about Pran. He told me, with a calm that was the reverse of my excitement, that he had been approached by Pran near the temple complex of Angkor Wat on February 15. Pran took Leo aside where they could not be overheard and, in French, asked him to take the message to me. "It will make him happy," Leo quoted Pran as saying. Pran also told Leo his general background—that he had worked for *The Times*, that he had evacuated his wife and children before the Khmer Rouge came, and that he had survived under the Khmer Rouge by passing himself off as a member of the working class.

All this took place shortly after the Vietnamese army swept through Cambodia in January 1979, pushing out the Khmer Rouge government and installing their own client regime; the dozen Soviet-bloc journalists were there through the auspices of the Vietnamese and their Moscow allies. Leo apologized for the two-month delay in getting me the message but explained that, after visiting Cambodia, he had gone back to Vietnam to cover the Chinese invasion of that country and had only just returned to Paris.

He said Pran seemed to be in "relatively good health." Moreover, Pran had asked Leo to take a picture of him and send that to me, too. That photograph—of Pran in Vietcong-style black pajamas standing in front of some lesser Angkor Wat temples—has been sitting, framed, on my office desk ever since.

Having a picture of him in front of me served wishfully—but not realistically—to mute my fears. From all the refugee reports, it was clear that being alive on one day in Cambodia was no guarantee of being alive the next.

Yet despite these constantly depressing reports, neither I nor Ser Moeun—as we kept our long-distance vigil—could have conjured, or wanted to conjure, the true misery and madness of the life that had been imposed on Pran inside Cambodia.

+

On April 20, 1975, when Pran and his group left the French Embassy and headed to the northwest in the chaos of the forced exodus, he still held some hope that life under the Khmer Rouge would be tenable. But within a day or so, he knew differently. The Communist soldiers were treating people like livestock; they were slashing the tires on cars to force people to walk; they used ideological words he had never heard before; they seemed totally alien. By the fourth day, when he reached the river town of Prek Kdam, twenty miles out of Phnom Penh, he had decided on his plan.

He threw away his regular Western-style street clothes and put on a working-class disguise, that of a lowly taxi driver—dirty shirt, short pants, sandals, a traditional Cambodian neckerchief. He also got a shorter haircut and threw away the twenty-six hundred dollars I had given him, since money was useless in the new Cambodia and it could only incriminate him.

"I could tell they were lying to the people to get them to cooperate," he says. "They told us we were only going to the countryside for a few days, because the Americans were going to bomb Phnom Penh."

"If you tell the truth, or argue even a little, they kill you" was Pran's simple rule of survival. "They told us people are one class now, only working-class, peasants." So he censored his thoughts and watched his vocabulary, keeping it crude and limited, to conceal his education and journalistic past. He talked as little as possible, and then softly and obsequiously. "I make myself a quiet man, like a Buddhist monk." He feigned total ignorance of politics. "I did not care if they thought I was a fool," he says. Inner discipline was a tenet of his survival. "I must resist in every way until I have victory." "Resist" is a word he uses constantly in telling his story.

Not every Cambodian—or even every journalist who had worked with Westerners—was as astute as Pran. At Prek Kdam, Pran met Sophan, a cameraman for CBS, sitting calmly by the side of the road with his two wives, four children, and sister-in-law. "Sophan was happy," Pran recalls. "When the soldiers asked him, he told them who he was and turned over his camera and film. He believed they were going to let him be a cameraman for the new government."

Wary, Pran exchanged only a few words with Sophan, told him he did not trust the Khmer Rouge, and shuffled quickly away in his new lower-class guise. Some time later, friends told Pran that Sophan and his entire family had been executed.

The first major Khmer Rouge checkpoint Pran encountered was at Phao, about forty miles out of Phnom Penh. Here the Communists were screening everyone meticulously. "They talked gently," Pran recalls. "'Tell us the truth about who you are,' they said. 'No one will be punished.' Most people believed them. They caught many big officials and military officers this way at Phao."

Pran told them his by-now polished tale of being a civilian taxi driver, and the Khmer Rouge accepted it. "They asked me where my wife and children were, and I told them that in the confusion we became separated and they were lost to me."

Pran received an identity card and moved on. Within a month, he reached the village of Dam Dek, about twenty miles east of his hometown of Siem Reap. He stopped there—and stayed for two and a half years—"because villagers told me the Khmer Rouge farther on were very brutal."

They were hardly benign in Dam Dek. Pran witnessed many beatings, with heavy staves and farm implements, and knew of many killings. "They did not kill people in front of us," he recalls. "They took them away at night and murdered them with big sticks and hoes, to save bullets." Life was totally controlled, and the Khmer Rouge did not need a good reason to kill someone; the slightest excuse would do—a boy and girl holding hands, an unauthorized break from work. "Anyone they didn't like, they would accuse of being a teacher or a student or former Lon Nol soldier, and that was the end."

Famine set in right away in Dam Dek, as it did across the entire country. The war had disrupted all farming and the next harvest would be too little, too late. Pran believes that maybe 10 percent of the Cambodian population of more than seven million died of starvation in 1975 alone, especially older people and children.

Early on, Pran secretly bartered his gold wedding band for some extra rice— but it didn't last very long. Eventually, the rice ration in Dam Dek was reduced to one spoonful per person per day. The villagers, desperate, ate snails, snakes, insects, rats, scorpions, tree bark, leaves, flower blossoms, the trunk of banana plants; sometimes they sucked the skin of a water buffalo. Reports reached Pran's village that to the west the famine was even more severe and that some people were digging up the bodies of the newly executed and cooking the flesh.

By October 1975, Pran—then part of a work gang planting and tending the rice fields—had become so weak that he needed a wooden staff to keep himself standing. He could not raise his legs high enough to cross the knee-high embankments around the paddies, so he would lower his body onto these knolls and roll himself over. His face grew puffy with malnutrition, and his teeth began coming loose. He feared he was dying. So he took a very grave risk.

One night, during the harvest season, he slipped out of his hut of tinder wood and thatch, crawled into a nearby paddy, and began picking rice kernels and stuffing them into his pocket. Suddenly, out of the darkness, two guards rose up. Pran tried to run, but his legs gave out and he fell. He pleaded with them, saying he was only stealing a little rice because he was starving. They called a dozen members of the village committee—ten men and two women—who began beating him with long, bladed implements used for cutting bamboo. He crumpled to the ground. They continued pounding him, shouting, "You are the enemy. You were stealing rice from the collective." "I thought they were going to cut my head off," he says.

They paused in their beating only to tie his hands tightly behind his back and lead him away to a more desolate spot. "Let's kill him," the leader of the group said. But another Khmer Rouge cadre, who liked Pran because he was a good worker, urged mercy. No decision was made, and Pran, trussed and swollen and bleeding, was left kneeling in the open all night to await his fate. It began to rain. "I prayed and prayed to Buddha for my life," he says. "I said if my mother's milk had value, my life would be saved."

By morning, the man who had counseled against the death penalty had persuaded the others. Pran was paraded before the entire commune of six hundred and denounced for his "crime." He was forced to swear that he would never again break the commune's rules. The oath he was made to pronounce was, "If I break the rule, I will give my life to you, to do with as you please."

Once released, he took another risk. Following Buddhist custom, he shaved his head as a sign of gratitude for his salvation. The practice of religion had been forbidden by the Khmer Rouge; all statues of Buddha had been destroyed; monks had been either killed or made to work in the fields as common laborers. Pran's act could have brought another death sentence down upon him.

Somehow, he got by again. When the Khmer Rouge asked him why he had cut off all his hair, he told them he had been having severe headaches and thought this might help. In this land of primitive medical practices, the Communists believed him.

This behavior may seem paradoxical to us, but not to Pran. Although for four years he went to extraordinary lengths to hide his background from the Khmer Rouge in order to stay alive, he never in heart denied himself or his upbringing. He prayed silently all the time. And he never changed his name, the one obvious mark that could have given him away, should anyone have recognized him and turned him in.

"Your name is given to you by your mother and father and by Buddha," he says. "If you are a good person, your name will be lucky and Buddha will protect you."

From 1975 through late 1977, Pran remained in Dam Dek, working at a series of arduous jobs: carrying earth to build the paddy embankments, harvesting and threshing the crop, cooking for a district cooperative of eighteen blacksmiths who forged farm tools, plowing with a team of horses, cutting and sawing trees in the jungle, fishing with hand nets in the Tonle Sap Lake. The workday ran from 4 a.m. to 6 p.m. and during the harvest season, in December and January, a few extra hours at night for threshing. The Communists called these the "assault" months, because everyone had to work faster and harder.

The Draconian rules of life turned Cambodia into a nationwide gulag, as the Khmer Rouge imposed a revolution more radical and brutal than any other in modern history—a revolution that disturbed even the Chinese, the Cambodian Communists' closest allies. Attachment to home village and love of Buddha, Cambodian verities, were replaced by psychological reorientation, mass relocation, and rigid collectivization.

Families were separated, with husbands, wives, and children all working on separate agricultural and construction projects. They were often many miles apart and did not see each other for seasons at a time. Sometimes children were separated completely from their parents, never to meet again. Work crews were sex-segregated. Those already married needed special permission, infrequently given, to meet and sleep together. Weddings were arranged by the Khmer Rouge, en masse; the pairings would simply be called out at a commune assembly. Waves of suicides were the result of these forced marriages. Children were encouraged, even trained, to spy on and report their parents for infractions of the rules. "The Khmer Rouge were very clever," Pran says. "They know that young children do not know how to lie or keep secrets as well as adults, so they always ask *them* for information." Informers, old and young, were everywhere; betrayal could be purchased for a kilo of rice.

Sometimes Khmer Rouge youths were ordered to kill their teachers or even their own parents. Some carried out these acts without apparent qualm. Others were devastated. Pran remembers a case in his district in which a man was identified as an enemy of the commune, and his son, a Khmer Rouge soldier, was told to execute him. He did so, but later, alone, he put the rifle to his own head and killed himself.

Pran says he was always most afraid of those Khmer Rouge soldiers who were between twelve and fifteen years old; they seemed to be the most completely and savagely indoctrinated. "They took them very young and taught them nothing but discipline. Just take orders, no need for a reason. Their minds have nothing inside except discipline. They do not believe any religion or tradition except Khmer Rouge orders. That's why they killed their own people, even babies, like we might kill a mosquito. I believe they did not have any feelings about human life because they were taught only discipline."

Outsiders have asked, in the years since 1975, how a people known as the "smiling, gentle Khmers" could have produced such a holocaust. The image of a bucolic, carefree people was, of course, simplistic—an illusion that foreigners preferred to see. All cultures are complex and all have their hidden savage sides waiting to erupt. The Nazi horror in World War II and the 1947 partition of India in which Hindus and Moslems slaughtered each other by the thousands are but two vivid examples. Nonetheless, the Khmer Rouge terror may have touched a level of cruelty not seen before in our lifetime. It was Cambodians endlessly killing other Cambodians.

Even the victims could not fathom whence the Khmer Rouge had come or how they had been created. "I look at them and do not know them," Pran says. "To me, they are not Khmers."

With their cruelty, the Khmer Rouge brought a new language—words with a dehumanized ring, a mechanical robot-like quality, euphemisms for atrocity, words that people had never heard before. There was the omnipresent *Angka*— the word for the Khmer Rouge regime itself. It means simply "the organization." No explanations were ever given for policy, just *"Angka* says" or *"Angka* orders." People were called *opakar*, or "instruments." The Khmer nation was called "machine," from the French or English—strange for a government trying to erase the colonial past.

And then there was a sinister word, a word with a deceptively polite sound, *sneur*, which means "invite" or "ask." The Khmer Rouge would come to someone's house, Pran explains, and *sneur* someone's son to study or to be educated. Lulled by the gentleness of the request, many went without a protest. But people quickly realized that those who had been *sneured* never came back; the word took on a new meaning: "take away and kill."

Fear and suspicion became the essence of existence. To trust anyone was to risk one's life. People stopped having meaningful conversations, even secretly, even inside their own family. (In July 1979, when Pran decided to make his escape attempt, he was too fearful to tell his mother or sister, who were the only survivors in his family. He was not afraid they would inform on him, but maybe the conversation would be overheard. Or maybe his family would say something inadvertently that would spell trouble for him. "You get used to keeping secrets," he says. "You decide it's better not to tell anything to anybody. I was afraid. Maybe my mother tries to talk me out of it. She worries, she loves me, I am her only son left. What if someone hears her talking?")

In the spring of 1977, a group of "moderates" in the Khmer Rouge leadership plotted a coup. They were discovered by the ruling group and wiped out. But *Angka* did not stop there. Fresh troops were sent to every district to replace and sometimes execute "untrustworthy" ones. The search was intensified for people like Pran, educated people from the Western-oriented past. The cold and wooden teenaged troops did not need evidence; their slaughter was wholesale— teachers, village chiefs, students, sometimes whole villages.

In late 1977, Pran made a move to another village, spurred by these fresh upheavals throughout the country, a new wave of purges and killings, and disquietude on his part that some fanatic villagers in Dam Dek were growing suspicious of him. "There were more killings in 1977 than in 1975," Pran says. "I saw many arrested in my village, hands tied behind their backs, crying for their lives. I got chills down my back, like fever. I kept on talking softly, pretending to support *Angka*. I prayed every day and every night, in my mind." As the radical fervor grew in Dam Dek, Pran looked for a way out.

During 1976 and 1977, he had become acquainted with the commune chief and others in the village of Bat Dangkor, four miles to the north. They seemed to him "not so pro-Communist and more compatible."

Movement from place to place was rigidly controlled and rarely allowed by the Khmer Rouge, but somehow, through gentle pleading and by playing the empty-headed worker, he got permission to move.

Life immediately improved for Pran. Though his work regimen remained severe and food was still not plentiful, his commune chief, a twenty-seven-year-old named Phat who had lost his love for the Khmer Rouge, took a liking to him. Pran became his houseboy, carrying water, chopping firewood, bathing the children, building the fire, washing clothes, and cooking. The days were long, but Pran felt somewhat protected. "I did everything to please him," Pran says. "I was like a slave."

This commune chief had a radio, and sometimes at night—maybe once a week—Pran and four or five trusted friends would gather around it with him and surreptitiously listen to the Voice of America. The V.O.A. came on at 8:30 p.m., and it was on these broadcasts that Pran learned of the fierce fighting throughout 1978 between the Khmer Rouge and the Vietnamese army along the border with Vietnam.

Though both governments were Communist, the Cambodians and Vietnamese were centuries-old ethnic enemies, and now the Chinese were supporting the Khmer Rouge and the Russians were supporting the Vietnamese. Vietnam, in its propaganda broadcasts, called Cambodia "a land of blood and tears, hell on earth," and announced the formation of a new "front" to "liberate" Cambodia. Pran took some hope from this; anything was better than the insane Khmer Rouge.

Finally, in December, he learned on the V.O.A. that the Vietnamese had invaded Cambodia in force. On January 7, 1979, they took Phnom Penh. Three days later, they reached the Siem Reap area, and the Khmer Rouge units around Pran's village took flight.

After a week of careful watching, Pran was persuaded that the Vietnamese were not killing civilians and were allowing people to return to their home villages. So, his spirits up but still cautious, he left Bat Dangkor by moonlight and, smiling a lot at his "liberators" on the way, he walked the twenty-odd miles to the town of Siem Reap to search for his family.

What he found was what most Cambodians found when they returned home: a few survivors but most of their family members dead. Of his mother and father, three brothers, two sisters, and numerous nephews and nieces, only his sixty-three-year-old mother, one sister, a sister-in-law, and five nieces and nephews were alive. One brother, nineteen, had been executed for being a student, the other two for being military officers in the Lon Nol army. One sister had been killed for being the wife of an officer. The sister who survived still had three children; a fourth child was lost to starvation.

Pran's father, a retired public-works official, had died of starvation in late 1975, about the same time that Pran was caught and beaten for stealing the pocketful of rice in Dam Dek. As he lay dying, he called out for Pran's wife, Ser Moeun, who had been close to him and had often brought him special treats from her kitchen. "Ser Moeun, Ser Moeun," he rambled deliriously as his life slipped away, "bring me some of your food and cake."

As Pran re-explored Siem Reap, people kept walking up to him in astonishment, saying, "I thought you died. How did you stay alive?" "Because of my education and background," he says, "no one could believe I could survive."

The reasons for their disbelief lay all around Siem Reap; they were called the "killing fields." "One day soon after I came back," Pran recalls, "two women from my village went looking for firewood in the forest. They found bones and skulls everywhere among the trees and in the wells. When they came back they told me about it and said they would take me there and show me. They asked me, 'Are you afraid of ghosts?' I told them, 'No, why should I be afraid? The ghosts may be my brothers or my sister.'"

So Pran went to see the killing fields. Each of the two main execution areas alone, he says, held the bones of four to five thousand bodies, thinly covered by a layer of earth.

"In the water wells, the bodies were like soup bones in broth," he says. "And you could always tell the killing grounds because the grass grew taller and greener where the bodies were buried."

Similar reports have come from every village in Cambodia: tall green grass and choked wells.

The Vietnamese "liberators," having seized the main towns, set up a client Cambodian government in Phnom Penh and were looking for administrators to help them govern throughout the country. In Siem Reap, local villagers who knew Pran's skills asked for him as their administrative chief, and the two Vietnamese governors of the province agreed. He became, in effect, the mayor of Siem Reap township, which held about ten thousand people. "I took the job out of pity for my people," he says. "They wanted a Cambodian in charge, so I take it to lift them up. There were so few intellectuals still alive. If I don't do it, who will lead and help my people?"

In his new job, Pran wore a khaki uniform with a Soviet-style military cap and carried an AK-47 automatic rifle. Every week he had to give a speech, cleared first by the Vietnamese, to a different section of the population in his township. "I don't talk politics," he says. "I just talk about nationalism, about how you have to work for food. I urge people to work because of the starvation and the low economy."

The two Vietnamese governors, Nhien and Linh, praised him often and showed him considerable respect, "because I helped them a lot to set up the administration. Sometimes they even embraced me." But Pran never stopped thinking about escape. It was during this period that he had cautiously approached the East German correspondent Gerhard Leo and asked him to carry that message—"Dith Pran survivor"—to me. The Vietnamese governors had directed Pran to arrange a welcoming committee of fifty villagers for the journalists, which is how Pran came to be there.

While cheered somewhat by the arrival of the foreigners, he was reluctant at first to approach the group, out of fear that giving away his *New York Times* background might put him in jeopardy. But then he saw Leo walking away from the main group to take some pictures and heard him speaking in French mixed with English. "I was afraid by now of all Communists," he said, "but when he was alone I decided to take a risk because he's a long-nose [Westerner]."

Five months later, Pran's fears were realized. His Vietnamese superiors somehow discovered, perhaps through an informer, that he had worked for American journalists. They called him in, told him he was politically "unclean," said his mind was tainted by "unrevolutionary thoughts," and forced him to resign his job. On July 15, 1979, an election was held in Siem Reap to fill Pran's post. He grew increasingly nervous about what the Vietnamese might do to him now that they had found him out.

✦

The news about Pran from Gerhard Leo in April 1979 put me in a state of euphoria, but it also made me desperate. I knew he had been safe on February 15, but I had no clue as to what was happening to him now. So I began exploring every possible way to get further news of him, to get a message to him, to get him out of the country. Through friends, I quietly sounded out the Vietnamese, but they were unwilling to help, saying it was a domestic Cambodian matter.

I renewed my contacts with international agencies, some of whom were just then making efforts to open relief programs inside Cambodia. The next several months were marked by many long-distance telephone calls, cables in coded language, the passing of money to my contacts in the event bribes were necessary on Pran's behalf once they got inside Cambodia, and, throughout, the private help of Henry Kamm, *The Times'* correspondent in Bangkok, whose dedicated and gifted reporting—perhaps more than any other factor—had made the world aware of the enormity of the refugee problem in Indochina.

In July, my contacts, who were now in Phnom Penh but who could not get to the Siem Reap area, reported that third parties had seen Pran again there on May 7. A later report, in August, said he was okay in the latter part of July, working in some vague capacity for the Vietnamese-installed province committee. Also in August, my contacts sent a cautiously worded letter to Pran through a third party who was going to Siem Reap. It said that I had received his message of survival from Gerhard Leo, that I and his family were "anxious" about "your health," and that if possible he should send either a verbal or written reply back to my contacts in Phnom Penh. My sources were convinced that Pran received this letter—which would have been the first confirmation to him since April 1975 that I had been searching for him and now knew he was alive. But no reply came back from him as I waited nervously through August and September; my contacts were due to come out of Cambodia in early October, and I kept reassuring myself that they would be carrying direct news from Pran.

Pran never did get that letter. In fact, until our reunion on October 9, I was never able to get word to him that his message had reached me or to give him any sign at all of my long search for him. We were functioning in two different worlds, each darkened to the other. While I was counting on his remaining safe and fixed in Siem Reap as I maneuvered through my contacts to extract him from the country through official channels, he took the step he had been planning and dreaming of for four and a half years—he made his move for the border.

On July 29, his relationship with the Vietnamese having broken down, he slipped quietly out of Siem Reap for the village of Phum Trom, forty miles to the northwest. He headed for Phum Trom because he had heard that the anti-Communist resistance, known as *Sereika* (liberation), was active there and was helping people to escape. After six weeks of preparation in that village, he and eleven other men set out before dawn on a morning in mid-September.

In a straight line, the border with Thailand to the north was only about thirty-five miles away. But their route was as the snake crawls—sixty miles—weaving and turning and climbing across brambled jungle and rocky hills to avoid roving bands of Khmer Rouge guerrillas, Vietnamese patrols, deadly punji traps (sharpened bamboo stakes smeared with toxic matter and covered with leaves and brush) and unmarked minefields.

At noon on the second day of their exodus, they stopped briefly to rest. When they rose to start again, Pran, who had been toward the end of the single file, by happenstance began walking third in line. A few minutes later, the two men in front of him, only fifteen feet ahead, were dead; they had stepped on a mine. A piece of shrapnel hit Pran in the left side, but it was only a flesh wound and he was able to run on with the others.

They reached the border on the fourth day. Pran's companions had clandestine contacts there; he did not. So, afraid of being arrested by the Thai authorities if he crossed over, he waited for seventeen days just a few hundred yards on the Cambodian side—in a no-man's-land where he was reasonably safe—watching for the right moment to get across and into the sanctuary of a Cambodian refugee camp fifteen miles away. (During this frustrating wait, he sent letters to me through a courier, who was supposed to mail them from the nearby town of Prasat. Only one ever reached me, and it arrived long after our reunion.)

On the seventeenth day—October 3—with the help of friends who provided him with a uniform worn by the Cambodian resistance, which satisfied the Thais, he crossed the frontier and made it to the refugee camp.

Although finally free, he was still insecure because he was an "illegal"—an unregistered refugee—and could technically be pushed back into Cambodia (the Thais had done this to several thousand Cambodians some months before). Pran instantly searched out an American relief official in the camp, Ruth Ellison, told her his history, and asked her to get word to me through the American Embassy or *The Times*' correspondent in Bangkok. Miss Ellison, who, with her mother and father, had been working in the camp for years, representing a missionary group, called an embassy official as soon as she reached her home in Surin that night. He called Henry Kamm, who called my office. It was Thursday morning, October 4, I was not in yet, and he left no message except that I should call him. My attempts to reach him through the day were unsuccessful, and I was jumpy and tense all day, one moment conjuring up my wildest hope, that Pran had escaped, and the next moment trying to curb my excitement and ease the letdown should the news be innocuous or worse.

✦

At 7:50 p.m., I try to phone Henry again. I get him this time and he says quickly, "Pran is out. He's in Thailand, in a refugee camp at Surin." Skyrockets go off in my head. I can hear Henry saying something about what he is doing at the American Embassy to speed up Pran's entry into the United States, but then I can't grasp it. I'm crying at my desk, and it doesn't matter.

I call Ser Moeun as soon as the Bangkok call is over. It is only 5 p.m. in San Francisco and she is not home yet from her job as clerk in a bank. I get the eldest son, Titony, and blurt out the news. "Hey!" he shouts, as American as a fifty-yard touchdown pass, "aaaaaaaaaallll riiiiight!" Then he turns to his sister and two brothers: "Hey, you guys! Our dad is out of Cambodia! Our dad is out of Cambodia!" They cheer and yell and bang on something. Then I call the Drypolchers and my wife. A few hours later, I get Ser Moeun. The telephone holds a lot of happiness that night.

The next few days are like a dream. I leave on the first available plane for Bangkok to get to Pran. I am high on the miracle but still full of anxiety about getting him across the last bureaucratic barriers, into this country. My plane is three hours late taking off, and it looks as if I have no chance to make my connecting flight in Athens, but that plane is very late, too, and I get on it just in time. I start believing in omens and symbols, for everything is going my way. As I enter my Bangkok hotel room on Sunday afternoon October 7, the first thing my eyes light on is a magazine called *Business in Thailand* lying on an end table. On the cover, its lead article is billboarded in large bold type: PRAWN ON THE WAY.

There is more good fortune at the American Embassy's refugee office, where Pran's case has been given priority and the staff is being spectacularly helpful. By midday Monday, Pran has been put on a special list that will get him out of the refugee camp on Wednesday and down to Bangkok for final processing. With that done, I can leave for the border area, three hundred miles and six hours to the northeast. But without Thai government papers authorizing me to visit the camp, I shall have to wait until the next morning, Tuesday, when the relief worker, Ruth Ellison, can take me in "unofficially" with her. I go to bed in a run-down hotel in Surin shortly after midnight, but I cannot sleep. Finally I give up the attempt and rise at 4 a.m.

On the twenty-mile drive south to the camp, I make small talk to hide my nerves. At 8:40 a.m., we pass through the camp gates, and in five minutes we are outside the hut where Pran is staying with another family. I jump out and run inside, sputtering in French as I ask where Pran is. He's in the long house on stilts fifty feet away, and a young man runs to get him, shouting in Khmer, "Brother, brother, someone's here. You have a chance now. You have a chance." Then Pran comes running out of the long house—I remember in that fraction of a second thinking how hurt and vulnerable he looked—and literally leaps into my arms, his legs wrapped around my waist, his head buried in my shoulder. "You came, Syd, oh, Syd, you came." The words come sobbing out with the tears. We stand like that for several minutes until his thin frame stops shaking and his legs slip to the ground.

He looks at me then and says, "I am reborn. This is my second life."

Arms around each other's shoulders, we walk slowly into the hut and begin talking nonstop, ricocheting from one subject to another in chaotic sequences, as we grope for the meaning of our lost four and a half years.

We talk of his wife and children, of how he disguised his identity to survive the savagery of the Khmer Rouge, of old Western journalist friends, of old Cambodian friends who are now dead, of the members of his family inside Cambodia who were executed, of the Seiko digital watch he has just bought from another refugee in the camp, of the time in 1975 when he was almost beaten to death for stealing a pocketful of rice, and of the letter he wrote to me only two days before, still unaware that I had received any of the messages from him. (That letter arrives at *The Times* on October 24, a week after Pran and I reached the United States. It says in part, "Need see Schanberg. At least a cable from him. We have many things to write.") Restless, pent-up, we walk through the barren camp, sipping an orange soda, holding hands, looking long at each other. There is much waiting to be said.

With trepidation, I ask the question that has been churning inside me since that distant April in 1975. "Can you forgive me for not being able to keep you safe in the French Embassy, for leaving Cambodia without you?"

"No, no," he says, gripping my hand hard. "It's not like that. Nothing to forgive. We both made a decision. We both agree to stay, no one pushed the other. You tried all you could to keep me, but it didn't work. Not your fault. We stayed because we did not believe in a bloodbath. We were fools; we believed there would be reconciliation. But who could have believed the Khmer Rouge would be so brutal?

"We both made mistakes, both of us," he goes on, in a torrent of words that has been locked up so long. "Maybe we should have tried to buy a French passport. We had a lot of money. But I was never angry at you, even when the Khmer Rouge beat me near to death. I always missed you; sometimes I cry in the forest, thinking of you."

Why did Pran wait so long to try to escape? "My brain was always thinking how to get out," he says, "but Khmer Rouge patrols were everywhere and they had mine fields all along the border and traps made of punji sticks. I must build relations in each place where I live. I must take care with each step, to make sure I have good information and at least fifty-fifty chance of not getting killed. One time I was going to try for it but then I heard the Thais were pushing refugees back into Cambodia so I stopped the idea." When he talks about life under the Khmer Rouge, he uses phrases very unlike him—"true hell," "more than insane," "below zero."

The camp loudspeaker suddenly calls his name, summoning him to the camp office. He ignores it. I tell him that probably the embassy document has arrived, clearing him for departure to Bangkok on the following day. It has, but he is uneasy and tells me a friend of his will check it out instead. In his viscera, he is still not convinced he is free. Maybe the Thais, he thinks, will yet force him back into Cambodia. (Even when we reach Bangkok and meet old friends around the hotel pool, Pran's eyes narrow and his voice fades to a whisper whenever he talks about the Khmer Rouge and their policies. "There's no one here," I say. "You can relax." He laughs self-consciously, but he is not persuaded and looks around to see if anyone is listening.)

We start talking again about our separate thoughts and dreams since 1975. They are not very separate. Pran tells me, "I think of you all the time inside Cambodia. I imagine that you adopt one of my sons—probably Titony, the eldest—because you have only girls."

Then he adds, in a rush of memory, "Every month, under the Khmer Rouge, I have dream that you come to get me in a helicopter. I have a radio on the ground and you radio me your position." I tell him I repeatedly had the same fantasy, like a waking dream.

It all seems uncanny and it makes us both elated and yet discomposed. We laugh to break the spell and bring us back to the gritty dust of the camp. Now, more than ever before, we have lionized each other, given each other heroic dimensions. It is mystical, but it is also unreal, and we know that in the times to come we will have to deal with our respective warts and flaws and humanness.

But not just yet. He tells me he always knew I would be loyal to him and to my promises. "In Cambodia, I tell myself," he says, "if I die, I die with my eyes well closed, because I know you will always take care of my family. I trust you one hundred percent."

I tell him I prayed for him often. "Ohhh. Ohhh," he says, marveling. "That explains it. That's why I was so lucky."

I have with me the many joyous written messages from Pran's friends on *The Times*. Some of the writers had met him only through my constant tales. I now take these messages from my briefcase—the same briefcase that still carries that scruffy silk rose I squeezed for luck on the day we were captured in April 1975—and give them to Pran. As he reads, his eyes turn moist again.

Abe Rosenthal, *The Times*' executive editor, writes that "all these years . . . you have been in the minds of all *Times* men and women" and that the news of his return to freedom had brought "rejoicing throughout the paper."

Jim Clarity, whom Pran had shepherded to many scary battle sites, says, "Pran, you are a true hero. I am proud to know you. Now that you are safe, thanks again for keeping me safe."

Al Siegal, whom Pran also guided on a trip to Phnom Penh, writes, "With all my heart and all my love . . . you have given all of us another reason—the most wonderful of reasons—to be proud of our paper and our profession. We embrace you, Pran."

Joe Lelyveld, another of Pran's flock: "I feel freer today because you are free . . . I pray that the rest of your days will be filled with peace."

And so many more.

As Pran folds the last of the notes and puts it away, he murmurs, "They were all thinking of me. Oh, how wonderful."

Pran's mood goes up and down wildly that first day; he weeps at some unspeakable memory and then bursts into laughter over the wonder of our reunion and the good news I bring him about his family thriving in San Francisco. Yet he is concerned about how Westernized they may have become and how he will adjust to them, and they to him, after all this time. "Do they still speak Khmer?" he asks. I tell him I think they speak it often at home.

Suddenly, Pran asks me, "What about your book? Did you finish it?"

"How did you know I was writing a book?" I reply, taken aback.

"Oh," he says, "I was sure with all the notes you take and papers you save you must be going to write a book." I tell him I had become stymied on the project for many reasons, and he looks upset. But then I tell him of the Pulitzer I won and that I accepted it on his behalf as well as mine, and his face becomes incandescent.

He starts talking ebulliently and zanily about going back to work right away with me. "Can I get an American passport?" he asks. "There are many stories to do here. We could work along the border. My people are in trouble. If I had a camera, I could take pictures, too—like the old days." I remind him, laughing, that first he has to get to San Francisco just to get his American refugee-status papers and to rejoin his family, and that I have a family and job in New York. "You're crazy," I say warmly. He remains a driven reporter.

He chortles, too. "Yes, sure, I'm crazy," he says. "I still want to work as a journalist."

We also discuss the medical care he will need. His legs and feet are scarred from his march out of Cambodia. Many of his teeth are loose and rotting from malnutrition; there is a large gap between his two front teeth where porcelain fillings fell out in 1976. He keeps his hands in his pockets much of the time because when he holds them out, they shake like those of a palsied old man—also from malnutrition.

On the drive back to Bangkok the next day—October 10—we stop for breakfast at a hotel in Korat. Pran orders only milk and coffee, saying his stomach is not ready for a big meal. He is uncomfortable in the modern dining room. When he has to go to the toilet, he asks me to take him. "I feel like a monkey," he says, embarrassed.

We arrive in our hotel room in Bangkok at 2 p.m. At exactly 2:03, the message button on the telephone lights up. The post office has just delivered a large envelope from Pran's wife. In it are letters from his family and the first pictures of them he has seen since their evacuation from Phnom Penh on April 12, 1975. He opens the packet, reads the letters with tears in his eyes, and then examines the color photographs incredulously. Titonel, the youngest, was only three when they parted. Titony, now fifteen, has grown bigger and taller than his father from his rich American diet. Pran scans the pictures again and again, holds them at arm's length, and shakes his head. "I don't think I would know them if I saw them on the street," he says, in wonder. "I am sure I would not know Titonel."

Pran's first telephone call to his family is both jubilant and uneasy. The electronic reunions that occupy the first part of the call are ecstatic. But then Pran tries speaking in Khmer to the children and comes away a little distressed when he realizes that the two youngest, Titonel and Titonath, understand almost nothing of what he has said. The traditionalist father in him is troubled.

But there is something more important on his mind. He gets Ser Moeun back on the phone and tells her of the fortune-teller in Cambodia who, in early 1979, read Pran's "numbers" and told him that the forecast for his eldest son was zero—which means death or the threat of death. Pran has been worried about Titony ever since, and now tells Ser Moeun to take him immediately to a Buddhist priest, get some holy water, and have Titony drink it. She agrees and has it done before we get to the States.

✦

Culture shock is too mild a phrase to describe what overtook Pran in Bangkok. This was his first trip outside his own country, and Bangkok is a much more modern city than once-graceful and somnolent Phnom Penh. During his ten days in the Thai capital Pran did many things he had not been able to do for four and a half years, such as sleep in a real bed, eat a full meal (his first entrée was *escalopes de veau cordon bleu*), wear a shirt tucked inside his pants, and use a mirror in which he could see his whole body. But other phenomena he was experiencing for the first time in his life: a department store (where he bought Wrangler corduroy jeans), a divided highway, pancakes and syrup.

Other things were traumatically new, too. When my story about his escape appeared on the front page of *The Times* on October 12, calls and cables began streaming in. Some were from elated old friends. Others were from people who wanted him to go on lecture tours, write a book, make a movie, appear on television, give interviews for magazines and newspapers.

From total disguise and anonymity and silence behind Cambodia's bamboo curtain, Pran had stepped into the blaring media age. But what possibly overwhelmed him most was the realization—from the correspondence and clippings and letters I had brought him and from the fresh communications arriving at the hotel—of how many people had been aware of him and his plight and of how many people had cared about him through his four and a half years of misery. Though baffled by it all, he was warmed by the celebrity attention. He asked me to handle all the inquiries, and I became his press secretary. Our roles were changing, I was somewhat disoriented by it. In fact, I wasn't sure I liked it.

Among the cables was one from Jon Swain, the British journalist whose life Pran had saved along with mine when we were captured by the Khmer Rouge. It read, "Sydney, this is the most wonderful, wonderful news. Please give Pran my love and a big hug from someone who owes him everything." Pran's reply to Jon read something like a Cambodian proverb. "Hi, Jon. The world is round. Now I meet you again. Pran was in bad shape, but the life is remained. Love, Pran."

After a few days, I noticed that Pran had begun to hum and even sing again, pleasures that were not allowed in Cambodia. He was coming alive. His health, however, remained fragile. As we pushed through the many days of medical exams, security checks, and governmental procedures—both Thai and American—necessary for final clearance to leave for San Francisco, Pran was hit by periodic waves of high fever. We both eventually suspected it might be malaria, but, afraid that detection in Thailand could lead to a long period in quarantine for Pran, we decided to treat it through the easygoing hotel doctor and with store-bought antibiotics.

The first time it happened—the night of October 12—we thought it was some kind of flu or viral infection. We didn't have a thermometer, but his body was burning up, so I threw a pile of ice cubes into a tub and made him take a cold bath. It brought the fever down somewhat, but he ached all over, so I got him back into bed, put a cold cloth on his sweating forehead, and gave him a back and head massage. I also gave him fruit juices and antibiotic tablets.

By morning, the fever had broken, and we sat around joking about the "counactional movement" developing in our hotel room. "*You* used to see to *my* needs," I told him, as he laughed. "Now things are reversed. What's going on?" I was getting rid of some of my pique over our changed roles; it was a healthy development.

Later, on another night when I was feeling achy and he was massaging *my* back, he told me that he had, on occasion, been ordered to give massages to Khmer Rouge troops when they were sick. "Just think of me as the Khmer Rouge," I said, continuing our jesting.

In between his fever bouts and forays into bureaucratic red tape, Pran spent his time resting, eating, and giving interviews to television and print journalists. He also kept pulling out the pictures of his children and staring at them for long periods of time.

Though he was groping with his radically changing life and moving into the future, the past was never too far away. One morning, during a break in an interview with Australian television on the hotel's broad lawn, he saw a line of red ants marching up the trunk of a coconut palm. "That's what we used to eat for food when we had nothing else," he said in a monotone. On another morning, I felt like a swim in the pool and asked Pran to join me. "No," he said with a grimace. "I was out in the sun for four years in the rice paddies. I don't need any more."

In the middle of one night, we were startled awake by the phone. It was Sylvain Julienne, a French freelance photographer who had taken in an orphaned Cambodian infant in the days before Phnom Penh's fall and had been with us in the French Embassy. He was overjoyed by Pran's escape, but there was a shadow in his mind as well. He was desperate for news of Sou Vichith, a Cambodian photographer he was very close to. He asked Pran nervously if he knew anything about Vichith. Pran told him ruefully that the reports he heard were that Vichith died of some illness in Kompong Cham Province in the early days of Khmer Rouge control.

Our flight home to San Francisco on October 19 was an anxious eighteen-hour journey—anticipation and agitation in equal doses, as the family reunion neared. On the last leg of the flight, I turned to Pran and asked him, just out of curiosity, what was the first thing he wanted to do when he saw his family. His face spread into an elfin grin and then he just buried his head in my right shoulder and giggled and giggled in embarrassment. I told him that I had asked the question innocently, not thinking at all about marital pleasures, but he just kept giggling.

A few hours from San Francisco, the fever struck again. He popped another handful of the hotel doctor's pills into his mouth, and his temperature subsided. As we neared the shores of the United States, he became very nervous, his right knee jiggling up and down like a telegraph key gone wild.

The reunion at the airport was sweet trauma—a crush of flowers, deep hugs, tears and television cameras. After that day, Pran would have no difficulty recognizing his children on the street.

We departed for Ser Moeun's modest attached house in the Sunset section, near the ocean, where Pran's first American meal awaited. It was Kentucky Fried Chicken; Ser Moeun had been too excited to cook. The television set was turned on to a puppet show. The family album, holding all the photographs of the years he had been away, was brought to him. He could not absorb it all, and I left with the Drypolchers for their house, so that the family could be alone.

During the night, Pran's fever flared anew. Ser Moeun called us at 1:45 to say that his temperature had risen to 105 degrees. We rushed over and took him to the emergency room of Kaiser Permanente Hospital. I stayed with him all night, as blood, urine, and sputum tests were made. He couldn't sleep. His mind—as it had repeatedly since our reunion—raced over the past and he chattered in a stream of consciousness about our adventures in the good old days.

About the day our car broke down past the airport in desolate emptiness—almost into Khmer Rouge territory—and we frantically tried to push it back toward Phnom Penh and finally got a push from a government truck whose driver was as nervous as we were. And about the day the Khmer Rouge seized Phnom Penh and trained their rockets on the Hotel Le Phnom and ordered all the Westerners out and we took pictures of them with their rockets and Pran joked about getting the pictures developed at our regular photo shop, My Ho, and mailing them to the Khmer Rouge. And on and on he went.

By midmorning, his illness was definitely diagnosed as malaria. Prescriptions were written for chloroquine and primaquine, and we took him home. Later he told me, "When you were in the hospital that night, you were exhausted, but still you took care of me. I look at your face and I think, you and I, it seems like we are born from the same mother. I kept talking about everything else," he explained, "because it was very difficult to tell you these things."

✦

A few days later it is time for another difficult parting, for I must return to New York, while he recovers his health.

Even though the leave-taking is only temporary, it is disquieting nonetheless for both of us. It is my turn now to manufacture diverting conversation, choosing a tone of avuncular guidance, as I tell him to follow the doctor's orders, open a checking account, take long walks, eat well, et cetera.

Then, in a futile attempt to hide my feelings and lighten the moment, I tease him about our old argument in Phnom Penh on that day when I pushed him hard to tell me "the whole truth," an argument that had since become a kind of special folklore between us. That argument had ended with Pran saying he could not tell me the entire truth, only eighty percent of it, because "twenty percent I have to keep for myself."

"Is it still only eighty percent?" I ask now, gibing at him fondly.

"No, not anymore," he says, in a tone as solemn as mine was airy. "There is nothing to hide. No more secrets. No more camouflage. We both have the same blood."

◆

Author's Note: After Dith Pran escaped from Cambodia in late 1979, he became a successful news photographer for The New York Times. *When* The Killing Fields *film was made of his story of captivity and my search for him, he also became an international crusader for his Cambodian people—and for all people who suffer and die in wars and genocides. He was a peacemaker. He was endeared around the world. After twenty-eight happy years at* The Times, *he was suddenly seized by pancreatic cancer and died on Sunday, March 30, 2008—at the age of sixty-five—with friends and Buddhist monks and all his family around him. He will not be forgotten. He will always be my brother.*

CHAPTER THREE

East Pakistan Fights to Become
Independent Bangladesh

All articles in this chapter were published in The New York Times.

PAKISTAN'S MILITARY CRACKS DOWN ON EAST PAKISTAN
FREEDOM MOVEMENT
March 21, 1971

DACCA, Pakistan—"If you are united, there is no power on earth which can prevent you from getting Pakistan."

These words were spoken to a Bengali crowd in East Pakistan 25 years ago by Mohammad Ali Jinnah, head of the Muslim League and father of the unlikely two-part country known as Pakistan, whose east and west wings are separated not only by 1,000 miles of Indian territory but also by their different cultures and languages.

Pakistan came into being in 1947, a year after the late Mr. Jinnah's speech. But if the East Pakistanis ever shared any of his feelings of unity, that day is long past. The two wings are now confronting each other like two enemy countries.

In this recent escalation of animosity, the 75 million Bengalis of East Pakistan, led by Sheik Mujibur Rahman, have taken de facto control of their province, defying the martial-law regime imposed here by the central government in West Pakistan and obeying only the directive of the Sheik and his Awami League party.

The armed forces, an instrument of West Pakistan, have reinforced their garrisons in the East; tension is high and many Bengalis fear an army bloodbath to prevent them from gaining independence, or even a large measure of self-rule. Clashes between civilians and West Pakistani soldiers erupt occasionally.

Gen. Yahya Khan—Army Commander-In-Chief and the President of Pakistan since he took over as martial-law ruler after the fall of the Ayub Khan Government amid bloody riots two years ago—has flown here from the West to try to resolve the crisis through talks with Sheik Mujibur.

The talks are really moving now, after several days of little discernible progress. But few details are known, and it is difficult to tell what formula of self-rule will emerge to satisfy East Pakistan's determination to end the long domination and economic exploitation by West Pakistan.

The Sheik's student and worker followers have been screaming for total independence since early this month, when West Pakistani troops killed scores of Bengali civilians.

The Bengalis had been staging protest demonstrations against President Yahya's last-minute postponement of the National Assembly, in which more populous East Pakistan had won a clear majority in national elections last December.

Sheik Mujibur would settle for something just short of independence—perhaps for two largely self-ruling regions and a central government with powers restricted to defense and some foreign policy matters.

The present speculation—and in this mercurial situation it could change overnight—is that the talks will produce some temporary arrangement for transferring power from the military to civilians. This could mean the establishment of interim governments in each of the five provinces (the four provinces of West Pakistan, plus East Pakistan) until the National Assembly, now re-scheduled to convene on Thursday, adopts a new constitutional structure for the country.

After the Army killings early this month, the Sheik made some new demands, including immediate transfer of power to the people's representatives and the lifting of martial law. It is expected that martial law will be softened, if not lifted, during the interim period.

The confrontation across the bargaining table in Dacca is ironic in that Sheik Mujibur and President Yahya are not enemies. General Yahya was the first Pakistani President to acknowledge the West's exploitation of the East and to try to do something to end it by holding elections according to the one-man, one-vote procedure, which gave East Pakistan the dominant voice.

That comprehension of East Pakistan's grievances is one reason for hope for a break in the deadlock.

PAKISTANI ARMY SETS DACCA ABLAZE
March 28, 1971

Editor's Note, March 27, 1971—Mr. Schanberg was one of 35 foreign newsmen expelled Saturday morning from East Pakistan. He cabled this dispatch from Bombay, India.

DACCA, Pakistan—The Pakistani Army is using artillery and heavy machine guns against unarmed East Pakistani civilians to crush the movement for autonomy in this province of 75 million people.

The attack began late Thursday night without warning. West Pakistani soldiers, who predominate in the Army, moved into the streets of Dacca, the provincial capital, to besiege the strongholds of the independence movement, such as the university.

There was no way of knowing how many civilians had been killed or wounded. Neither was any information available on what was happening in the rest of the province although there had been reports before the Dacca attack of clashes between civilians and West Pakistani soldiers in the interior.

The firing here was at first sporadic, but by 1 A.M. yesterday it had become heavy and nearly continuous and it remained that way for three hours. Scores of artillery bursts were seen and heard by foreign newsmen confined to the Intercontinental Hotel on threat of death.

From the hotel, which is in North Dacca, huge fires could be seen in various parts of the city, including the university area and the barracks of the East Pakistan Rifles, a paramilitary force made up of Bengalis, the predominant people of East Pakistan.

Some fires were still burning and sporadic shooting was continuing early this morning when the 35 foreign newsmen were expelled from Dacca.

"My God, my God," said a Pakistani student watching from a hotel window, trying to keep back tears, "they're killing them. They're slaughtering them."

On the ride to the airport in a guarded convoy of military trucks, the newsmen saw troops setting fire to the thatched-roof houses of poor Bengalis who live along the road and who are some of the staunchest supporters of the self-rule movement.

"Bangla Desh is finished, many people are killed," a West Pakistani soldier at the airport said in a matter-of-fact tone. Bangla Desh, or Bengal Nation, was the name adopted by leaders of the autonomy movement in East Pakistan.

When the military action began on Thursday night, soldiers, shouting victory slogans, set ablaze large areas in many parts of Dacca after first shooting into the buildings with automatic rifles, machine guns and recoilless rifles.

The firing started at about 11 P.M., but at first it was intermittent and it was not clear that a full-scale military operation had started.

When the foreign newsmen, all of whom were staying at the Intercontinental Hotel, tried to go outside to find out what was happening, they were forced back in by a heavily reinforced army guard and told they would be shot if they tried to step out of the building.

Telephone calls to friends and news sources in the city brought reports of scattered shooting and civilians putting up barricades in the streets. At 12:20 A.M., a call to the home of Sheik Mujibur Rahman, leader of the independent movement, was answered by a man who said he was an official of the Awami League, Sheik Mujib's political party.

"The situation is very bad," he said, and he added that Sheik Mujib was in his bedroom. The Pakistan radio reported later that Sheik Mujib was arrested at 1:30 A.M. The report said that five of his colleagues were also arrested.

The firing began to increase in the vicinity of the hotel and at 1 A.M. it seemed to become very heavy all over the city. Artillery opened up, but it was difficult to tell where the shells were landing. Some, however, seemed to be falling in the areas of the university and the East Pakistan Rifles headquarters.

At 1:25 A.M., the phones at the hotel went dead, shut down by order of the military guard outside. The lights on the telegraph office tower went out at about the same time. Heavy automatic-weapons fire could be heard in the university area and other districts.

Occasionally there would be an answering report, perhaps from one of the old rifles that some of the militant students were reported to have been collecting. But at no time was there any significant answering fire.

At about 2:15 A.M. a jeep with a mounted machine gun drove by the front of the hotel, turned left on Mymensingh Road and stopped in front of a shopping bazaar, with its gun trained on the second floor windows. A dozen soldiers on foot joined those on the jeep, one group carrying some kind of rocket piece.

From the second floor suddenly came cries of "Bengalis, unite!" and the soldiers opened fire with the machine gun, spraying the building indiscriminately. The soldiers then started moving down an alley adjacent to the bazaar, firing into, and then overturning cars that were blocking the alley. The scene was lit by the soldiers' flashlights, and to the newsmen watching from the 10th floor of the Intercontinental, it was an incredible drama.

As the soldiers were firing down the alley, a group of about 15 or 20 young Bengalis started along the road toward them, from about 200 yards off. They were shouting in defiance at the soldiers, but they seemed unarmed and their hands appeared empty.

The machine gun on the jeep swung around toward them and opened fire. Soldiers with automatic rifles joined in. The Bengali youths scattered into the shadows on both sides of the road. It was impossible to tell whether any had been wounded or killed.

The soldiers then turned their attention back to the alley. They set a spare-parts garage on fire and then moved on to what was apparently their main objective, the office and press of *The People*, an English-language daily paper that had strongly supported Sheik Mujib and ridiculed the army.

Shouting in Urdu, the language of West Pakistan, the soldiers warned any persons inside that unless they surrendered they would be shot. There was no answer and no one emerged. The troops then fired a rocket into the building and followed this with small-arms fire and machine-gun bursts. Then they set fire to the building and began smashing the press and other equipment.

Moving farther along, they set ablaze all the shops and shacks behind the bazaar and soon the flames were climbing high above the two-story building. Then they came back down the alley toward the street, waving their hands in the air and shouting war cries.

They were shouting "Narai Takbir," a Moslem cry meaning "victory for God," and "Pakistan Zindabad!"—"Long Live Pakistan!"

In the distance, fire that looked as though it extended over at least an acre lighted the sky. Pakistani journalists in the hotel said two dormitories at the university appeared to be on fire.

Shortly after 4 A.M. the shouting eased somewhat, but artillery rounds and machine-gun bursts could be heard occasionally. Tracer bullets from a long way off flew by the hotel.

At 4:45 A.M., another big fire blazed, in the direction of the East Pakistan Rifles headquarters.

At 5:45, in the hazy light of dawn, six Chinese-made T-54 light tanks with soldiers riding on them rumbled into the city and began patrolling main thoroughfares.

The intermittent firing and occasional artillery bursts continued through yesterday and early today, right up to the time the newsmen were expelled.

Helicopters flew overhead yesterday morning, apparently on reconnaissance. Four helicopters given to Pakistan by Saudi Arabia for relief work after last November's cyclone and tidal wave in East Pakistan were reported being used for the military operation in the province.

At 7 A.M. the Dacca radio, which had been taken over by the army, announced that President Agha Mohammad Yahya Khan had arrived back in West Pakistan and would address the nation at 8 P.M.

A West Pakistan brigadier who came into the hotel was asked by newsmen what the military operation was all about. "We've taken over, it's as simple as that," he said.

A military vehicle with a loudspeaker went through the streets issuing a warning. People immediately went to their roofs to remove the black flags that had been one of the symbols of the non-cooperation movement.

Shortly after 8 A.M., a black 1959 Chevrolet with an armed escort of troops in jeeps and trucks pulled up in front of the hotel. This convoy was to take Zulfikar Ali Bhutto and his party to the airport to fly back to West Pakistan.

Mr. Bhutto, the dominant political leader of West Pakistan, opposed Sheik Mujib's demands for East Pakistan autonomy.

It is generally accepted that his opposition, supported or engineered by the army and business establishment in West Pakistan, was what forced the crisis. Mr. Bhutto, who is aware that the Bengalis largely blame him for their present troubles, came into the lobby flanked by civilian and army bodyguards with automatic weapons. He looked frightened and brushed off all newsmen's questions with, "I have no comment to make."

Just before he left the hotel, the Dacca radio said that anyone who violated the curfew would be shot. It then went off the air for an hour and a half, signing off with the Pakistan national anthem sung in Urdu. One of the clerks at the hotel desk leaned on the counter, his hands clasped and shaking in front of him, his eyes brimming with tears.

At 10 A.M. the radio announced the new martial orders that were said to be necessary because "unbridled political activity had assumed an alarming proportion beyond the normal control of the civil administration."

Every time newsmen in the hotel asked officers for information, they were rebuffed. All attempts to reach diplomatic missions failed. In one confrontation, a captain grew enraged at a group of newsmen who had walked out the front door to talk to him. He ordered them back into the building and, to their retreating backs, he shouted, "I can handle you. If I can kill my own people, I can kill you."

No information was available on what role was played by the East Pakistan Rifles, the Bengali paramilitary force, and the East Bengal Regiment, a heavily Bengali army unit stationed 25 miles north of Dacca.

The Bengali population considered these units potentially sympathetic but the army insisted that they were loyal to the Government.

Shortly after noon, as artillery bursts and automatic fire could be heard in the city, the Dacca radio announced: "The general situation in the province has been brought under control."

The British Broadcasting Corporation reported at 5 P.M. Friday that Calcutta had monitored a clandestine broadcast saying that Sheik Mujib was calling on his people to carry on the fight against the "enemy forces."

Shortly afterward, the military Government sent word to the hotel that foreign newsmen must be ready to leave by 6:15 P.M. The newsmen packed and paid their bills, but it was 8:20, just after President Yahya's speech, before their convoy of five trucks with soldiers in front and in back, left for the airport.

Just before leaving, the lieutenant colonel in charge was asked by a newsman why the foreign press had to leave. "We want you to leave because it would be too dangerous for you," he said. "It will be too bloody." All the hotel employees and other foreigners in the hotel believed that once the newsmen left, carnage would begin.

"This isn't going to be a hotel," said a hotel official, "it's going to be a bloody hospital."

At the airport, with firing going on in the distance, the newsmen's luggage was rigidly checked and some television firm, particularly that of the British Broadcasting Corporation, was confiscated.

REPORTER'S NOTEBOOK: STICKS AND OLD RIFLES AGAINST TANKS
March 29, 1971

NEW DELHI—The people of East Pakistan, armed with sticks, spears and home-made rifles, are mounting a resistance movement against a military force from West Pakistan that is armed with planes, bombs, tanks and heavy artillery.

The resistance, which began after a surprise attack on the civilian population by the Government force three nights ago, sprang from a nonviolent drive for provincial autonomy.

The East Pakistanis tried to claim the majority political power they had won in the elections last December, and the army moved to prevent this.

Earlier this month, Maj. Saddiqui Salik, public relations officer for the martial-law administration in East Pakistan, was telling foreign newsmen about the role of the Pakistani Army in dealing with disobedient civilians.

"When you call in the army," said the tall West Pakistani officer, "it's a last resort. The army would shoot to kill."

The remark was prophetic. Two weeks later, starting last Thursday night, the Pakistani Army apparently began killing anybody who moved in the streets of Dacca or who shouted defiance from a window. The troops used artillery, machine guns, recoilless rifles and rockets against East Pakistani civilians to crush the Bengali movement for self-rule.

East Pakistan and West Pakistan are divided by the northern breadth of India. Their peoples have different languages, cultures, physical appearances. Ever since the country was carved out of the Indian subcontinent in 1947, on the basis of the Moslem religion shared by the two regions, the West has dominated the East.

The army comes from the West. Big business is concentrated there; the per capita income is higher; prices are lower. Everything is better for the 55 million West Pakistanis than for the 75 million East Pakistanis.

Many Bengalis, as the people of East Pakistan are known, had fled the city in the last few weeks for home villages in the interior.

Foreign newsmen, including this correspondent, were expelled from East Pakistan on Saturday. Their film and notebooks were confiscated in thorough body and luggage searches.

Most of the East's foreign exchange earnings and taxes went for development projects in the West and for the support of the army, which consumes more than 60 percent of the national budget. Fewer than 10 percent of the troops are Bengalis.

The army has acquired most of its weapons from the United States, the Soviet bloc and Communist China. So far, none of the major powers have criticized the army's action in East Pakistan.

✦

Heavy secrecy surrounded the political talks in Dacca, whose breakdown was followed by the army's surprise attack. But the bits and pieces that have come to light make it clear that the power establishment in the West never intended to let Sheik Mujib win a significant measure of autonomy for East Pakistan.

Many observers believe that the dominant political leader of West Pakistan, Zulfikar Ali Bhutto, was used by the army and major West Pakistan business families to sabotage the talks so that they could keep control of East Pakistan.

President Agha Mohammad Yahya Khan—whose image as a potentially decent general, sympathetic to the Bengalis' grievances, has changed drastically —said that the talks had broken down because Sheik Mujib refused to let an agreement be negotiated at a session of the newly elected National Assembly. But Sheik Mujib knew that he had to get an agreement in writing before the Assembly met.

✦

The talks dragged on for 10 days and the Bengali "bush telegraph" said that they were taking too long, that something was wrong.

During this time, Sheik Mujib and his Awami League defied the martial-law administration by leading a nonviolent movement of noncooperation with the virtually unanimous support of the population.

Sheik Mujib's followers took over certain Government agencies, closed others and ignored directives, such as the one that ordered civilian defense employees to report to work or face 10 years "rigorous imprisonment."

The green, red and gold flag of Bangla Desh—Bengali for Bengal Nation—was unveiled and militant students and workers began demanding complete independence, not simply semi-autonomy.

But those buoyant days for the Bengalis ended quickly. After initial reports of progress the talks slowed and fears of an army crackdown revived.

Troops were flown in daily from West Pakistan, and many Bengalis began to believe that the negotiations were being deliberately prolonged to give the Government in West Pakistan time to get heavy reinforcements to the East.

✦

Clashes between civilians erupted in several towns and a number of deaths were reported. Sheik Mujib denounced what he called "a reign of terror" in a statement distributed last Thursday just before 7 P.M. Four hours later the troops moved into the streets and began firing.

No one knows whether the 51-year-old Sheik Mujib is alive and free, as the clandestine radio of Bangla Desh asserts, or under arrest, as the army insists. But alive or dead, he is the symbol of resistance in East Pakistan.

In addition to the unconfirmed reports of organized operations against the West Pakistani troops, there are some clearer clues that there is resistance.

On Friday morning, 15 rigid new regulations were issued, including one aimed at the noncooperation movement. All Government employees were ordered to report to work by 10 A.M. Saturday or face trial in a military court.

At 12 noon Saturday, Radio Pakistan announced that all department heads had to submit the names of absentees to martial-law headquarters. There seemed no reason for this order unless large numbers of Bengalis were still staying away from their Government jobs.

✦

The exact number of West Pakistani troops in East Pakistan is unknown. Some diplomatic sources estimate that there were 25,000 before the crisis. Since then, troop ships have been dispatched from Karachi and one report said that some had reached Chittagong. Daily flights also carry troops from the West.

Fresh estimates place the troop strength at over 30,000 and some reports put it as high as 60,000, though this seems high.

Another problem for the West Pakistanis is the fact that all flights must take the long 2,800-mile route by way of Ceylon. India banned Pakistani flights over her territory in early February after two Kashmiris hijacked an Indian Airlines plane to Pakistan and blew it up there.

If Ceylon were to change her mind and deny Pakistan landing and refueling rights, the military offensive would be badly hurt. The Pakistanis are already low on airplane fuel and one recent report said they had asked Burma for supplies.

Yet in the end, the terrain may be the decisive factor, for while the army may keep a grip for some time on the cities—Dacca, Chittagong, Khulna and Rajshahi—it seems doubtful it could move effectively in the primitive interior.

BENGALI OFFICER FEIGNS DEATH AND ESCAPES EXECUTION
April 17, 1971

AGARTALA, India, April 13—On the night of March 25, Dabir recalls, he and the two other East Pakistani officers in the 53d Field Artillery Regiment were standing outside when they heard their commander tell the West Pakistani officers he had summoned to his office:

"All of you go now to the city, and by morning I want to see the whole of Comilla filled with corpses. If any officer hesitates to do so, I'll have no mercy on him."

Late in the afternoon of March 30, Dabir says, after five days of house arrest for himself and the two other Bengali officers, the West Pakistanis sent an officer to their room to execute them—but Dabir, wounded, escaped by feigning death.

He has now joined the forces fighting for the independence of Bangla Desh, or Bengal Nation, as the Bengali population has named East Pakistan.

Dabir's experience was apparently no exception. All over East Pakistan—according to Western evacuees, and Bengali soldiers and refugees—West Pakistanis, who dominate the armed forces, were killing their East Pakistani comrades in uniform to deny the independence movement a cadre of military leaders. The sources report that the families of many Bengali officers were also rounded up and killed.

The breakdown of the code of the soldier—officers and troops killing men with whom they had fought—perhaps depicts as well as any other facet of this conflict the depth of the racial hatred felt by the West Pakistanis, who are Punjabis and Pathans, for the 75 million Bengalis of East Pakistan.

The killing of Bengali soldiers began on the night that the army launched its effort to try to crush the independence movement.

Dabir, a slightly built second lieutenant who is 20 years old and unmarried, told his story of that night and the days that followed to this correspondent at a post in the eastern sector of East Pakistan.

Dabir is not his real name; he asked that a pseudonym be used on the chance that some members of his family—his parents, a brother and three sisters—might still be alive.

Talking in a soft, almost unemotional voice, he gave this account:

After the West Pakistani officers left the commander's office and headed for the armory to get their weapons, the three unarmed Bengali officers were called in and placed under what amounted to house arrest, although the commander said they were being given office duties.

That night, which they were made to spend in the room next to the commander's, Dabir could not sleep. At 1 A.M. seven or eight shots were fired somewhere in the compound.

During the next three days, as Dabir and the two others, both captains, answered telephones and shuffled papers under the watch of sentries, they heard the sounds of machine-gun, small-arms and artillery fire in the distance.

Through a window they saw the 60 Bengali soldiers of the regiment being taken off behind a building, their hands in the air, by West Pakistani troops. Then the three heard a sustained burst of firing and assumed that the Bengalis had been killed.

All pretense was dropped on March 29 and the three officers were locked in a room together. They passed the night in fear.

On the afternoon of the 30th a West Pakistani officer walked up to the door and broke the glass with the barrel of a submachine gun.

One Bengali captain fell to his knees and begged for mercy. The answer was a burst of fire. The West Pakistani then fired a second burst into the other captain.

Dabir pressed himself against the wall next to the door. The West Pakistani tried the locked door, cursed and went away for the key.

Dabir threw himself under his cot and covered his head with his hands. The man returned. "I shrieked," Dabir said. "He fired. I felt a bullet hit me. I made a noise as if I was dying. He stopped firing, thinking I was dead, and went away."

One bullet had struck Dabir's right wrist, another had grazed his cheek and a third had ripped his shirt up the back. He rubbed blood from his wrist over his face and held his breath when other officers returned to make sure all three were dead.

The West Pakistanis poked and prodded until they were satisfied. For the next two and a half hours soldiers kept coming into the room to view the spectacle. A Punjabi sergeant kicked the bodies of the two captains. Each time Dabir desperately held his breath.

"Time passed," Dabir continued. "The blood dried and flies gathered on my wound. The smell was bad."

After seven hours Dabir left by the window and dropped four feet to the ground. A sentry heard him and began firing, but it was dark and the shots went wild. Other soldiers in the compound also opened fire, but Dabir made it past the last sentry post, crawled through a rice paddy, swam across a small river and escaped. The next day a country doctor removed the bullet from his wrist and bandaged him.

Dabir looks like a boy—he weighs only 120 pounds—but his manner leaves no doubt that he is fully grown now, only three months after graduating fourth in his class from the military academy at Kakul, in West Pakistan.

His hatred for the West Pakistanis is intense but controlled. "Without any reason they have killed us," he said. "They have compelled us to stand against them."

CHOLERA, HUNGER AND DEATH AS REFUGEES FLEE TO INDIA
June 9, 1971

KARIMPUR, India—Sickness, hunger and death are common scenes now along India's 1,350-mile border with East Pakistan. Millions of Bengalis—unofficial figures put the number over five million—have fled East Pakistan to escape the Pakistani Army, which since late March has been trying to crush the movement for autonomy, and later independence, in East Pakistan.

The Bengalis have brought cholera with them. Official figures put the death toll here in West Bengal state at 3,600, but reports indicate that it is much higher—probably well over 5,000. A thousand or more others have died in the three other border states where the Bengalis have taken refuge.

Here, in this Indian town near the border, a mother had died of cholera an hour before but the infant, less than a year old, continued to nurse until a doctor came upon the scene and pulled him gently away.

A few feet away on the cold cement porch of the health center another person had just died—a 70-year-old grandfather, Abinash Malakar.

His son sat crumpled and crying beside the stiffening emaciated body. Flies had begun to gather. A granddaughter hung, wailing, in the arms of an aunt. This family, from the Jessore district in East Pakistan, had walked for 13 days to reach India.

The toll rises steadily and, with new waves of refugees pouring into India daily, there is no way to predict when the epidemic will end.

Along the roadsides lie the bodies left by those too frightened of the disease themselves to take the time for burial.

Vultures, dogs and crows fight. Skeletons already picked clean bleach in the sun. A few bodies have been buried in shallow graves but the vultures have torn the graves open.

The roads leading from the border are a trail of clothes and bones. A body floats in a marsh or stream. The stench is acrid and villagers cover their faces as they hurry past.

In some towns, attempts have been made to bury the bodies in mass graves. Here in Karimpur, 120 miles north of Calcutta by road, five relief workers buried several hundred in a 24-hour period. But even at these sites, packs of stray dogs dig in the earth.

In many ways the scene is a repetition of the horror of the cyclone that killed hundreds of thousands in the Delta area of East Pakistan last November—leaving bodies for days in marshes, streams and bays.

The tiny, jammed health center at Karimpur—it has 20 beds and over 100 cholera patients—is typical of the overworked health stations along the border.

The sounds of the epidemic—coughing, vomiting, groaning and weeping—echo through the small brick building and across the lawn, also crowded with victims.

Shatish Matabbar—the father of the infant who had gone on nursing after his mother died—stood on the porch in tattered clothes, sobbing out his tale.

"No words can describe what has happened to me," the 45-year old rice farmer wailed. "My wife is dead. Three of my children are dead. What else can happen?"

The infant and an 8-year-old have survived, although the older almost died of cholera. He sat on the floor near his father—naked, staring blankly, underfed.

The family came to India a month ago from their farm in the Faridpur district of East Pakistan.

Why had he left East Pakistan? a visitor asked.

"Why, you ask?" he said, crying again. "Because the Pakistani soldiers burned down my house."

In the last day or two, the death rate in some areas declined a little. This is apparently because foreign medical and relief supplies have begun arriving in sufficient quantities—saline solution to treat the victims and syringes for mass inoculations. Hundreds of thousands have been vaccinated.

But doctors are reluctant to say that the epidemic will be under control soon. For one thing, though India's army medical corps has been called in, medical facilities and personnel are inadequate.

The epidemic is apparently much worse in East Pakistan than in India. Medical facilities in East Pakistan, even in normal times, are meager. In an average year, 150,000 die here of cholera, most of them because they never get any treatment. In a bad year, the toll sometimes runs as high as 300,000.

Dr. M. A. Majid, the chief medical officer of the Nadia district, the worst-hit area, said today that he expected the death rate to start climbing again. The cholera vaccine, he said, gives only 30- to 90-percent protection.

The weakened condition of the refugees helps explain the virulence of the epidemic. Many are on the verge of death when they arrive.

In addition, living conditions are little short of desperate. Though the Indian Government has marshaled all available resources to provide shelter and food, it is impossible to keep up with the influx.

Relief camps—even just tents made by throwing tarpaulins over bamboo frames—cannot be erected fast enough. It is estimated that 3.5 million refugees are either living in the open or in crude thatch lean-tos of their own making. The monsoon rains have arrived and many refugee towns are mud holes.

There are water shortages and sanitation facilities have virtually broken down. The main streets of border towns are avenues of garbage and flies.

Food lines stretch for hundreds of yards and it sometimes takes hours for a refugee to get his ration.

More refugees are moving toward Calcutta as the other camps become choked. New camps are springing up on the edges of the city—just past the airport and in the Salt Lake area.

About 50,000 to 60,000 refugees have entered the fringes of the city, and at least 60 deaths have been recorded in this group.

A few thousand refugees have moved into the heart of Calcutta and are camping in the Sealdah Railway Station.

Indian officials are worried that the refugee epidemic may spread to the people of Calcutta—an overcrowded, tense city of eight million that has its own fairly serious periodic cholera problem.

A BRUTAL OCCUPATION: ETHNIC CLEANSING, THOUSANDS MASSACRED
July 4, 1971

DACCA, India—"Doesn't the world realize that they're nothing but butchers?" asked a foreigner who has lived in East Pakistan for many years. "That they killed and are still killing Bengalis just to intimidate them, to make slaves out of them? That they wiped out whole villages, opening fire at first light and stopping only when they got tired?"

The foreigner, normally a calm man, was talking about the Pakistani Army and the bloodbath it has inflicted on East Pakistan in its effort to crush the Bengali independence movement.

Most of the foreign residents—diplomats, missionaries, businessmen—also talk the way this man does now. They are bursting with three months of pent-up anger and outrage. And they are very eager to tell what they know to those foreign newsmen who were permitted to reenter East Pakistan in the past fortnight and travel around unescorted for the first time since March 25, when the army began its suppression campaign.

Pakistan's military regime considers the foreign press implacably hostile, but it is desperate to prove to the world its claim that order has been restored, that the army is in control and that normality is fast returning to East Pakistan.

The army is, indeed, in control, except for a few areas near the border with India, where the Mukti Fouj, or "Liberation Army," is active and growing more so—with aid from India.

Yet, East Pakistan is anything but normal. For this is clearly and simply military occupation by an alien army.

Bengali police have been replaced by police from West Pakistan. West Pakistanis are also being flown in to replace officials in every Government department, in some cases even down to the level of typists.

Houses and shops of those Bengalis who were killed or fled to villages in the countryside have been turned over to Moslem non-Bengali residents of East Pakistan, who are collaborating with the army. The temples of the minority Hindus—the army's special scapegoats—are being demolished for no other reason than to demonstrate that those who are not part of the army's design of "Islamic integrity" are not true Pakistanis and will not be tolerated.

Bengali youths, who just over three months ago were exultantly marching through the streets and shouting their slogans of defiance at the military regime, now talk in whispers, slipping up to foreign newsmen for a few seconds to murmur some information about a massacre, the murder of a family member or the destruction of a village. Anonymous letters containing such details find their way every day into newsmen's mailboxes at the Hotel Inter-Continental.

The effluvia of fear is overwhelming. But there is also a new spirit. Many of the Bengalis—a naive and romantic people—realize now that no other country is going to save them, that they will have to do it all themselves and that it will take a long time.

Significant numbers of young men are slipping off to join the Liberation Army, which operates from border areas and from sanctuaries just across the border in India. Bengali guerrilla terrorism is increasing. A number of army collaborators have been executed, and more and more homemade bombs explode in Dacca. The resistance is still sporadic, peripheral and disorganized, but it is growing.

With each terrorist act, the army takes revenge, conducting reprisals against the nearest Bengali civilians. Several hundred were reported to have been rounded up and mowed down by the Army in Noakhali District recently after the Mukti Fouj executed a member of one of the army's "Peace Committees" and his wife and children.

The once widely held theory that the cost of the occupation would prove prohibitive and compel Pakistan to pull the army out fairly quickly has been discarded. Even without the World Bank consortium's massive annual aid, which has been suspended in censure of the repression, the Islamabad regime seems determined to keep its grip on East Pakistan.

President Yahya Khan's speech to the nation last Monday was supposed to have unveiled his long-awaited plan for returning Pakistan—East and West—to civilian rule. It turned out to be exactly the opposite—a declaration that the military dictatorship would continue, with a handpicked civilian government as camouflage.

In his speech, which Western diplomats here described as "a disaster," the President, who is also army chief, heaped praise on the army for rescuing the country from "the brink of disintegration . . . by the grace of Allah." He also extended his "fullest sympathy" to the six million Bengalis, mostly minority Hindus, who have fled to India because of "false propaganda by rebels," he said. He appealed to them to "return to their homes and hearths for speedy rehabilitation."

Just the day before President Yahya's speech, an army platoon stormed into several predominantly Hindu villages 30 miles from Dacca, killing men and looting and burning homes. Reports of similar pogroms come from other parts of the province. No one knows exactly how many Bengalis the army has killed, but reliable foreign sources here put the figure somewhere over 100,000—and possibly much higher.

The East Pakistani economy, which used to provide the national treasury not only with half its exports and foreign exchange but also with a captive market for West Pakistan's manufactured goods, has been badly crippled by the upheaval. However, the military regime seems willing—at least for the present—to pay the severe economic price of holding East Pakistan as a colony, no matter how sullen or resistant the population.

"It's a medieval army operating as if against serfs," said one Westerner here. "It will use any method just to own East Pakistan and keep milking it dry. Even if the Bengalis are serious about the resistance, it will take five to 10 years to make a dent."

HINDUS BECOME SPECIAL TARGETS OF PAKISTANI TERROR
July 4, 1971

FARIDPUR, Pakistan, June 29—The Pakistani Army has painted big yellow "H's" on the Hindu shops still standing in this town to identify the property of the minority eighth of the population that it has made its special targets. Members of the Moslem majority—who, though not exempt from the army's terror, feel safer than the Hindus—have painted on their homes and shops such signs as "All Moslem House."

The small community of Christians, mostly Baptists, have put crosses on their doors and stitched crosses in red thread on their clothes.

Compared with some towns in East Pakistan, Faridpur—which sits 85 miles by road and ferry west of the capital Dacca—suffered only moderate physical damage when the army struck here in April. The attack was part of the offensive begun March 25 to crush the Bengali autonomy movement.

Though a number of shops, most of them belonging to Hindus, have been razed in Faridpur, most of it is physically intact. But every other aspect of life has been shattered, and the hate and terror and fear that wrack the town make it typical of virtually every community in this conquered province of 75 million people.

Only about half of Faridpur's 35,000 people have returned, although the flow has been growing. Recently the army eased up on its executions and burning of villages in an attempt to demonstrate that normality has returned. The change in tactics began in mid-June, just before the central Government announced that it was allowing foreign newsmen back into the region.

An undetermined number of Faridpur's 10,000 Hindus have been killed and others have fled across the border to predominantly Hindu India.

Some Hindus are returning to Faridpur, but it is not out of faith in a change of heart by the army but rather out of despair. They do not want to live as displaced persons in India and they feel that nowhere in East Pakistan is really safe for them, so they would rather be unsafe in their own town.

A Hindu barber said that he was still in hiding but that he sneaked into Faridpur every day to do a few hours work to earn enough to eat. "I come into town like a thief and leave like a thief," he said.

Those Hindus who have slipped into town keep guards posted at night. "None of us sleep very soundly," a young carpenter said. "The daylight gives us a little courage."

A 70-year-old Hindu woman who was shot through the neck said that as bad as conditions were and as frightened as she was, "this is our home—we want to stay in golden Bengal."

On April 21, when the army rolled into Faridpur, the old woman and her 84-year-old husband ran to seek refuge in a Hindu village, Bodidangi, about three miles away. The next day the army hit Bodidangi and, reliable local reports say, as many as 300 Hindus were massacred.

The old woman stumbled and fell as she tried to flee, she related, and two soldiers caught her. She said they beat her, ripped off her jewelry, fired a shot at point-blank range into her neck and left her for dead.

She and her husband had owned a small piece of property on which they rented out a few flimsy huts. Only the dirt floors are left, she said.

The campaign against the Hindus was—and in some cases still is—systematic. Soldiers fanned through virtually every village asking where the Hindus lived. Hindu property has been confiscated and either sold or given to "loyal" citizens. Many of the beneficiaries have been Biharis, non-Bengali Moslem migrants from India, most of whom are working with the army now. The army has given weapons to large numbers of the Biharis, and it is they who have often continued the killing of Hindus in areas where the army has eased off.

Hindu bank accounts are frozen. Almost no Hindu students or teachers have returned to the schools.

President Agha Mohammad Yahya Khan has appealed to the Hindus to return from their hiding places and from India—possibly four million of the six million Bengalis who have fled to India are Hindus—and has assured them of an equal role in East Pakistani life. However, army commanders in the field in East Pakistan privately admit to a policy of stamping out Bengali culture, both Moslem and Hindu—but particularly Hindu.

Although thousands of "anti-state" Bengali Moslems have been killed by the army, the Hindus became particular scapegoats as the martial-law regime tried to blame Hindu India and her agents in East Pakistan for the autonomy movement.

In Faridpur—and the situation was much the same throughout East Pakistan—there was no friction to speak of between Hindu and Moslem before the army came.

The army tried to drive a wedge between them. In April, as a public example, two Hindus were beheaded in a central square in Faridpur and their bodies were soaked in kerosene and burned. When some Hindus, trying to save their lives, begged to convert to Islam, they were shot as unworthy nonbelievers (in some cases, however, converts are being accepted).

The army also forced Moslems friendly to Hindus to loot and burn Hindu houses; the Moslems were told that if they did not attack Hindus they themselves would be killed. Most of the Hindu houses in the region around Faridpur— some say 90 percent—were burned as a result.

Still, there is no sign of a hate-Hindu psychology among the Bengali Moslems. Many have taken grave risks to shelter and defend Hindus; others express shock and horror at what is happening to the Hindus but confess that they are too frightened to help.

Many Bengalis, in fact, feel that the army has only succeeded in forging a tighter bond between Hindu and Moslem in East Pakistan.

INDIAN GENERAL: "WE WILL LET LOOSE THE HOUNDS OF WAR"

Author's Note: On November 23, 1971, I managed to talk my way from Calcutta to a checkpoint within a few miles of India's tense border with East Pakistan, where things were heating up. I watched as large Indian military convoys carrying ammunition, supplies, and soldiers armed for battle roared by—heading directly for the border. The Indian government had consistently denied that its troops had entered Pakistani territory. Officers at the checkpoint barred me from proceeding any farther, but they made no effort to hide or deny the evidence that these troops were indeed crossing the border to support the Bengali insurgents. "My men have been waiting to move forward for a month," one smiling officer at the staging area said. "Their spirits are high." My story ran the next day on page 1, raising a hullabaloo at the United Nations, where Pakistan accused India of invading its sovereign territory. Embarrassed, India considered expelling me but, in its democratic tradition, didn't. Ten days later—see the story below—war was officially declared.

December 4, 1971

CALCUTTA, India—The forces of India's eastern command are poised for an all-out drive into East Pakistan against the Pakistani troops there.

"We will take necessary action; we will take whatever action an army is supposed to take," a military source said here last night after the Government had reported that planes from West Pakistan had attacked Indian airfields in the west and that the Pakistanis were shelling Indian units on the western border.

Pakistan insisted that India had attacked first with ground troops all along the western border. "That's a bloody lie!" said the Indian military source.

"I give you my word there was no attack."

However Indian units here in the east, supported by tanks and artillery, have been jabbing and probing at the Pakistani troops in East Pakistan for several weeks.

The Indian operation was designed to help the Bengali insurgents oust the West Pakistani troops who have occupied East Pakistan since March, when they moved to crush the Bengali autonomy movement.

"As far as I'm concerned, it's a war," said the Indian military source. "We now have to take certain steps, which will be apparent in the morning."

"We will set the machine in motion," another military source said angrily. "We will let loose the hounds of war."

Many diplomatic observers believe that the main war will be fought on the eastern front. Their view is that with the reported Pakistani attack in the west, the Indians will push directly into East Pakistan to accomplish their objective—the creation of a friendly, independent East Pakistan that will take back the nearly 10 million Bengali refugees who India says have fled to her soil during the eight months of strife and who pose a threat to her stability.

The observers believe that Pakistan, by her military actions in the west, may be trying to bring about international intervention as a means of freezing the situation and holding on, however tenuously, to East Pakistan.

"The United Nations may be able to stop the fighting in the west," said a Western diplomat, "but no one on this side is going to stop to listen to the U.N. bray. They're going to push right in."

Even without the United Nations intervention, independent observers think the major action may be in the east.

A key objective is the city of Jessore and its cantonment, which are only about 20 miles from the border with West Bengal State, in India.

It was clear last night that, at least to officers of the eastern command, the Pakistani move came as a surprise. "We were not expecting war so soon," a military source said.

Calcutta, the overcrowded capital of West Bengal that sits less than 50 miles from the border, was calm last night. Diplomats attended their usual parties, the brightly lit Park Street nightclubs were humming and the movie theaters were full. The diplomatic mission of the insurgent government—which calls itself Bangla Desh (Bengal Nation)—was quiet, its iron gate locked.

The only sign of crisis was a blackout at the airport, where large sandbag fortifications have been erected in the last week to protect military aircraft. No seats were being booked on domestic flights in anticipation of the suspension of all flights.

Prime Minister Indira Gandhi addressed a political rally in Calcutta before the crisis broke, speaking from 5 P.M. to nearly 6. The Pakistani air attacks were said to have begun shortly after 5:30 P.M. Mrs. Gandhi was not told the news until after her speech.

"Pakistan is talking about war," she told a crowd of about 500,000 on the Brigade Parade Ground. "We do not want to fight. I hope they will not follow up their talk, but if they do we are prepared."

The Prime Minister flew back to New Delhi after her speech. Shortly after midnight, in a nationwide radio broadcast, she told her people that Pakistan had launched a "full-scale war" on India and declared a state of national emergency.

INDIAN VICTORY AND PAKISTAN SURRENDER
December 17, 1971

DACCA, Pakistan—On a broad grassy field in central Dacca known as the Race Course, the Pakistani forces formally surrendered today, 13 days after the Indian Army began its drive into East Pakistan.

It was at the Race Course on March 7 that Sheik Mujibur Rahman, in a speech to thousands of Bengalis, called for the end of martial law and the transfer of power to his autonomy-minded Awami League, which had won a majority in national elections.

Today there were no speeches—just two men sitting at a single table on the grass—Lieut. Gen. Jagjit Singh Aurora, chief of India's Eastern Command, and Lieut. Gen. A. A. K. Niazi, commander of the 70,000 Pakistani troops in East Pakistan—who signed the formal papers of Pakistani surrender.

The final hours of the Indian drive, which ended with the ceremony at the Race Course, were punctuated by artillery and machine-gun fire as the troops pushed across the Lakhya River, just outside Dacca proper.

Seven Western journalists, including this correspondent, were the only newsmen and only foreigners to ride into Dacca with the Indian troops.

The population turned out in quiet droves to sit and watch the Indians rain artillery shells on the Pakistanis. Such was the case this morning in a field of rice paddies at Barpa, about nine miles from Dacca, where a battery of six 75 mm. mountain guns was firing on Pakistani positions across the river.

A few hundred villagers sat 100 yards back as the guns roared for an hour.

"Good shooting!" an officer from the command post yelled across after getting a report from the forward observer. "We got some vehicles."

The gun crews applauded. So did the villagers.

It was 10 A.M. A cease-fire was in effect but the Indian officers said it applied only to firing on Dacca City and they were firing short of it. Besides, no one in this brigade advancing on Dacca from the northeast knew anything about the Pakistan surrender that was being arranged at that very time.

The Pakistanis opposite them were also in the dark, for soon afterward a tank, artillery and infantry battle was raging a few miles farther down the road to the regional capital.

Two light Indian tanks captured from the Pakistanis in an earlier fight moved into position, one in a mango grove and the other 200 yards to the left by an embankment.

As the tanks were getting set, Indian artillery shells whistled overhead on their way to an enemy position in Demra, a couple of miles to the northwest. Columns of smoke rose from burning buildings there.

Then the tanks opened up, pummeling the eardrums of those nearby and much more devastatingly pummeling the factory complex in the distance across the Lakhya River, where some Pakistani troops were impeding the Indian advance. Smoke columns began to mushroom from the factory buildings, too.

After 20 minutes of pounding the area with shells, the tanks also opened up with machine guns, peppering the area in front of the buildings where the Pakistanis were dug into bunkers.

A column of Indian infantry then began making its way forward along the bottom of the embankment and then turned right and began crossing a marsh toward the river.

At about 12:30 P.M., under the bright sun, the officers with the Indian units decided to take the press party forward to watch the infantry in action.

Now there was no answering fire from the Pakistanis. We climbed up the embankment to the road, and silhouetted against the azure sky, we walked confidently forward. For about one minute.

A Pakistani machine gun began spitting and bullets whizzed by. We flew unsmartly down the opposite embankment, sending up gravel and dust in the wake of our slide. An Indian major, to assure us, said the bullets had passed 10 to 15 yards away.

Carefully tucked below the ridge of the road, we walked forward as the Pakistanis kept firing. They hit a baby goat gamboling in a culvert and the animal crumpled. In 10 minutes we reached an Indian platoon lying at the top of the embankment, their rifles and machine guns pointing at the Pakistanis, who then began firing at them instead of us.

The Indians opened fire. As the staccato continued, the major with us got a message over the field radio that the Pakistanis had surrendered. The Pakistanis opposite had obviously not been told. Some Pakistani units had lost communications with their headquarters.

That was 12:40. For an hour more the Pakistanis kept the Indians pinned down. Then at 1:45, a Pakistani soldier—apparently an officer—came into the open on the opposite bank waving what looked like a big handkerchief.

The Indian major, M. S. Dhillon, climbed over the embankment and moved toward the river, stopping behind a wall. He then began shouting at the Pakistanis to surrender immediately.

"Are you moving or not?" the major yelled. "I want you to move in just one minute! Before I lose my patience, I want you to get a move on. Get your men round you and move to that little boat and start crossing. Put your weapons down. Put your damn bastard Sten gun down. Don't compel me to plaster you with artillery. I'm telling you again. Start moving, start moving!"

The newsmen had followed the major to the wall but were crouched behind it and could not see what was happening. The major obliged with a narrative: "There's an officer standing there. He's got four chaps. He's waving his white hankie. They have surrendered now. There seem to be about 15 chaps."

The rest of the Pakistanis, however many there were, had apparently fled.

This scene—ending what may have been the last battle of the war in the East—took about 20 minutes to unfold, during which a wounded Indian soldier was groaning where he lay in a shallow lily pond. As the major was preparing to gather in the surrendering platoon, a cloud of dust on the road signaled that the brigade was suddenly moving up toward Dacca.

Though small-arms fire could be heard far off, serious resistance had ended. Indian infantry columns—happiness writ on the face of every soldier—were advancing on the regional capital. Bengalis joined the column, pulling artillery pieces. This correspondent hitched a ride on one of the tanks that had been blasting the Pakistanis only a few minutes before.

The road was filled with jubilant Bengalis and troops heading for Dacca on tank, truck, scooter, bicycle, rickshaw and foot. Everyone was hitching rides to get to the liberated capital—it was more of a circus parade than a military convoy.

All along the army's route fathers held their infants up in the air and waved the infants' hands at the Indian soldiers.

At the Lakhya River, the tank, an amphibious vehicle, had to jettison some passengers to be able to motor across. I caught a country boat and, when we got across, joined 17 other people—officers, soldiers and newsmen—who clambered onto a jeep driven by the brigade commander, Brig. R. N. Misra.

As the mustached commander drove slowly toward Dacca, trying to see the road through the mass of passengers on the hood, we passed through a countryside only slightly scarred by the war. It has been the same all over. A burned-out vehicle here and there on the road hit by artillery or mortar fire. A blown-up Pakistani bunker. And in those towns where the Pakistanis made a stand, a lot of blackened and razed buildings and huts.

By and large, except for the road and rail bridges the Pakistanis blew up as they retreated, the territory has not been severely damaged. In some areas, as kingfishers dive for minnows in the streams along the paddy fields and cows graze near lush coconut and banana groves, it is difficult to tell—except for the silence of the dead and of those who have not yet trekked back—that war has touched this country.

Yet there was one clear sign of the war—the Pakistani troops at the roadside who had surrendered. There had not been enough time to take away their weapons or move them near surrender areas, and they came near the road carrying their arms—a slightly chilling sight for those of the passersby who had seen them use them on unarmed civilians last March 25, when the army began to try to crush the Bengali autonomy movement.

The Pakistanis looked slightly dazed and seemed demoralized. They badly needed a word of reassurance, which they are not likely to get from a people that had suffered so under their rule by bullet. When a passerby raised a hand in greeting, they waved feebly back and smiled just as feebly.

Brigadier Misra stopped his jeep outside a Pakistani barracks to tell the officer in charge to keep his men inside until Indian troops arrived to take them to surrender areas. "Don't go on the road," he warned. "The Mukti Bahini might be there."

Many members of the Mukti Bahini, or Liberation Forces—the Bengali insurgents who had been fighting alone for independence—are eager for revenge. Their potential targets are not only the Pakistani troops but the razakars, or home guards, trained by the troops and the civilian collaborators, most of them non-Bengalis who did a lot of the dirty work for the army.

"If we don't protect the Pakistanis and their collaborators," said an officer in the brigadier's jeep, "the Mukti Bahini will butcher them nicely and properly."

As the jeep proceeded directly into Dacca, a throng of several hundred Bengalis suddenly materialized and—in the throes of happiness—started walking fast toward the approaching Indian troops, shouting welcome slogans.

But a Pakistani jeep with a .50-caliber machine gun was also moving toward the crowd. The uneasy Pakistani crew, thinking the crowd was coming at them, fired a few bursts. Two people fell and the crowd carried off these wounded as it melted away.

Brigadier Misra and other Indian officers, in a rage, stripped the four Pakistanis of their weapons and shouted vilification at them until they looked so frightened they probably thought they were going to be shot. They were taken off to be placed under guard to face courts-martial.

Near the scene was a bus overflowing with Pakistani troops and their families, some sitting on the roof. The women and children huddled next to their men like terrified refugees.

Because the Pakistanis surrendered before the Indians had to storm Dacca, the capital did not suffer any major damage except for the scars from heavy bombing of the airfield and the military cantonment.

The road to the airport is still full of craters. The airfield runways have been repaired, but off to one side are the charred heaps that used to be fighter planes. The windows of the terminal building have been blasted out by the raids.

Many houses and shops are still shuttered, awaiting the return of their occupants. Still, the crowds gathered quickly, as if from nowhere. They swarmed over our vehicle—shouting greetings, calling us "brother" and trying to touch and hold another human being.

Near sundown, 10 Indian helicopters in formation descended on the airport. They carried General Aurora, other Indian officers and newsmen from Calcutta—all flying in for the surrender ceremony. General Niazi, his face a mask of determined dignity, was waiting on the tarmac wearing a black beret and carrying a collapsible hunting seat, though he never opened it to sit down.

Beside him stood General Aurora's chief of staff, Maj. Gen. J. F. R. Jacob, who just a few minutes before had been embarrassed by the frenzied embraces of Bengalis who had come to the airport.

The two walked out to greet General Aurora's helicopter and after being surrounded by microphones and cameras, they drove off to the race course field for the signing of the surrender documents.

After signing, the two generals rose and shook hands. General Niazi rode off in a jeep and General Aurora in a staff car.

Sporadic small-arms fire was still crackling in the city when the Indian military party drove back to the airport, as darkness fell, to fly back to Calcutta. There had been sporadic street fighting throughout the day in Dacca, including a gun battle between Mukti Bahini guerrillas and Pakistani soldiers outside the Inter-Continental Hotel, which had been declared a neutral zone for the war.

At the airport tonight, long lines of West Pakistani troops seemed eager and relieved as they marched off to surrender areas where they will be protected by Indian soldiers from Bengali crowds.

REPORTER'S NOTEBOOK: WITH THE INDIAN ARMY ON ITS PUSH TO FREE BANGLADESH
December 21, 1971

CALCUTTA, India—Jottings from the notebook of one correspondent who covered the Indian Army in the 15 days of the war with Pakistan:

Dec. 5
The army public relations office arranges a trip in East Pakistan for some newsmen. It takes five hours to drive to the war over bad roads. We arrive in Uthali, a small, dusty village about three miles inside, which was taken by the army on the first night of the war.

Nothing to see except empty Pakistani bunkers and discarded ammunition boxes until an Indian soldier standing about a hundred yards away starts yelling "Hands up!" at us.

We think he's joking but put our hands up anyway. He keeps yelling and walking forward and pointing his Sten gun at us. I grow uneasy. He looks drunk. Some photographers start taking pictures of him and this enrages him. He walks faster toward us, gets within 25 yards and cocks the Sten gun. Our escort officer, a major, yells, "Stop, stop!"

The soldier drops to one knee and aims the gun at us. We scatter and hit the dirt. The major, screaming at the soldier, rushes forward and pulls the barrel down. The crisis is over and the soldier is led away. This is not the action we came for.

✦

We go to another liberated town nearby, Darsana. Lieut. Col. Bhupal Singh tells us about the battle there and shows us his battle scar—a graze at the base of his spine. As the television cameras grind, he turns his back, bends over and pulls up his shirt. He stays in that position until the television people tell him they've got enough film of his back.

At the deserted railway depot the last entry in the stationmaster's book is for the morning of March 26—the morning after the Pakistani reign of terror began.

A crippled old man, Mazzam Hussein Mia, hobbles onto the station platform. He says he has been in hiding for nine months near the town because, unlike the other residents, he could not flee fast enough to get to India when the Pakistani soldiers came.

We return to Colonel Singh's headquarters for further briefing. He gets fed up with newsmen asking questions and wandering around on their own, so he orders the troops in some nearby emplacements to fire a few rounds to scare us and make us leave. They start firing. The television crews swarm to the emplacements to take pictures of the firing.

"Please control these fellows!" the colonel yells at our escort officer. The officer is equally exasperated. "I told you not to let them go there," he replied. "You let them go and now you tell me to control them!'

As we leave the escort officer is mumbling to himself: "Fighting the press is worse than fighting the war."

✦

We head for a village about 15 miles away, Suadih, where a battle has just ended. It is still burning when we get there, the mud huts knocked down and the thatch roofs set ablaze when Indian artillery tried to flush out the Pakistanis who had retreated there. Grimly, silent villagers carry water from the village pond and pour it on the flames. An old man weeps uncontrollably.

In a field a few hundred yards away, 22 Pakistani soldiers lie dead in their bunkers—some in positions of repose, others broken and twisted grotesquely by the artillery bursts. One bunker is caved in—a burial mound with two booted feet protruding.

In Calcutta, when we get back that night, Firpo's Restaurant is holding "An Evening With Miss Calcutta 1971." She was chosen in a contest the night before.

Calcutta is disturbed only superficially by the war. The blackout annoys some people and buses bear placards with slogans such as: "Don't Panic or Listen to Rumors" and "Be United Against the Enemy." But the crowds of Sunday strollers are of normal size as are the armies of beggars.

Dec. 8

A trip to Jessore, whose people are celebrating their first full day of liberation. On the 80-mile jeep drive from Calcutta, village crowds come out to cheer us and touch our hands.

Almost no young women can be seen, for they have been the objects of Pakistani sexual brutality and will be the last to return from their hiding places and refugee camps in India.

Some fields are unsown; others overgrown with uncut sugarcane. The big road bridge at Jhikargacha, over the Kabathaki River, is blown up—the Pakistanis' last act before retreating to Jessore.

We cross the river on small boats as the army goes about building a pontoon bridge with hundreds of villagers eager to help. On the other side small, newly made Bangladesh flags are selling for 75 paise in Indian money, or about 10 cents. On our arrival the price goes up to a rupee, or about 13 cents.

The countryside is not badly scarred by the war, except where set battles took place, and even there the debris does not remain for long. Villagers strip the Pakistani bunkers for building materials—wooden beams and corrugated metal sheets. They also strip the occasional burned-out Pakistani vehicles. The next rains will blur any remaining scars.

Squads of guerrillas of the Mukti Bahini march or bicycle down the road, their faces serious. They are not being used much in the front lines, but it was they who harassed and demoralized the Pakistani troops and they are determined not to let their dignity or morale slip.

✦

We enter Jessore and drive to the military cantonment. No sign of fighting here. The big battle was fought north of the city. Maj. Gen. Dalbir Singh, commander of the Ninth Division and a very round and hefty man, gives a briefing at which he says the Jessore troops are retreating down the road to Khulna. "They'll surrender or otherwise we'll destroy them. I'm endowed with a gentle nature."

Asked to reconcile his capture of Jessore with the statements made by officials in New Delhi that the plan was to bypass it, he replied, "Some are destined to die for their country and some are destined to lie for their country!"

With the general's permission, we go down the road toward where Indian forces are attacking the retreating Pakistanis. Pakistani bedding and belongings are scattered at the roadside, left behind in the pell-mell retreat. A letter from a boy in West Pakistan to his soldier-father tells him to "crush India."

The bodies of two Bengali civilians are in a field nearby—being gnawed on by dogs. Villagers say the retreating Pakistanis killed them. Another Bengali lies not far away, his left arm cut off and the flesh of his chest torn away.

We start back. Driving through Jessore again we see enraptured crowds of Bengalis hail an incoming column of Indian troops. The Bengalis cheer and embrace and kiss their liberators. A bus drives by, full of jubilant Mukti Bahini, some of them dancing on the roof. Their guns poke out of every window, so the bus looks like a rolling pincushion.

Dec. 9

The evidence is growing that the Pakistanis are slaughtering Bengalis as they retreat and that the Mukti Bahini and other Bengalis are, in turn, taking vengeance on the Pakistanis and their civilian collaborators. The Indian Army issues strict orders against reprisal executions by the Bengalis in the hope of avoiding massacres.

An army captain says he has seen several mutilated bodies of Pakistani soldiers along the route, their fingers and nipples chopped off and their throats slit.

Dec. 13

I take a drive with another reporter toward Khulna to see how that battle is going. My driver, Mr. Singh, gets nervous as we approach the booming artillery guns. We are still a few miles away, but his speed drops to almost zero. "If you don't want to drive, Mr. Singh," I tell him, "I'll drive." "You drive, Sahib," he says as he gets out, smiling and relieved.

"Welcome to Khulna," says the road sign. Long columns of infantry carrying everything from cooking pots to bazookas are walking down the road.

We walk too. My colleague inquires about the possibility of mines. "No bloody mines, sir," says a soldier in a foxhole, laughing.

A medium tank rolls by toward the front; the commander waves. It's a friendly war. The Indians at least are happy and friendly and brimming with confidence.

A jeep carrying Indian wounded comes back from the fighting. In the back a man's legs are sticking up in the air, as though he'd been tossed in head first.

It's tough slogging for the Indians. The Pakistanis are dug in well and fighting bitterly. As the brigade commander, Sandhu Singh, spoke, a couple of incoming artillery shells exploded about 200 yards away. Heavy Pakistani machine-gun fire offers a pizzicato in the background.

On the way back people who fled the shooting are returning to their homes. The Bengalis are never more than a mile or two behind, filling the vacuum the army leaves in its wake. Some of the returnees are from the refugee camps in India, carrying their pathetic sacks of belongings. They look uncertain, nervous.

Dec. 14

The Indian Army has picked 11 newsmen, including me, to accompany the troops on their final push into Dacca.

We leave Calcutta for Agartala, an Indian border city on the eastern side of East Pakistan, in an Indian Air Force DC-3 with no door.

We are flying across the breadth of East Pakistan, the first Indian military plane to do it since 1947, when India and Pakistan were born in mutual hatred. There seems no danger, for Pakistan's entire air force in the East has been shot down and the only antiaircraft guns left are in Dacca, and we are flying north of the capital.

As we land, a work crew is repairing runway damage inflicted by the Pakistanis at the start of the war.

Dec. 15

Our riverboat leaves Brahmanbaria, pushing a pontoon raft carrying two 5.5-inch artillery pieces. The Indian troops on the riverbank clown and pose for pictures.

After a long-delayed trip by road to brigade headquarters at Bhulta, about nine miles from Dacca, we spend the night in a prosperous farming village of 300 called Bhaila. The mosquitoes are large.

Dec. 16

The artillery fire grows heavy at 5:15 A.M. With the guns as a leitmotif, the villagers serve us—on china and glassware that must have been dug out of someone's trunk—a superior breakfast of flat wheat bread, beef and chicken curry, hard-boiled eggs and tea. The village gathers to watch us eat.

We are greeted at the headquarters of the Fourth Battalion, Brigade of Guards, by the commander, Lieut. Col. Himmeth Singh. Sitting in a haystack, a map on his lap, he orders tea for us and then lays out the battle plan. He hasn't shaved since the war began and says that, as a lucky charm, he won't until it's over.

✦

After the chaotic surrender ceremony in Dacca, small-arms fire punctuates the night. People are taking revenge on the collaborators and some of the collaborators are firing back.

We hitch our final rides—first on a helicopter to Agartala and from there on a plane. The helicopters whirring behind us in the night look like giant fireflies.

In Calcutta, on our return, Indian Bengalis are celebrating the birth of Bangladesh with fireworks and brass bands. The blackout has been lifted. Mr. Singh can drive again without squinting.

THE PRICE OF BENGALI INDEPENDENCE—GRAVEYARDS, ONE AFTER ANOTHER
January 24, 1972

DACCA, Pakistan—"On this graveyard, we shall build our golden Bengal." So reads a cardboard sign hung on a flagpole in the city of Khulna.

Not far from the flagpole, human bones, picked clean by vultures and dogs, still litter the roadside at various execution sites where the Pakistani Army and its collaborators killed Bengalis.

Bloodstained clothing and tufts of human hair cling to the brush on these killing grounds. Children too young to understand play grotesque games with the skulls and other bones.

This correspondent found on a recent tour of the countryside, that almost every town in East Pakistan had one or more of these graveyards, where the Pakistanis killed hundreds of thousands of Bengalis, apparently often on a daily basis, throughout their nine months of military occupation. The killing ended last month when the Pakistani forces, all from West Pakistan, were defeated by the Indian Army and Bengali guerrillas in a 14-day war.

Sheik Mujibur Rahman, the Bengali leader who was recently freed from Pakistani imprisonment and came to Dacca to become Prime Minister in the Government of Bangladesh, has estimated that the Pakistanis killed three million of his people. While foreign diplomats and other independent observers do not generally put the figure this high, all say it was at least several hundred thousand and many put it at more than one million. The Bengali leader has ordered a house-to-house census to get a precise figure.

In Khulna, one of the Pakistani execution sites was a road on the edge of town that leads west to Satkhira. Though truckloads of skeletons have recently been carried away for proper burial, bones are still scattered along the gray roadside for over a mile. Both Bengalis and foreigners who live in Khulna say that at least 10,000 people were killed at this site alone.

The execution area was off limits to the public, but the Khulna radio station is less than 100 yards from the road, and Bengali employees at the station, who say they were kept working at gunpoint throughout the occupation, witnessed most of the killings either through the windows or from the front steps of the station.

"They killed some people every day," said Mokhlesur Rahman, a 26-year-old technician. "Sometimes five or six. Sometimes 20. On one day, they killed 500.

"On Sept. 3, they killed the most—1,000 people. They fired with machine guns almost continuously for three hours. Then they threw many of the bodies into the river, and they were carried out to sea."

Their voices were choked and their fists clenched as the radio station employees recalled the murders and told of victims begging for mercy and screaming in pain before they died.

One engineer said that sometimes the Pakistanis had put seven or eight Bengali prisoners in a tight queue and then, to save ammunition, fired one bullet through all of them. Sometimes, he said, they killed the Bengalis with bayonet charges.

Another engineer, Mazedul Haque, 25, vividly remembered the day the Pakistanis killed 500 people—July 25—"by shooting and by cutting their throats with long knives and bayonets.

"First the soldiers came and told us to come out and watch," he said. "They said, 'Come and see how we kill your people.' They were sharpening their knives on the stones. It was their way of torturing us mentally."

"All those months," Mr. Haque went on, "thousands of vultures were flying overhead here. Now they are gone."

It almost seems, as one goes from place to place, that each story of the killings is more gruesome than the one before.

In Jessore, a 12-year-old boy, Habib Ramatullah, said he had seen Pakistani soldiers beat a man to death after hanging him upside down from a tree in front of the district courthouse. The boy said one of the judges had died of a heart attack as he watched.

All the evidence now indicates that the killings were on a wider scale and more sadistic than foreign newsmen and other independent observers had earlier thought.

According to confirmed reports, the Pakistani troops in nearly every sector kept Bengali women as sexual slaves, often making them remain naked continuously in their bunkers. After the Pakistanis surrendered on Dec. 16, the mutilated bodies of many of these women were found.

Other independent reports established that the Pakistanis also killed many, if not most, of the Indian soldiers they took prisoner. In these cases, too, bodies were mutilated.

Maj. Gen. M. S. Brar, commander of India's Fourth Infantry Division, lost some of his men this way at Kushtia. He says that at the time of the surrender, the opposing Pakistani commander, a Maj. Gen. Ansari, said he was unaware of the killing of any Indian prisoners. "I told him," General Brar declared, "'Either you lost complete control of your troops or you are a bloody liar.'" It seemed obvious that General Brar believed the latter.

A Baptist missionary from the Mymensingh district, Ian Hawley, reported that the Pakistani troops, as they retreated before the Indian forces and the guerrilla fighters, killed their own wounded in a hospital there. Other missionaries in the same district say the Pakistani troops also killed several hundred razakars— the home-guard collaborators they had trained and armed—by locking them in a building, throwing kerosene on the building and then setting it on fire.

In a few areas, the local Pakistani commanders were apparently not in accord with the mass-killing policy and tried to keep down the amount of slaughter. In Faridpur, for example, residents say that the officer who was in charge of the district for the last two months of the occupation, Maj. Ata Mohammed, "was a comparatively good man."

But the officers who preceded him were evidently different.

At a Hindu temple on the outskirts of Faridpur, which the Pakistanis had half destroyed with dynamite, almost the entire stone floor around the altar bears a dull red stain. The stain is from blood, for this was one of the places of execution.

In the weeks since the fighting ended, local Hindus and their Moslem friends have tried many times, without success, to scrub out the stain.

The minority Hindu community was a special target of the Moslem Pakistani Army.

"Many times during those months," said Jagodish Guha, a Hindu gas station manager who fled from Faridpur to hide in the interior, "my mind was disturbed. What is the answer? Only that they were animals. There were no religious troubles here. The Moslems and Hindus and Christians were brothers."

An old Moslem laborer was helping clean up the debris at the Hindu temple compound. Asked about relations between Hindus and Moslems in Faridpur, he said softly, "I watched the Hindu priests at this temple feed the poor of all faiths for 40 years. And then the Moslem soldiers came and killed them. How can they call themselves Moslems? That is why I am helping now."

The yellow "H's" that the Pakistanis painted on the doors of Hindu homes and shops are still there, but the Hindus are slowly returning to Faridpur and other towns—the men first to survey the situation.

In every village and town, shuttered shops and houses and fields lying fallow are testimony to the number of people who were killed or who fled and have not yet returned.

Many of the elite were murdered, some in the last few days before surrender, apparently as part of official Pakistani policy to try to decimate the Bengali leadership.

Professors, students, political activists, journalists, engineers and railway technicians were all targets.

Every day, new mass graves are discovered. Every day, the newspapers run long lists of notices asking for information about missing persons.

In the capital, Dacca, many execution grounds have been found—particularly in sections like Mirpur and Mohammedpur, which are populated largely by non-Bengalis who collaborated with the Pakistanis.

One corner of the zoo in Mirpur is strewn with skeletons with hands tied behind backs. Many of the animals were also killed.

In the Sialbari neighborhood of Mirpur, skeletons seem to lie behind every bush and down every well. On the floor of a Bengali peasant's ruined house stands a large pile of bones crushed, apparently, to prevent identification. A well 60 feet deep is filled to within two feet of the top with human bones.

Zebed Ali, a 35-year-old father of seven who fled Sialbari in the early days of the occupation, has come back to try to revive his small firewood business. His hut no longer exists, and he and his family are sleeping under a tree—but they have picked a tree some distance outside Sialbari. "It is too frightening to sleep there," Mr. Ali says.

A nine-year-old, Nazrul Islam, guided an American visitor to a field in

Sialbari and said he thought his father was buried there, but he did not know just where.

His family fled Sialbari when the army came, he said, but his father returned later to try to harvest their rice, and that was when the Pakistani soldiers shot him.

As dusk descended, the boy wandered through the field, pointing out clumps of bones with scraps of clothing and hair clinging to them. His eyes grew larger and his behavior was nervous and odd as he seemed to look for his father.

"Dig anywhere here," he whispered, "you will find more bodies."

U.S. PROLONGED THE WAR BY DELAYING PAKISTANI SURRENDER MESSAGE

Author's Note: The slaughter in East Pakistan and the Indian military victory that ended it carried elements of the long Cold War between Moscow and Washington that was still intact.

India and Pakistan were enemies who had already fought two wars. In the Cold War, India—a democracy—generally leaned toward Moscow, while Pakistan— essentially a military autocracy—lined up with Washington. Pakistan, for example, had been the covert link used by Richard Nixon and Henry Kissinger to restore relations with China.

Washington gave Pakistan substantial military aid, including arms and equipment used in the killing spree in East Pakistan.

During the December 1971 war, the United States sent a large naval armada ominously into the Bay of Bengal, on East Pakistan's southern border. Washington said this was merely a precaution, in case Americans, missionaries, and others needed to be evacuated from the war zone. India saw it as a threat to its security.

In elaboration, here is an excerpt from a story of mine published on December 19, 1971:

The United States has called for the withdrawal of the Indian Army from Bangladesh—which the Nixon Administration insists on still calling East Pakistan—but the unfortunate truth is that if the army pulled out right now, the sporadic executions would become full-blown massacres.

President Nixon also continues to enrage the Indians by keeping a task force of the Seventh Fleet in the Bay of Bengal, apparently as a form of pressure on India because of her alliance with the Soviet Union.

Anti-American sentiment is running high here. The American consulate in Calcutta, under heavy police protection, has been besieged by angry demonstrations. "If he doesn't get that fleet out of here," said one American working in Calcutta, "he'll have to use it to evacuate us from India."

The final hostile act by Washington is described in the story below, about the White House decision to delay turning over to Pakistan a surrender message to India. The Pakistani commander in Dacca, his communications broken, sent the message through the American consulate to be passed immediately to India. We will never know how many needless casualties were caused by that unexplained one-day delay.

January 26, 1972

DACCA, Pakistan—The brief war between India and Pakistan last month was prolonged by a day because the Pakistani message of surrender, conveyed to India through the United Stales, was held up in Washington, according to authoritative reports.

The reason is not known, but authoritative sources in New Delhi and Calcutta—and informed visitors to Dacca—confirm that there was a gap of more than 20 hours between the time the message was sent by the Pakistanis and the time it was given to the Indians by the Nixon Administration.

These sources report that the message was sent by radio from the United States Consulate in Dacca to Washington—where all messages from the consulate have to go—shortly before 7 P.M. Dacca time on the night of Dec. 14. This was shortly before 6:30 P.M. Indian time.

The message was received at the State Department almost instantaneously and was acknowledged.

But, the sources added, it was not given to the Indian Government until 2:30 P.M. Indian time the next day, Dec. 15, when the United States Embassy in New Delhi—which had apparently just received it from Washington—passed it to Gen. S. H. F. J. Manekshaw, the Commander in Chief of the Indian Army.

The message was from Lieut. Gen. A. A. K. Niazi, commander of the Pakistani forces in East Pakistan. According to the sources, it said that he was ready to surrender and wanted to discuss the terms and arrangements.

General Manekshaw, on receiving this message, is said to have consulted with Prime Minister Indira Gandhi and other top Indian officials. Less than nine hours later, at 11 P.M. Indian time on Dec. 15, the sources said, he communicated the terms to General Niazi, by way of the United States Embassy in New Delhi. The embassy transmitted the message immediately to the consulate in Dacca, which telephoned it to General Niazi.

The surrender negotiations then began, and were completed the following morning, Dec. 16. The formal surrender documents were signed that afternoon in a brief ceremony in Dacca.

The war, which lasted 15 days, ended totally on the next day, Dec. 17, when Pakistan accepted a cease-fire on the western front—the border between West Pakistan and India.

American diplomats on the subcontinent—in New Delhi, Calcutta and Dacca—will not comment on this episode, but the details have become known, for one reason, because General Niazi, now a prisoner of war of the Indians, has related the story to others.

On the evening of Dec. 14, General Niazi rode from the military cantonment a few miles away to the downtown office of the United States Consul General, Herbert D. Spivack. With him, the sources said, was Maj. Gen. Rao Farman Ali Khan, the No. 2 man in his headquarters.

According to the sources, the general said he wanted to surrender and asked Mr. Spivack if he had "quick communications" to reach the Indians. The Consul General said yes, and General Niazi and he then sat down to work out the message, in which the Pakistani commander asked the United States to use its "good offices" to bring about a cease-fire.

The message was transmitted by the consulate radio on a "flash" basis, the fastest message category. It was acknowledged by Washington within 20 minutes, the sources said.

Several pieces of the puzzle are still not in place, for example, why General Niazi chose the Americans to act as his messengers.

Another unanswered question, and the most crucial one, is why Washington reportedly held the message for more than 20 hours before passing it to the Indians.

Some sources say it may have been because the Americans were trying to clarify their own position in the complex situation, to keep from being drawn into the surrender negotiations as a participant.

Indian officials, including some key generals, have complained privately that whatever the reason for the delay of the message, it prolonged the war by a day and caused unnecessary loss of life on both sides.

CHAPTER FOUR

Vietnam, 1972

All stories in this chapter appeared in The New York Times.

Author's Note: In 1972 I was shifted temporarily from my post covering South Asia, as bureau chief for The New York Times *in New Delhi, to our Saigon bureau to assist with the coverage of the sudden "Easter Offensive" by the North Vietnamese. The major assault on numerous fronts, which lasted several months, seemed at times to come close to threatening the fall of the Saigon government. It was finally blunted by massive American bombing, which inflicted heavy casualties and eventually caused the Communist forces to pull back.*

SAIGON DIVISION MUTINIES AND FLEES COMMUNIST OFFENSIVE
May 3, 1972

HUE, South Vietnam—Thousands of panicking South Vietnamese soldiers—most of whom did not appear to have made much contact with the advancing North Vietnamese—fled in confusion from Quangtri Province today, streaming south down Route 1 like a rabble out of control.

Commandeering civilian vehicles at rifle point, feigning nonexistent injuries, carrying away C rations but not their ammunition, and hurling rocks at Western news photographers taking pictures of their flight, the Government troops of the Third Infantry Division ran from the fighting in one of the biggest retreats of the war.

No one tried to stop them; their officers were running too.

The battlefront north of Hue was thus left solely to a brigade of a few thousand South Vietnamese marines.

The Third Division had fallen back before, at the beginning of the enemy offensive a month ago, but the commander, Brig. Gen. Vu Van Giai, had managed to scrape it together again and put it back on the line around Quangtri until yesterday.

But today, according to American advisers, virtually the entire division—about 10,000 infantrymen plus 1,000 rangers—was in rout, not even stopping at the checkpoints where military policemen were supposed to halt runaways and turn them around.

It was the force that was supposed to have defended the city of Quangtri, which was abandoned yesterday and which had been the northernmost town held by the Government.

There does not seem to be much now between the North Vietnamese and their next and more important objective, the city of Hue, whose residents are already packing up and fleeing farther south in large numbers.

Many of the retreating troops are not even stopping in Hue, which is about 40 miles south of Quangtri, but are continuing on, taking their rifles, artillery pieces, tanks and armored cars with them.

The province chief went on the radio tonight, appealing to the people of Hue not to panic and flee and promising that the Government would defend them. As he spoke American advisers in Hue were calling Saigon to ask for every available aircraft to evacuate the thousands of refugees from the north who have flooded the city.

Bowling down Route 1 from Quangtri, the Government soldiers, their guns bristling at anyone who tried to interfere with them, clung to the sides and roofs and hoods and trunks of every available vehicle.

With horns blaring and headlights glowing in the midday sun, they raced down the center of the road, pushing other vehicles out of the way. They used trucks and tanks and they took over big buses and three-wheeled minibuses. They stole motorcycles, riding as many as four to the bike. There were also many on foot, particularly walking wounded.

Their anger at those who watched them running seemed born of their shame. Until the Third Division can be pulled together again, it hardly exists as a fighting force.

The South Vietnamese marines, the only units that have fought well on the northern front, are still holding three bridges on Route 1 between Quangtri and Hue. They are trying to slow the enemy advance, the first bridge being about 30 miles north of Hue and the last only 20 miles away.

No one expects that they can hold the positions very long. After those the only major defense before Hue is a large military base known as Camp Evans, or Hoa My, about 17 miles from the city. The new headquarters of the Third Division, it is packed with artillery pieces, which are constantly firing.

At the southernmost of the bridges, at a village called Photrach, the South Vietnamese marines watched with pained faces as the army men fled. They would not talk about it, but their embarrassment was plain.

Their American advisers were not so inclined to silence. "This is really sickening," a Marine lance corporal said.

"It's unbelievable," said an American Marine major, Robert Sheridan, as he leaned on a jeep at the side of the road. "It's hard to comprehend. To stand here and watch this when you've seen the same people in your own units fight well because they have different leadership."

"You see the troops," he went on, waving his hand at the road. "But I don't blame them. Where are their officers? There's no one to tell them 'stop' and to pull them together."

The major said the Vietnamese marines in his unit were "very sad and very angry" at the army retreat. "They are embarrassed because I am standing here watching it," he added.

The marines stopped a thousand fleeing rangers last night as they tried to cross the northernmost bridge, he related. The reason for blocking their flight, he said, was that "we couldn't tell if they were enemy." At daylight they were allowed to pass because the marines had no authority to stop them.

The marines fought "a hell of a battle" at the forward bridge this morning, the major said, knocking out 18 tanks with the help of artillery and air strikes.

The major said that last night, when the Communists started moving in the area, he wanted to call in naval gunfire from American vessels standing off the nearby coast, but that South Vietnamese officials held off the fire, apparently because they thought it might hit the retreating forces.

Many of those on foot had inexplicably thrown away their boots and were limping along barefoot. Some had bandaged their feet with rags. All were tattered and muddy. Even those who were riding had had to plod for 10 miles through the countryside during the night before they got to the first bridge held by the marines, where transport was available.

Whether riding or walking, the fleeing men had no time for anything but their own escape.

The body of a soldier lay on the road just outside Camp Evans under the baking sun, a victim, perhaps, of a road accident. His gear lay strewn about him. The troops passed without a glance.

As this correspondent turned back toward Hue today with three other correspondents, an interpreter and a driver in an old Citroën, South Vietnamese soldiers waving automatic rifles and pistols forced the car to halt. Fifteen pushed in and on, blanketing the roof, hood and trunks. All appeared panic-stricken.

One was a major, Nguyen Van Niem, 45, commander of an ordnance company that had fled Quangtri. Laughing with embarrassment, he said he had no idea where his company was.

Like many of the fleeing men, Major Niem said that when he left Quangtri last night he had not seen any enemy troops, nor had he seen Government troops exchanging fire with the enemy. That apparently means that the Government force fled before it was attacked on the ground, although Quangtri had been under intense shelling by heavy artillery for three days.

Major Niem said he was going to Danang, 50 miles south of Hue, to join his parent unit. He said of the retreat, "We do not feel ashamed. The enemy fought very strongly and we have to withdraw from a new front."

As the Citroën went on toward Hue, the driver craning out the window because the windshield was blocked, the soldiers brandished their weapons and uttered threats to keep others along the way from climbing on.

The ordnance major, who pushed his way into the car with great vigor, had developed a severe limp by the time the car reached Hue. He explained that he had been wounded by a rocket, and when he stepped out of the car he hobbled a few paces and collapsed into the arms of a military policeman, who carried him off.

Another soldier had a small neck wound that appeared to be healing nicely. Just before he got off in Hue he unwrapped his first-aid field bandage and asked that it be tied around his neck. A wounded man has a better chance of escaping shipment back to the battlefield.

Some of the retreating troops reached Hue early enough this morning to find time for relaxation and refreshment. A mud-splattered armored personnel carrier clanked through the gate of the main hotel at 9 A.M. and parked on the grass. A dozen soldiers and their captain clambered out, smiling, climbed the three flights to the terrace restaurant overlooking the Huong River and ordered an ample breakfast of omelets and French coffee.

REPORTER'S NOTEBOOK: MUTINOUS SOLDIERS SOW FEAR IN A FIERY RAMPAGE IN HUE
May 8, 1972

HUE, South Vietnam—The young American helicopter pilot, rescued by another helicopter after having been shot down by North Vietnamese ground fire, was badly cut and bruised and in a state of shock.

"It's a dream. It's a dream," he kept repeating incredulously. "It's not happening to me. It's happening to someone else and he's got inside me."

With his words of stunned disbelief, he could have been talking about what happened on the whole northern front this past week—an entire South Vietnamese division was put to rout, thousands of soldiers deserted and went on drunken looting sprees and tens of thousands of civilians fled southward to escape the enemy advance, leaving Hue a city of empty streets and nervous soldiers.

✦

A little girl was found on the road about five miles above Hue. Her mother's body lay nearby, blown apart by a North Vietnamese rocket. The rocket gashed and burned the child's face and arms and broke both her legs, but she lived.

When she was brought to the Hue hospital, her eyes seemed sealed shut. But two days later she was able to open them.

The hospital authorities do not know her name or where she comes from. They think she is nearly 3 years old.

She has been given an orange to try to pacify her, and she grips it in both hands desperately. But it is no pacifier.

"I want to go home," she wails constantly. "I want to go home with my mother."

She also calls for her aunt. Maybe she is calling to the middle-aged woman— also a wounded refugee—who sits on the edge of the child's bed all day long, stroking her head and cooling her with a bamboo fan.

"I want to go home," the child cries again.

"We'll go home tomorrow," the woman says, to soothe her.

"Yes, yes. Please," whimpers the child with no name, gripping her orange.

✦

Quangtri, a city about 40 miles north of Hue, had just fallen—a serious defeat for the South Vietnamese—but the news had not reached many people in Hue yet. At the American compound—whose offices are decorated with such signs as "It's always a good day in Hue" and "We have no problems, only interesting situations"—the music system in the dining room was softly wafting "I'm Dreaming of a White Christmas."

That night, Brig. Gen. Thomas W. Bowen, a disillusioned American adviser whose advice to hold Quangtri had been ignored by South Vietnamese commanders, watched the evening movie—"Shaft."

Interviewed afterward in his trailer, where he was reading a book titled "Imperial Tragedy," about the last days of the war against Japan, the general talked gloomily of the fall of Quangtri and the threat now to Hue, and said, "This hasn't been my most jolly day."

✦

The fleeing civilians came first down Route 1 toward Hue—before the government soldiers—when it seemed Quangtri would fall soon. The river of refugees stretched unbroken in some places for three miles or more. Silhouetted against a darkening and drizzly sky, they plodded south with their sacks and babies and animals. Piglets squealed. Chickens chattered. The people were silent.

Though frightened, the peasants seemed stoic and pragmatic. There was no panic. Some of them had been through it all many times before and some only a few weeks ago, when they fled their homes in the first enemy push. Later they had returned to Quangtri when they mistakenly thought it was safe again.

"We tried to get away from the shells coming down to Quangtri," said a woman who was fleeing with her two children for the second time in a month, "but the shells were everywhere and we had to leave the city."

✦

A South Vietnamese soldier who ran away on March 31, the second day of the enemy invasion, hitches a ride in our car. Asked if he is returning to fight with his unit, he says no, he is only returning to try to collect his pay. What if he gets arrested for desertion, he is asked. "I would rather go to jail than to the battlefield," he replies.

✦

A day later, two members of the Popular Force, a kind of home guard, discussed their fright frankly as they clambered onto a bus for Hue. "We are scared of the shelling," one said. "Let the regular troops fight."

A few miles farther on, three regular soldiers fleeing from overrun Dongha, a town north of Quangtri, said they were heading for Hue to get out of the fighting. Asked why they did not stop in Quangtri to help defend that city as they retreated, one of them said, "We have already fought hard. Quangtri is not safe for us."

These three soldiers and several others commandeered a bus at rifle point and forced many refugees off, hurling their meager belongings after them. Pots of rice and greens splattered on the road. As the bus sped to Hue, it passed a sign that reads, "Drive defensively. Your country needs you."

✦

On the official level, there is an unreality in the language used to describe the fighting—a devotion to euphemism. When a key fire support base called Bastogne, about 15 miles west of Hue, was taken by the North Vietnamese, an American adviser insisted, "We weren't overrun. We just withdrew."

He said the loss of Bastogne was on balance a good thing because it made the defense line for Hue tighter and more viable. He explained the actions of the Army of the Republic of South Vietnam by saying, "The ARVN had been defending Bastogne like it was some kind of national shrine. Actually, it was a pain in the butt to resupply."

✦

After one ambush was temporarily beaten off on Route 1, there was a respite in the fighting. The South Vietnamese troops scavenged through the belongings of the enemy dead. One soldier sniffed at a handkerchief he pulled out of a North Vietnamese pack and giggled.

Letters were strewn in the sand. One, from an enemy soldier's girlfriend, told of the death of her father and her sadness. She added, "But I forbid you to be sad, because you are at the battlefield and that needs all your courage and zeal. Besides, you don't have the right yet to be sad for me. You are still only my boyfriend, not yet my husband."

Another North Vietnamese soldier had a letter from his brother, also a soldier. It read, "We are now ready to make a drive. We hope we can do something for the country. We leave in a few weeks for the South. This is my second time. I'll try to do better this time."

✦

The South Vietnamese marines are the only government troops fighting well on the northern front. An American marine adviser—a huge, blond and grubbily unshaven major—led his battalion to a new position along Route 1. He beamed as he greeted an American newsman with a thumbs-up gesture. "We had two contacts this morning," he chortled, "kicked the . . . out of them. We got 40 of them, lost only three ourselves. It was great. Outstanding!"

✦

The South Vietnamese soldier long ago adopted G.I. slang for his scale of values. When something is "Number One," it is the best. "Number Ten" is the worst. But the recent defeats have added new dimensions to the low end of the scale.

"Everything Number One?" a passerby yelled to a South Vietnamese soldier standing by his truck, as other troops retreated past him. "Yeah," he replied sardonically. "Number One Thousand."

✦

Some of the retreating troops of the Third Division shed their rank and insignia. When they reach Hue, many turn ugly, taking things from shops and stalls without paying. They are deserters now, ashamed and surly—and armed.

They curse their officers for having abandoned them at Quangtri—many officers ran away first—and to express their rage they set fire to the central marketplace. Neither the police nor the fire department dare to intervene, and the blaze becomes a Cecil B. DeMille spectacular.

✦

The next morning people are leaving Hue by the tens of thousands, fearing the enemy attack might be imminent. Because most of the market was destroyed during the night, there are no eggs or bread for breakfast at the hotel occupied almost exclusively by journalists. Much of the staff has fled—the laundry crew among them—causing a brief panic among the more fastidious newsmen.

The drivers of rented cars have also fled, so it becomes a war to cover on foot.

Transportation out of Hue becomes chaotic. For the poor, there is nothing to do but walk. But for those with some money, there is bargaining. Owners of cars are demanding 40,000 piasters (about $100) for the 50-mile trip to Danang.

At the airport Air Vietnam flights are booked three weeks in advance, but scalpers have bought up blocks seats and are extorting enormous sums from panicking families.

There is also a Chinese clock maker who will arrange boat transportation down to Danang in large but often leaky sampans—for 5,000 piasters ($12) a head.

✦

This city—which had been swollen by refugees to a population of over 350,000—has shrunk to maybe 50,000.

One of those still wandering the streets is a tank commander who escaped from Quangtri and now seems unable to comprehend what has happened. Asked where he was going, he said, "I don't know. Maybe some coffee shop where there is soft music. When I was a kid, I used to sit for hours in a coffee shop listening to soft music. It was so good."

He could find no coffee shop open in Hue, nor any soft music.

✦

At night, the city streets are eerie and walking back from the American compound, where a newsman can telephone his story to Saigon, is a nervous experience. North Vietnamese infiltrators have reportedly slipped into town and every shadow is a lump in the throat.

South Vietnamese sentries are just as nervous, for they fire at shadows. The late walker whistles and sings and shouted "*bao-chi*" (newsman) every 30 seconds or so.

✦

In the morning, Hue was very still. The city was nearly empty. The police and a few other civil servants were left, as were the regrouping Government troops and some civilian diehards.

The Quangtri province chief who had fled to Hue and set up a "government in exile" there fled further south to Danang and once again announced his exile administration.

✦

The Americans' Armed Forces Vietnam Network comes on with a revised call sign. It used to say "This is AFVN, serving the American fighting man 24 hours a day, from the delta to the DMZ." Now that the North Vietnamese have pushed their border 30 miles south of the demilitarized zone, the military network says simply that it serves the fighting man all day, with no reference to geography.

✦

A professor of French at Hue University opens a conversation with a news-man at the telegraph office. His wife had taken their three children to safety in Danang, and he is waiting for her to come back before they move the last of their belongings.

"How long do you think I can stay in Hue?" he asks. "Will it be safe for five days, maybe a week? I must wire for my wife and I have not heard from her."

The newsman says he has no way of knowing when the enemy will attack, but the distraught professor keeps asking how much time he has. Finally, he lowers his voice to a desperate whisper and asks, "Will the American troops come back? Will the marines come to help us?"

He pauses, then adds woefully, "If they don't Hue is finished, and the country is finished."

✦

On the street outside, a deserter tries to sell me his M-16 rifle. When I de-cline, he says, "No sweat, man."

✦

At the military compound inside the old walled section of Hue known as the Citadel, there is a mammoth hospital complex for the thousands of army wounded. What will happen to them when the North Vietnamese attack, a doctor is asked. He shakes his head disconsolately. "They'll never get them out of here in time."

✦

A young policeman on duty at one of Hue's bridges has sent his family away.

But he says, "I've got my back to the wall. If I run away now, the government might arrest and shoot me. And if I stay, maybe the other side will kill me."

✦

It all sounds hopeless and irretrievable. But when a student friend in Hue is asked what will be his people's fate, he smiles and replies stoically, "We'll survive. That's all I know. We'll survive."

VIETNAM'S QUEEN MOTHER AGES ALONE, SAYS SON IN PARIS DOESN'T WRITE
May 16, 1972

HUE, South Vietnam—She is part of Vietnam's past, though probably not its future.

"If the Communists come, I will have to run away because I cannot live with Communists." The tiny woman pauses, then adds, "And because they will kill me."

The queen mother of the Vietnamese royal family, Tu Cung, is 84 years old. The last time North Vietnamese troops occupied Hue—for three weeks during the Lunar New Year offensive of 1968—she stayed here through the fighting. But then the attack came as a surprise. This time the enemy's preparations for an assault on the former imperial capital of Vietnam are well known.

Tu Cung's only son, Bao Dai, now 60 and living in exile in France, was Vietnam's last Emperor. He was deposed in 1955 by Ngo Dinh Diem, who became the first president of South Vietnam.

The queen mother, who speaks very softly, drops her voice even lower, when she talks of her son. She is hurt, it seems, that he does not write more often. "I get letters sometimes after two weeks, sometimes after two months," she says. "You know, a mother and a son are tied tightly together."

She seems to crave news of Bao Dai, for she asks her visitor several times if he will be stopping in Paris soon, and if so, will he please drop in on her son.

"He lives in Paris," she says, "but he is always thinking of Vietnam, and especially Hue."

When her son was deposed, the queen mother left the spacious palace in the walled imperial section of Hue. She now lives in a two-story French colonial-style house beside a moat in a well-to-do section of the city.

It is grand by Vietnamese standards, but not palatial. The house sits in a two-acre compound lush with coconut palms and mango trees. A pagoda bell and gong graces the second-floor balcony. A television aerial sprouts from the roof.

The local government has provided a guard of about a dozen soldiers—largely symbolic protection for the queen mother.

The queen mother welcomed her visitors graciously at short notice. "I do not normally receive visitors at this hour," she said, "but because you must return to Saigon this afternoon, I have agreed." She showed them into a sitting room filled with heavy wooden furniture inlaid with marble and mother of pearl.

The furniture dwarfs the queen mother, a miniature woman who has become frail and whose little gold-slippered feet now walk in a halting shuffle. Her graying hair is thinning toward baldness, her teeth are lacquered black according to local custom and wrinkles seam what must have been a pretty face.

Paintings and photographs surround her—of Bao Dai, of his father and her husband, Khai Dinh, the previous Emperor, and of herself, on a throne.

She was dressed in a golden silk ao dai—the traditional long Vietnamese gown—with the imperial dragon design. The effect is elegance, yet somehow faded.

When her visitor asked her what she thought would happen to South Vietnam now, she answered with a plaintive question: "Do you have any good ideas to help save Vietnam and the Vietnamese people from the present crisis?"

Throughout the interview, she repeated this appeal. "The situation is very cruel," she said. "It is worse than ever before. Many people are being killed, civilians as well as soldiers. The Vietnamese people do not like Communism. Is there no way the great powers can end this suffering without Communist domination?"

She talked incessantly of the importance of Hue, its history and tradition as the royal seat. "This city is the face of Vietnam," she said. "If it falls, Vietnam will lose its face before the world and will fall, too."

She sidesteps all political questions about the Government in Saigon, but complains bitterly that she was never compensated for the damage done in 1968 to one of the huge houses her husband left her.

About her daily regimen, the queen mother, a devout Buddhist who observes a vegetarian diet half of the year, said, "I cannot work because I am too old and weak. I pray all day. I pray for everybody, for all of living life and nature."

She refused to allow her picture to be taken, but said that if her visitor got written permission from Bao Dai in Paris and brought it back to Hue, it would be all right then.

She was asked if her son, whom she has not seen for 17 years, had any plans to try to return to Vietnam. "It's not a good time, even if he wanted to," she said. "It depends on the wishes of the people. They must be willing."

She was silent for a moment. Then, wistfully, she said, "I am always waiting for him."

DOWNED U.S. PILOT CELEBRATES HIS RESCUE FROM THE GULF OF TONKIN
May 20, 1972

ABOARD U.S.S. CONSTELLATION, in the Gulf of Tonkin—Thomas R. Wilkinson's A-7 Corsair jet was hit by antiaircraft fire on a bombing mission over North Vietnam today, but the Navy pilot managed to make it out to sea. He parachuted and was later plucked from the Gulf of Tonkin by a rescue helicopter as shells from enemy shore batteries pocked the water around him.

"From the lion's jaws back to life again," the exultant squadron commander said a few hours later, after the helicopter had returned him to his base, this aircraft carrier steaming about 60 miles off North Vietnam.

His narrow escape typified the fears and risks shared by all the pilots on this and the four other attack carriers that are part of the 60-ship flotilla of the Seventh Fleet operating off Vietnam.

Before today, Commander Wilkinson, a 42-year-old veteran of five tours in Vietnam, had flown 125 bombing missions over North Vietnam "through flak you could walk on and I always managed to skate out."

He told his story to a group of newsmen aboard the Constellation—after changing into his tropical khakis and paying a visit to the flight surgeon. The surgeon had ordered him to take a 24-hour rest and had celebrated his rescue with a prescription of medicinal spirits.

Commander Wilkinson said his plane was hit at about 9:30 A.M., just as his group was beginning its mission against targets northwest of Donghoi. The shell hit just behind and below the cockpit and, he said, the plane quickly became a "flaming hulk."

Though the cockpit was filling with smoke and the pilot was gulping for air, he was able to turn the plane toward the coast, about eight miles away, and was four miles over the sea when the situation became untenable and he pressed the ejection button. "All I could think of at first was to get over water," he said.

The coastal guns began firing at him even before he and his parachute hit the water. One of the first things he did in the water was light an orange smoke flare to mark his position. But he quickly realized that this also marked him for the enemy guns. So he snuffed out the flare, shed all his gear, took off his boots and deflated his life vest somewhat—to make himself as inconspicuous as possible.

Shells fell within 100 yards of him. "I could see the shrapnel peppering like rain around me," he said.

Meanwhile, his buddies were circling in eight or nine jets trying to protect him and knock out the coastal guns with bombs. Eventually, these guns fell silent but antiaircraft batteries kept firing at the jets that continued to circle until the rescue helicopter, which they had called in from the nearby carrier Kitty Hawk, arrived.

"Time passed very slowly," Commander Wilkinson said.

Finally, after he was in the water for about half an hour, the helicopter, which had taken antiaircraft fire coming in, hovered at about 30 feet and lowered the rescue cable. A paramedic dived into the water, attached a cable to both their harnesses and signaled the helicopter to haul away.

Less than an hour later, the copter landed on the flight deck on the Constellation and Commander Wilkinson, wearing someone else's fatigue uniform, hopped down—his face lit like a Christmas tree. He punched a deck crewman on the shoulder and embraced another.

"Tom, welcome aboard," the captain's voice boomed over the public-address system.

Since the North Vietnamese offensive began, the Constellation has lost only three planes and two fliers.

Her 75 jet bombers and fighter-bombers have flown well over 1,000 missions and are estimated to have dropped 2,000 tons of bombs.

The Constellation's Captain J. D. Ward, said today that he was "very pleased and happy" with President Nixon's decision to mine enemy ports and to begin heavy bombing of communications and supply lines. The carrier's planes were reportedly involved in laying the mines, but the captain declined to comment.

The mining and the bombing, said Captain Ward, "are the best move in the whole war toward stopping the supply flow and defeating North Vietnam."

Many of the pilots share his enthusiasm for the wider air war.

"A lot of us felt the war was being pursued with no view to winning," said Allan Junker, a 27-year-old lieutenant from Nashville who flies an A-7. "The enemy lived in a sanctuary," he said. "The restriction on the war meant we were losing men needlessly. Now there's a shining light on the horizon."

Another, pilot, Lieut. David Garcia, also 27, of Modesto, Calif., who flies F-4 Phantoms, decried antiwar demonstrators "who just want to tear things down."

"I feel what I'm doing now is constructive," he said. "If the war ends tomorrow, I can look at myself in the mirror and say, okay, I did my part."

While some of the pilots are committed to winning the war, others are simply committed to flying—the enjoyment and excitement of it, the technical thrill of hitting a given target.

Their commitment is also related to their being volunteers and career men. Several of them, in many conversations today, seemed to need the catharsis of talking to an outsider—to explain why they do what they do, in the face of what they regard as hostility to the bombing in the American press and public.

"I do enjoy the challenge of seeing if I can hit something on the ground," said Douglas Ball, a 26-year-old F-4 pilot from Seattle. "Not people. I don't enjoy the idea of killing people. It happens sometimes. But that's not our primary purpose. That's not the satisfaction I'm talking about."

What about the risk of being hit by antiaircraft guns or missiles, and being either killed or taken prisoner?

"Being shot at is terrifying," Lieutenant Ball said softly, lowering his eyes.

But after a pause, the young pilot blurted out, almost convulsively, "I can't recall a period of my life when—I wouldn't call it excitement—but you see the SAM's coming right at you—the big balls of fire blowing from the tails—and then you come out of it alive. Well, you're elated. You're elated."

THE SAIGON FOLLIES, OR, TRYING TO HEAD THEM OFF AT CREDIBILITY GAP
November 12, 1972, The New York Times Magazine

SAIGON—Not long ago, a key officer in the military office of information told a newsman that his previous job in Washington—he had come from a high information post at the Pentagon—had been much harder. In Washington, he explained, there were continual "leaks" from Capitol Hill that had to be reacted to and denied quickly so as to get the denials into the next morning's newspapers, whereas in Vietnam things were simpler because "there's no competing line."

Before this officer arrived in Saigon a few months ago, one of his franker colleagues-to-be was asked what kind of man he was. "He's got a reputation," the man said wryly, "as a leading graduate of the Pentagon school of escape and evasion." Escape and evasion about sum up the attitude that most American officials in Vietnam have taken toward newsmen most of the time—an attitude that, notwithstanding areas of guarded coexistence, generally consists of suspicion, distrust and sometimes outright animosity.

Recently, when two reporters from the same American publication arrived for an interview, a high embassy official physically pushed one of them out of his office on the ground that he was hostile to the story the embassy was then marketing. Usually the relationship between the American Establishment in Vietnam and the press has been more civil than this, at times even cordial, but the outcome has been the same: very little information has been dispensed. The Establishment has been "nothing but a huge fact-suppression machine," says one seasoned American newsman.

There is absolutely no reason to believe that obfuscations and falsehoods would suddenly cease with a cease-fire. On the contrary, there is every reason to believe that until love and brotherhood break out in epidemic form all over Indochina there will be no public frankness about what is going on here.

I am not an old hand in Vietnam—my reporting here consists of a brief 10-day stint in 1970 during the American incursion into Cambodia and most recently a four-and-a-half month tour to cover the North Vietnamese offensive— so I cannot personally compare what it was like to cover the war in, say, the nineteen-sixties to what it is like today. Yet from all accounts—though the American Establishment has always tried to suppress unhappy facts—it would seem that with more of the American involvement becoming hidden from the press (such as the air bases in Thailand that are usually closed to newsmen), American officials in Saigon have been more secretive and more obstructive.

News stories from Saigon almost never use the word "lie" about American press releases and reports—perhaps because of the need for coexistence and because softer words will get the idea across. But there is really no other word for some of the stories the Americans put out. For example, when the number of bombing raids against North Vietnam increased markedly in the period from November 8, 1971, to March 8, 1972, the American command explained it by saying the weather had improved. It later turned out that this explanation concealed the fact that the Seventh Air Force commander, Gen. John D. Lavelle, frustrated by the restrictions on bombing of North Vietnam, had ordered unauthorized raids on military targets in the North and called them "protective reaction" attacks. The raids suddenly stopped from March 8 until March 30, the day the current North Vietnamese invasion of South Vietnam began. The command said the weather had closed in again.

What had happened had nothing to do with the weather. General Lavelle's activities had been exposed by the Air Force intelligence specialist who wrote to his Senator about the unauthorized raids—and all missions over the North had then been halted while an investigation was under way. General Lavelle was recalled to Washington, demoted and relieved of command.

This is but one of almost daily instances of distortions and omissions of facts—a practice that stems more from official embarrassment over the course of events than from reasons of military security. The South Vietnamese information apparatus is even less truthful—their briefers occasionally announce victories that simply have not occurred and often omit all mention of defeats but foreign newsmen do not generally expect Vietnamese officials to tell the truth about how the war is going. It is appreciated that, unlike the Americans, they have more at stake than failure of a foreign policy.

The idea of the press as an adversary to government is certainly not new. All governments try to control the news, especially in crises. But I for one have never been in a reporting situation quite as frustrating as the one in Vietnam. Reporters can, from time to time, obtain interviews with all the top American officials—with Ambassador Ellsworth Bunker and also the commanding generals—but none will speak for the record. No names can be used. No one accepts personal responsibility for what he says. What this means is that these men can get things in print as the official American view—sometimes outrageous things—and never have to answer for them personally if events prove their analyses totally wrong. How many times did we "turn the corner" in Vietnam or sight that famous light at the end of the tunnel? Usually these officials do not assume this cloak of anonymity out of venality but rather out of fear, and presumably because of instructions from Washington. Toward the end of April, when Brig. Gen. Thomas W. Bowen spoke frankly and on the record to reporters in Hue about the deteriorating situation on the northern front, he was admonished and silenced by his superiors in Saigon, who had apparently got the word from Washington.

Few of the reporters I know in Vietnam, though they often get frustrated, ever get truly angry at being treated hostilely or with suspicion by American generals or embassy officials. They accept that this hostility is born of the failure of American policy here and of the inability of those whose careers have become so entwined with Vietnam to admit it. Some of these men have been in Vietnam for a decade. They know virtually no other life but the one of trying to make American policy come out right. To admit defeat would be to throwaway the linchpin of their existence. But the press has reported their failures for them, and under such circumstances no one can be surprised at their distrust and dislike of newsmen.

Typical of such men was the American general advising on the northern front who agreed to talk off the record with a half-dozen Western reporters one day. He immediately made it clear that he considered us unpatriotic, because he assumed, correctly, that we had been writing stories saying the war was not going well for the allied side.

"I want you to get something straight," he said, pointing an accusing finger. "You're talking to a hawk. You know that. The only solution possible is a military solution. It's going to take a military victory to end it. We've got to prove to the North Vietnamese that they can't invade and take over." The general then said that the North Vietnamese high command does not put the same value on life as Americans and South Vietnamese do. "They've already determined they can expend 100,000 men this year on the offensive and they don't care if they come back or not. A North Vietnamese officer has the power of life and death over his men. They shoot a man if he refuses to go on attack." Saying these things seemed to console the general.

He then repeated what had become a standard allied briefing note—"The North Vietnamese are chained inside their tanks. They are also chained together in their bunkers." But he acknowledged that he had never seen this himself nor did he know anyone who had. There were no pictures either of such forced military service among the Communists. If this had been a popular war, perhaps the relationship between the generals and the press would have been a more salutary one, as it was in World War II. But most of the generals blamed the press largely for the war's unpopularity and this made *détente* impossible.

For a reporter, talking with the generals can be an unsettling experience, for there is often no communication, as if two people from different planets had just met. Naturally each believes the other is not addressing reality. Actually both are wrong: They are simply dealing in different realities. Many of the military men still cannot grasp why the rules of war have been changed for them between World War II and Vietnam. They have not understood the seriousness of the social stresses triggered by this war on the people back home. They cannot cope with the fact that Air Force aces are no longer welcomed as dashing young heroes when they go home these days but as shadowy, questionable figures whose bombs may have killed or maimed civilians. In short, these men are bitter.

"We wiped out whole cities, whole cities, in World War II," an Air Force general fumed in a recent interview, "and there wasn't a single protest. Now one bomb falls outside the target area and they scream in righteous moral indignation. It's all baloney." This general, another anonymous member of the American hierarchy, became greatly exorcised during the interview, frequently pounding his desk and raising his voice in exasperation. I rather doubt whether anything I said was responsible, for I said very little—the interview was largely a monologue. It was just that his frustration was terrible and he needed someone to rail at, and I was a newsman and per se a culprit.

"The thing that's played up is the alleged wrongs of the military, the bombing of the dikes, when it's not being done," he said. "It's the big lie. We haven't done any of these things you read about. That's why we introduced 'smart bombs.' I look at every photo like a hawk. This thing is on my desk at all times [waving a large magnifying glass]. I've never seen a picture of a hospital hit. I have a hard time finding any misses. I think you'd be hard-pressed to find 3 percent of the bombs outside the target area. And then they're not very far out." He refused to talk about civilian casualties. Or to discuss the war in human terms at all. At one point I said that his press releases used a jargonized form of language that made the bombing sound like a clean surgical operation instead of the mess and horror that war actually is. He was polite but in his next sentence he talked of bombing "on a surgical precision basis." We were discussing two different realities.

In criticizing the American Establishment for being less than frank, I am not suggesting that the press corps in Saigon has no warts. Some reporters suffer from the same malaise that seems to grip their readers—a sense of weary *déjà vu* about Vietnam and maybe a hardening of viewpoint. Judging from the readers' letters received by me and my reporter friends, and from the reactions reported by other newsmen who have returned from home leaves in the States, most Americans seemed to have made up their minds and taken sides on the war long ago and haven't wanted to read or hear anything that might interfere with their point of view. It's not hard to understand this, but it is difficult to write for an already locked-in audience and even more difficult to read their letters.

Consider a letter from a young antiwar activist in Maine who wanted to help a wounded and orphaned 3-year-old girl I had written about. He wrote "as an American whose Government is the prime mover" behind the war and behind this particular incident, ignoring what I had clearly written in my story—that this little girl had been wounded and her mother killed by North Vietnamese troops who had fired deliberately on civilians trying to flee south out of embattled Quangtri province. Or consider the letter from a doctor in New Jersey who began his epistle, "dear S---berg" and then went on to accuse me of working for the Communists.

I think some reporters do come to Vietnam with their opinions, like the letter writers', already formed, but I would contend that these are a small minority. The press corps in Saigon, as in Washington or any capital, is hardly a corps at all in the sense that its members think or act in a uniform manner. Many reporters, if not most, have spent a lot of time in the field, seeing the fighting and its consequences for themselves. If the bulk of reporting from Vietnam over the past decade has suggested the existence of a chasm between optimistic official pronouncements and actual events in the field, it is because reporters, separately, have personally observed that chasm, not because they sat in bars in Saigon and cooked it up to be perverse.

One myth fostered by supporters of United States policy in Vietnam is that the Saigon press corps is a monolithic body whose members, to a man, are antiwar ideologues who spend their days searching sedulously for negative things to write about. These people would be pleased to learn that there are prominent reporters in Saigon who have been sympathetic to American policy—and they are the only ideologues this reporter met while in Vietnam.

Item: A British correspondent, who has earned a reputation as a hawk, not only writes for a leading London newspaper but also prepares reports for Sir Robert Thompson, the guerrilla-warfare specialist who receives huge fees for advising the United States Government. Sir Robert's reports have generally told the Americans the light-at-the-end-of-the-tunnel things they wanted to hear, and the one report I saw done by the British correspondent for Sir Robert did much the same thing. Presumably it was passed on to the Nixon Administration as expert analysis. That correspondent almost never moves out of Saigon and his report was based on developments in combat theaters he had never been to. He asked my opinion of the report and I pointed out several major errors of fact about battles I had covered—errors that made his conclusions ridiculous. But I got the impression that he had no intention of changing a word.

Item: The acting bureau chief of a major American publication, whose sympathies with the American Embassy and the Saigon Government are well known, first allowed one of the bureau reporters to prepare a story on the torture of political prisoners by the Government and then successfully killed the story by telling his editors in New York that the subject was old hat and had been well covered before. But he acknowledged to the reporter later that the real reason he had scotched the piece was that "this is a sensitive time for [President Nguyen Van] Thieu and I don't think we should add to his troubles."

At the moment, there are more than 350 newsmen in Vietnam accredited by the South Vietnamese Government and the American command known as MACV (Military Assistance Command, Vietnam). This includes both freelancers and full-time salaried correspondents. Of the total, about 150 are Americans and the rest are about evenly divided between third-country nationals and Vietnamese newsmen working for foreign news agencies. The press corps was larger in the early weeks of the Communist offensive that began last spring. It reached 490 in late May. The record was set during the Communist Tet offensive of 1968, when the number reached 647.

It goes without saying that not all stories written from Vietnam are prize-winners. There cannot be a reporter in Vietnam who doesn't cringe at the memory of some of the stories he wrote in the innocence of his early days in the country or on the basis of information that looked absolutely solid at the time. I would give a lot to be able to redo a story I wrote in late July reporting that South Vietnamese units were making progress in clearing Communist troops off Route 13 between Saigon and Anloc—which was true at the time. But the story also suggested that the road might be opened up soon—which never happened. Route 13 has been cut since early April and it remains so.

Newsmen also suffer occasionally, from real and imagined pressures. There is the pressure of competition, felt most keenly by the international wire services, each of which has had to put out a combat story every day and then face a rating system by its editors according to the play the story received around the world. And some newsmen feel a compulsion, when they haven't written a story for several days, to sit down at the typewriter just "to get something in the paper." Right or wrong, reporters often feel their editors are grading them, at least partly, on quantity.

And then there are the pressures from melodramatic editors. A correspondent for a popular British paper received the following cable from his home office last April 25: "In view of rapidly worsening Vietnam situation, editor wants you to give top priority to big piece on the plight of Saigon. He sees it as Berlin-type situation with Red forces closing in from all sides. The city built up on American money, where one could get anything from a missile to a beautiful girl. Now the whole infrastructure likely to be dismantled. David wants good, hard, color-packed copy which would make spread. Repeat, must be serious but perhaps cynical to match mood of nation facing defeat and mood of Nixon in almost hopeless dilemma." This cable would be laughable if it were not so professionally disgraceful. At no time in the North Vietnamese offensive has the city of Saigon been directly threatened. I do not know if the reporter wrote a story along the lines suggested.

There was also an Italian correspondent who received this cable on Aug. 23: "*Mandaci un pezzo sull'offensiva di Giap l'assedio che stringe Saigon.*"—"send a piece on Giap's offensive and the siege that squeezes Saigon."

These reports are extreme cases, and fairly rare, but moderately misguided cables from editors are common. It is up to the reporter, who is not always willing to risk a fight with his desk, to resist writing such poorly conceived stories. However, as often as not, the clinkers from Vietnam have been the result of something doled out in a press release or briefing by the American or South Vietnamese commands. For instance, one wire service, United Press International, went along with the Government claims in reporting the recapture of Quangtri Citadel in early July, and did not back off the story for nearly a week. The citadel was finally retaken, but not until September. Such episodes underscore one of the basic difficulties with coverage of Vietnam and one of the caveats the reader of Vietnam news should be apprised of: the core of the combat story that many American newspapers run as a daily staple comes from an afternoon briefing in downtown Saigon that bears about as much relation to reality as a trip through a funhouse at an amusement park.

The briefing, which has become known as "the Follies," begins at 4:15 P.M. in a sweltering unair-conditioned auditorium that is part of a euphemistic operation known as the Press Center. Press releases are passed out beforehand—one from MACV, a separate one from the American Navy that expands on items already in the MACV release (the Air Force also puts out a separate one but distributes it in news-agency mailboxes), and one from the South Vietnamese armed forces, prepared by their Political Warfare Department. Political warfare is perhaps as good a way as any to describe what the American and South Vietnamese officers do at the briefing, which lasts anywhere from five minutes to half an hour. The Vietnamese military briefer steps to the lectern first, adding late developments to the press release, if there are any, and then accepting questions. The MACV briefer who follows conducts a similar performance.

Their releases and answers are notable primarily for their omissions. Entire battles have gone unreported. In early September, an Associated Press correspondent, through other sources, had learned of and written about a major two-day clash that had taken place less than 40 miles north of Saigon in which 180 North Vietnamese were killed and about 200 South Vietnamese were killed or wounded. When the battle had gone unmentioned at the briefing for two days, the correspondent asked the reason for the omission.

The South Vietnamese briefer went shuffling through the mound of papers on his clipboard and finally announced, "Between noon and early evening on Friday, Sept. 1, ARVN [Army of the Republic of Vietnam] elements engaged an undetermined-sized enemy force 12 kilometers north of Laikhe; 83 enemy were killed. On the ARVN side, 76 were wounded." On the face of it, this report was preposterous—it would take a miracle to produce a battle in which 76 men get wounded and not a single one dies. ARVN was simply covering up its losses again. These lies and omissions have tended to increase whenever battle losses have.

The American briefers, who smile knowingly about ARVN's doctoring of battle statistics, have not been much more forthcoming themselves with the facts of war. Their language, which has no connection with everyday English, has been designed to sanitize the war. Planes do not drop bombs, they "deliver ordnance." Napalm is a forbidden word and, when an American information officer is forced under direct questioning to discuss it, he calls it "soft ordnance." In the press releases and the answers to newsmen's questions, there is never any sense, not even implicit, of people being killed, homes being destroyed, thousands of refugees fleeing.

What has made the briefers' job of obfuscation easier is that nearly all the American involvement in the war was gradually moved out of the sight of newsmen. With ground combat troops phased out, the air offensive became virtually the only American combat function left, aside from advisers in the field, and most of the air offensive has been conducted in secrecy. In mid-October, an estimated 800 to 900 jet fighter-bombers were involved in the air war and as many as 200 B-52 eight-engine heavy-load bombers. But of this armada of more than 1,000 planes, fewer than 50 were left in South Vietnam. Some of the B-52's were based on Guam, but all the rest of our planes flew either from seven bases in Thailand or from carriers off the Vietnam coast. Visits by newsmen to carriers could be arranged, but they were carefully controlled. And the Thai bases have been virtually closed to newsmen. After years of press appeals to the American command in Thailand and the Thai Government (which has paper jurisdiction over the bases), a one-day tour of two of the Thai bases was finally arranged for a group of reporters on Aug. 29. But it turned out to be even more controlled and deodorized than the carrier visits. A few selected American airmen were produced for interviews, but newsmen were not allowed to talk to any others.

"The main difference between then and now," Malcolm W. Browne, a *Times* correspondent in Saigon who won a Pulitzer Prize for his coverage of Vietnam for the Associated Press in 1964, said recently, "is that then they tried to persuade us. Now they don't bother. They just freeze us out." In short, newsmen have known little more about the air war than what they were told by official releases and briefers, and there is strong evidence that much has been left out. For example, Pentagon sources in Washington disclosed to a *Times* correspondent that, from the start of the North Vietnamese offensive on March 30, fighter-bombers on occasion attacked railroad targets in North Vietnam within 25 miles of the Chinese border, that is, inside the 25-mile buffer zone in which American planes were forbidden to strike without special permission from Washington. In two or three instances, these officials said, planes strayed very close to Chinese airspace before being warned back by radar controllers, and on at least one of these occasions, Chinese jets were scrambled, but there was no shooting.

None of these raids were ever reported by the American Information machine in Saigon. The operation was, in a sense, denied, in one recent four-month period, on every occasion when the vague geographical description of a strike in the press releases suggested that it might possibly have been inside the 25-mile buffer zone. *The New York Times* bureau in Saigon asked the command information office if this was the case, and the office flatly said no. When the story broke from Washington in late August, I called the information office and asked one of the briefers why the raids had not been reported and, rhetorically, I asked him if he didn't agree that this sort of thing seriously damaged MACV's credibility. He expressed regret and helplessness and finally said, "What can we do? Sometimes they just don't tell us things."

The credibility gap in Saigon makes other such gaps look like hairline fractures. Perhaps every story based on the official communiqués—such as those about the bombing of the North—should be preceded by a paragraph in italics telling the reader that since the allies' track record on facts has been so poor, we have no way of knowing whether they are telling the truth and therefore cannot advise him on how credible the following story is.

Of course, the North Vietnamese and Vietcong propaganda apparatus, broadcasting and publishing from Hanoi, can hardly be considered reliable either. And since the Communists have refused to allow foreign newsmen to cover the war from their side of the fighting lines in South Vietnam, a large piece is, unavoidably, missing from the coverage. This press blackout obviously suits Hanoi's purposes—the mystery about the Communists' military operations has tended to cast an aura of invincibility around them. This is reinforced by the fact that without air support of their own, the Communists, indeed, kept coming despite the awesome American bombing. In any case, the Hanoi broadcasts and press releases are not treated in the American press with the respectability given to the American command's communiqués. They are treated as propaganda, as they should be, and buried in a paragraph or two at the bottom of other stories.

All the obstructionism notwithstanding, it was never very difficult to find out how the war was going. All it took was traveling to the field. It is there that reporters, often at great personal risk, have used their eyes and ears and common sense to paint an accurate picture of Vietnam over the years. In any journalistic situation, no single story is ever the whole truth. But after the fallible reporter has written 50 or 100 stories on the same subject, a true pattern emerges and the reader, if he has been patient, will have been enlightened. This is what has happened in Vietnam. There is no place for sham in the field, where the possibility of death is always so near, and this is why the story gets "trued up" there.

"I don't kid myself," says a weary American Marine adviser whom I met on a recent visit to the northern front. "Our mission was to bring democratic representative government to South Vietnam. The fact is, we lost. The fact is, they're not going to get democratic government." South Vietnamese artillery batteries are pounding a Communist-held village less than a mile away, but the exhausted soldiers around this command post—knowing how precious are their minutes away from the fighting—have learned to sleep through it. Some are awake, however, writing letters home, playing Chinese checkers. In a makeshift lean-to, a private with a guitar sings a ballad for his buddies in which a South Vietnamese girl laments her lover's departure for the front: "I ask you, I ask you when will you come back. Please tell me, please tell me, that tomorrow or the day after you will return."

A few days later, a blond Marine major, James Dyer, orders a drink at an American canteen in Hue and tries to behave normally, but can't keep up the facade. His face twists in pain, as he fights back the tears. "Worst day in my life," he blurts to a complete stranger next to him. "My buddy got it. Dan Kingman. His chopper got hit. Oh, damn. Damn. Damn. They shot him out of the sky." His head drops to his chest. "Nothing's worth Dan Kingman," he says, almost in a whisper. "Nothing. He was a soldier. A soldier. That's all you've got to know."

The reporter returns to Saigon to sit through an interview with an embassy official, anonymous as usual, who tells him, in response to allegations of widespread torture of political prisoners in South Vietnam's prisons, that although there are 150 American "public safety" advisers working with the Vietnamese on police and prison matters, the embassy has no information one way or the other. Because he knows this sounds incredible, he adds that "all kinds of deplorable things may well be going on," but he quickly tacks on, in amelioration of this torture the embassy knows nothing about, that some of the people arrested are known anti-Government activists involved in terrorist activities—"and who aren't exactly the nice college kids next door."

Perhaps this official's peculiar morality touches the crux of the problem for reporters in Vietnam. As long as the Governments involved continue to portray the issue as a struggle between good and evil, then the conflict between the press and these Governments will continue. For there are no good guys or bad guys in Vietnam. There are only victims.

CHAPTER FIVE

Return to Cambodia: A Military Coup

POL POT'S POISON LEGACY

October 1997, Vanity Fair

Pot was already the world's most prolific living mass murderer, but this execution was special. The marked man was Son Sen, who had been part of Pol Pot's small inner circle since the beginning, before they built the Khmer Rouge into the most murderous guerrilla movement in history.

It was Son Sen who, in 1975, had led the final bloody drive into Phnom Penh and then, at Pol Pot's direction, forcibly evacuated two million of its inhabitants to the countryside—part of Rouge's agrarian "revolution," which in only four years killed more than a million Cambodians—one-fifth of the country's population. And it was Son Sen who had served as Pol Pot's chief executioner. In the late seventies he supervised the infamous prison known as Tuol Sleng, where more than 10,000 Cambodians were tortured into "confessing" political crimes and then executed.

Now, in the summer of 1997, the Khmer Rouge were suddenly fragmenting after nearly two decades of guerrilla resistance in the jungles of northern and western Cambodia. Weary of Pol Pot's ruthless, hard-line demands, factions had been splitting off for a year, defecting to one side or the other of the bizarrely bifurcated government in Phnom Penh. Tensions built between the government's rival prime ministers, Hun Sen and Prince Norodom Ranariddh, who had grown tired of their uneasy, U.N.-imposed power-sharing agreement. The Khmer Rouge were a major reason why.

Pol Pot had learned that Son Sen was negotiating a deal with Hun Sen, the dictator's blood enemy. He may have also learned that other Khmer Rouge officers were talking with Ranariddh's rival royalist side. Pol Pot, hidden in his forested enclave in Anlong Veng, 200 miles north of Phnom Penh, had grown increasingly paranoid and delusional. He called a meeting of senior leaders for the night of June 9.

When Son Sen didn't attend, Pol Pot coolly ordered his security chief, General Sarouen, to kill the "traitor" and his family. Sarouen and 20 to 30 of his men drove to Son Sen's house after midnight and shot him dead in the right temple and cheek. They then killed his wife with shots to her left ear and right back. A dozen other family members, including a five-year-old child, were also murdered. Afterward, all the bodies were run over by a truck.

A few days later, in Phnom Penh, the royalists displayed gory photographs of the bodies strewn like rag dolls, with their heads leaking blood. The royalists announced that all of Pol Pot's lieutenants (who were seeking a deal with the government in Phnom Penh and worried that the purge might include them) had turned against the dictator known as Brother Number One, who was now on the run through the jungle. Prince Ranariddh (son of King Norodom Sihanouk) announced that his aides were in touch with Pol Pot's pursuers. There was talk of a deal in which the Khmer Rouge officials would receive amnesty and a role in Cambodian affairs—if they turned in Pol Pot and swore allegiance to the country's constitution. One angry Western diplomat summed up the proposed deal this way: "It was as if Göring, Goebbels, and Himmler said to the Allies, 'Exonerate us and bring us into the mainstream and we'll deliver Hitler.'"

By June the international press corps had descended on Phnom Penh. I arrived on June 30, shortly after the media circus began. It was my third trip to Cambodia since 1975, when I covered the fall of Phnom Penh for *The New York Times*—reporting that became the basis for *The Killing Fields*, the 1984 film about my experiences with my colleague Dith Pran. Phnom Penh had been a sleepy colonial-era capital. By the time I left, Cambodia had been devastated by carpet-bombing, politically induced famine, and genocide.

Since my last visit, in 1991, the countryside was pretty much the same: poor and exploited. But Phnom Penh had been transformed into a seamy boomtown overrun by drug dealers, sex traffickers, and Asian organized crime. The U.N.-supervised elections of 1993 brought "stability"—and a flood of dirty money.

The world press generally ignores Cambodia unless it's the locus of a war fought by foreign powers—or unless Pol Pot enters the picture. This time was no different. Scores of foreign journalists began the Pol Pot Watch. How would Brother Number One be brought in? Would he be hidden from public sight or placed on view in a bamboo cage? Every day the story shifted as the royalists de-livered yet another version of Pol Pot's whereabouts.

There were reports that Pol Pot was gravely ill with malaria and other ail-ments, that his loyal bodyguards were carrying him through the jungle on a ham-mock. Then came the story that he had taken some of his comrades hostage to shield his escape. Finally we learned that he had surrendered or been captured by his own troops, and that his former supporters were going to deliver him for trial by the international community for crimes against humanity.

Washington said it would send a military team to airlift Pol Pot out of the jungle. Secretary of State Madeleine Albright asked her Canadian counterpart, Lloyd Axworthy, to hold the trial in his country.

A month later, in late July, the 72-year-old dictator finally appeared, in a vid-eotape broadcast on ABC's *Nightline*. It was Pol Pot's first public appearance in nearly two decades. There he was, the world's most infamous living murderer: feeble, gray, hunched over a bamboo cane, his eyes impassive. He was in Anlong Veng, sitting in a large, open shed as 500 Cambodian peasants sat in rows in front of him. He was standing trial for treason and "rebellious acts." This wasn't a trial, however—it was a public-relations ploy staged by his estranged lieutenants. They wanted to prove that by punishing Pol Pot they were no longer gangsters—and no longer deserved to be international pariahs.

"Our ultimate goal today," a local official shouted into a microphone pow-ered by a car battery set on the earthen floor, "is that the international community should understand that we are no longer Khmer Rouge and not Pol Potists."

The well-rehearsed peasants raised their clenched fists and chanted, "Crush! Crush! Crush! Pol Pot and his clique!"

Wearing green civilian clothes and sandals, Pol Pot appeared frail and defeat-ed. He held the cane in one hand, a rattan fan in the other. Three of his loyalists sat nearby, manacled and glaring at the crowd. They were also on trial, for carrying out the assassination of Son Sen and his family.

Pol Pot offered no defense and never spoke. It was a trial out of the Chinese Cultural Revolution—except that the penalty was conspicuously light for a con-victed traitor: house arrest for life. And the tribunal ruled out turning him over to an international court, where he could be tried for crimes against humanity. After the trial was over, when two young soldiers helped him walk to a waiting vehicle, they did so with great deference.

Then Pol Pot went back into hiding, perhaps for the rest of his life. Given the obsessive secretiveness and xenophobia of the Khmer Rouge, the outside world

may never know the full story of the events leading up to the trial or, more important, the motives and plots behind them. "In Cambodia," says an aid worker who
has been in the country for several years, "there are always levels and levels—and
then more levels—of intrigue and shadows."

Pol Pot is a meaningless nom de guerre. He was born Saloth Sar in 1925,
when Cambodia was a French colony, the eighth of nine children from a farming
family in rural Prek Sbov. In 1931 the boy was sent to live with relatives in Phnom
Penh, where he was a well-liked schoolboy with a love of French literature. He
spent a year at a Buddhist school before winning a scholarship in the early 1950s
to study in France.

Saloth Sar studied Marxism, joined the French Communist Party, and met
the fellow students who would later become his Khmer Rouge coterie. He returned to Phnom Penh in 1953, where he led a double life: popular schoolteacher
by day, active member of the Communist underground by night. In 1963, under
increasing scrutiny by Cambodian authorities, he fled to the jungle, changed his
name to Pol Pot, and, with his Paris colleagues, founded the Khmer Rouge.

By 1968 there were more than 500,000 American troops in South Vietnam
and a U.S. "secret" war in Laos. Prince Norodom Sihanouk had managed to keep
Cambodia out of the war, by privately making concessions to both sides. But the
U.S., having decided the war was lost, wanted an ally to aid its plans to withdraw
from Vietnam. The opening came in 1970, when Sihanouk was ousted in a military coup by his defense minister, General Lon Nol, who was instantly embraced
by Washington.

Within weeks, President Nixon had ordered American troops into Cambodia to find and destroy what he said was the Communist headquarters known as
COSVN. COSVN was never found, but the Vietnam War then spilled into Cambodia and engulfed it.

The Khmer Rouge were supported by Sihanouk, Russia, Vietnam, and China in the early years, and then, by 1973, solely by China. The group eventually
grew from a ragged band of 3,000 rebels into a brutal, disciplined force of perhaps 100,000. In 1975 they seized the capital, Phnom Penh, and launched Pol Pot's
pathological Maoist experiment.

Pol Pot saw Cambodia, which he renamed Democratic Kampuchea, as a
perfect agrarian nation. The country became a giant forced-labor camp the size
of Missouri. Those who were not *borisot*—pure—were candidates for torture or
death. "To spare you is no profit; to destroy you, no loss," was a Khmer Rouge
slogan.

The core of Khmer life—the family—was shattered; children were taken from parents and indoctrinated against them. Schools were shuttered, currency abolished, factories left to rust, intellectuals tortured, monks killed or set to hard labor in the fields. By the end of Pol Pot's four-year purge, Cambodia's population had been reduced from seven million to perhaps five million.

In 1979, provoked by repeated border raids by Pol Pot's troops, the Vietnamese army swept into Cambodia and pushed the Khmer Rouge back into the northern and western jungles. Then they installed a friendly government in Phnom Penh. Cambodia's new foreign minister was 27-year-old Hun Sen, a former low-level Khmer Rouge commander who had managed to avoid participation in their purges and Draconian policies. He had been wounded in the final Khmer Rouge assault on Phnom Penh, in 1975, and lost his left eye, which was replaced by one made of glass.

Hun Sen defected to Vietnam two years later, then returned home during the Vietnamese invasion, in 1979. His critics have scoured the records of the Khmer Rouge period, but no evidence links him to any massacres or genocidal activities. And most analysts agree that although Hun Sen has maintained close relations with the government in Hanoi he has never been a puppet of the Vietnamese; in fact, he has sided against them on certain issues.

After the Vietnamese invasion, Pol Pot and a group led by Sihanouk's son Prince Norodom Ranariddh formed a loose resistance coalition to fight Hun Sen's "occupation." It and another non–Khmer Rouge group were backed by Western governments led by the United States, which provided arms, supplies, intelligence data, and tactical guidance. But because the Khmer Rouge dominated the resistance coalition, Western aid ultimately flowed to them.

Washington's policy was frozen in the Cold War; it punished the victorious Vietnamese by imposing an economic embargo on Cambodia and impeding international recognition of the new government. As part of this effort, the United States made sure that the Hun Sen government was not recognized by the United Nations. The result was surreal: the Khmer Rouge, creators of the killing fields that Washington professed to revile, occupied Cambodia's seat at the United Nations, and their flag flew outside the Secretariat building in New York.

In 1991, peace talks were held in Paris. The major powers, including France and the U.S., decided that the Khmer Rouge had to be included in the negotiations as a full partner. To leave them out, it was argued, would guarantee that their guerrilla resistance would continue and that the country would remain unstable. To many analysts, it was the equivalent of inviting the Nazi Party to take a full role in the revival of post–World War II Germany. The Khmer Rouge were not just troublemakers; they were evil. Not only were the Khmer Rouge invited in, their genocide could not be mentioned in any document—the word could not be used. The accords called for disarmament on all sides, but that never happened. The Khmer Rouge returned to the jungle, from which they launched constant raids into government territory—on the orders of Pol Pot.

The 1993 election—boycotted by the Khmer Rouge—gave a brief, tantalizing taste of democracy to a people who had always lived under god-kings, selfish co-lonial rulers, and, since 1970, nothing but chaos and violence. When Ranariddh's party won, the volatile Hun Sen charged fraud at the polls and threatened action. He felt he had held the country together for the 14 years since the Khmer Rouge had been forced out (which was essentially true) and now it was to be handed over to the spoiled, privileged prince.

To prevent civil war, the international community agreed to a hopeless power-sharing plan which called for two of everything: two prime ministers (Hun Sen and Ranariddh), two heads of each Cabinet department (one for each leader), and so on down the line. Hun Sen retained control of key police and security units.

Predictably, the Hun Sen–Ranariddh relationship quickly soured, and both men began building private armies, sometimes with dissident Khmer Rouge units. Hun Sen was faster off the mark. By early 1997, he had more than 1,500 private soldiers—perhaps twice as many as Ranariddh. He also held the loyalty of a majority of the regular armed forces, which number 100,000. Ranariddh was frantically trying to narrow the gap through secret negotiations with key officials at the Khmer Rouge's central command in Anlong Veng, the last stronghold of the unraveling guerrilla movement. Then, in March, men believed to be Hun Sen henchmen launched a grenade attack on an opposition rally, killing 16 people and wounding 130 others. After that, a warlord atmosphere gripped Phnom Penh.

On the sticky, monsoonal night of June 17, a gun battle erupted in the capi-tal between the two leaders' bodyguard units. Most of the fighting occurred near Ranariddh's luxurious compound in an affluent neighborhood that includes the residence of the United States ambassador, Kenneth Quinn. A stray rocket crashed into Quinn's garden, shattering glass doors and knocking family mem-bers out of bed. The outbreak—small-arms fire, B-40 rockets, tracer bullets arcing overhead—kept the population huddled inside for two hours. Two of Ranariddh's men were killed and several others wounded.

In the following days, each side blamed the other for starting the violence. The clandestine Khmer Rouge radio, pledging allegiance to Ranariddh, issued an "appeal to all combatants" to "fight the nest of the Vietnamese genocidal enemy and its puppet Hun Sen."

On June 18, the day after the street battle, Hun Sen declared that Ranariddh had to choose either to "join the Khmer Rouge or [remain in] the government." A week later, Hun Sen and senior members of his Cambodian People's Party (C.P.P.) leveled fresh accusations at Ranariddh, charging that he had covertly moved illegally acquired arms and Khmer Rouge guerrillas into Phnom Penh. (Hun Sen failed to mention that he too had enlisted Khmer Rouge defectors.)

I arrived in Phnom Penh a few days later—just before fighting broke out between units of the opposing sides near a naval station on the Tonle Sap River, 15 miles northwest of Phnom Penh. The next day, about 200 of Hun Sen's C.P.P. military policemen halted and disarmed a motorcade carrying several of Ranariddh's top aides and bodyguards. Ranariddh's Cabinet director, Ly Thuch, who was in the motorcade, said, "They pointed all their guns at my car. It's getting crazy." On the Fourth of July, Ly Thuch told me that the prince "is out of the country," which was curious. The prince had been there the day before, so he must have flown out today. Why? And why was the trip not announced? Later, I learned that he'd gone to Paris.

That night the American Embassy threw its Fourth of July party at the Hotel Cambodiana. Ambassador Quinn, a 55-year-old career diplomat, stood in the receiving line with his Vietnamese wife, Le Son. Bunting and a string ensemble enlivened the ballroom, but the mood was foreboding.

Diplomats, politicians, and journalists weaved through the crowded room, exchanging anxious questions. Why, at the last minute, did Quinn move the party from his lawn to the enclosed, better-protected hotel? Could the coup rumors actually be true? Why is no one here representing Ranariddh?

Quinn stood on the podium, flanked by his wife and Hun Sen's defense minister, Tea Banh. The ambassador then made a Fourth of July wish for "peace without violence," adding, "like all birthday wishes, we hope this one comes true." To some, his words seemed cryptic, as if he knew something we didn't.

While I was at breakfast the next morning, my wife, Jane, brought me a phone message from a reporter friend who had called our room. It read, "An unusual number of tanks around the airport. Troop movements and the sound of gunfire nearby. A report of armored personnel carriers on the outskirts of the city."

Jane and I headed for our car. Over the radio, Hun Sen's party reported the presence of "illegal" troops at various sites near the capital and said that government troops were moving to disarm them. One of Hun Sen's senior aides came on. He ordered all soldiers and police throughout the country to "halt any unauthorized troop movements."

My interpreter and I headed to the airport, where several of Ranariddh's military posts were located. At first the road looked normal. But then, in the ditches alongside the highway, we saw Hun Sen's soldiers crouched and at the ready. Still, we heard no battle sounds, and the airport remained open.

We headed south toward Hun Sen's personal military compound at Takhmau, which was about 10 miles from Phnom Penh. At the guarded entrance to Hun Sen's compound, I asked to see the prime minister. (A formal interview request had been sent a few days earlier.) The guard called his superior officer, then he hung up and shook his head. "It's tense," he said.

Just then, pickup trucks filled with heavily armed soldiers came out of the compound and sped past us, spinning up clouds of red dust. They were carrying shoulder-fired rockets, rifle-propelled grenades, and automatic weapons. Then a white sedan with darkened windows pulled up and stopped. Hun Sen's media adviser, Om Yien Teng, got out and strode toward me, his face taut with anger. He chewed me out for being an *effronté*—a brazen person. Clearly, he was worried that I might have seen something I shouldn't have.

Hun Sen's compound—known as "the Tiger's Lair"—was about one square kilometer, making it one of the largest military bases in the country. According to those who'd been inside, it housed tanks, trucks, armored personnel carriers, a Russian Mi-26 helicopter, and sophisticated communications equipment. Hun Sen had lightheartedly boasted that he could easily rain artillery shells onto Ranariddh's compound in the center of Phnom Penh.

That afternoon Hun Sen accused Ranariddh of an "unforgivable betrayal" of the nation by "illegally negotiating with the Khmer Rouge ringleaders in Anlong Veng." If not blocked, he said, this would lead to "the return of the genocidal regime to massacre the people anew." He also blamed the prince for virtually all of Cambodia's social ills—"such as drug trading, artifact smuggling, ship robbery . . . armed robberies, murder and ransom, kidnapping . . ."

(Days later, we learned that Hun Sen had found out, on July 4, that Ranariddh's chief commander, General Nhiek Bun Chhay, had just concluded an agreement with the Khmer Rouge that would bring their troops into the royalist fold. In response, Hun Sen apparently decided to head off Ranariddh before the agreement was announced.)

By afternoon, skirmishes had been reported at Ranariddh strongholds on the outskirts of the city. Meanwhile, Hun Sen's soldiers were surrounding other royalist sites, including Ranariddh's heavily armed compound in the city. The U.S. Embassy warned all Americans to avoid "unnecessary movements."

Back in Phnom Penh, Hun Sen's defense minister, Tea Banh, summoned the diplomatic corps to explain what was going on. Things weren't critical yet—both Pizza Hot and Happy Herb's were still delivering.

The defense minister repeated Hun Sen's claim that this was not a coup. He called the fighting "an operation mopping those anarchic forces." The Japanese ambassador, falling victim to language confusion, asked the minister to explain the "mapping operation." No one laughed—they were diplomats.

"Most foreigners are here because they want to help Cambodia," Quinn said at the conference a bit later. "They don't deserve to be put in danger."

During this meeting, we heard a report that the airport had been shut down, raising the possibility that Hun Sen was duplicating the events of 1970, when Lon Nol had closed the airport to keep Sihanouk from flying back from France to try to reverse the coup. When we headed to the airport, the city was filled with soldiers. Roadblocks had been set up, no one was being allowed in or out of Phnom Penh, and all vehicles were being inspected. The airport had indeed been shut down.

We turned around and headed back. The road ahead was empty—in Cambodia, that's always a dangerous sign. Suddenly several Russian-made T-54 tanks appeared, followed by pickup trucks jammed with soldiers and weapons, not to mention Lucky Strike cigarettes and bottled water. The soldiers had little strips of red cloth on their rifles or uniforms, to identify themselves as Hun Sen's forces and thus cut down on friendly-fire casualties, since both sides wore the same camouflage uniforms.

Then, as suddenly as the road had closed, it opened again. We drove at 70 miles an hour in order to reach the city before the route closed again. By now the big explosions had begun—rockets and mortars, possibly tank fire. It was three p.m. and the constant battle noise was spreading apprehension throughout the city.

That afternoon CNN reported that Ranariddh had been taken prisoner by Hun Sen's troops. A half-hour later, the network quoted Ranariddh's aides as saying that he was in the capital and in charge. Neither report was true, since Ranariddh was in Paris. CNN, it seems, does not have a great reputation in Cambodia. Expatriates who watch it say viewers must always apply the "C.D.F."—the CNN Discount Factor.

In the early evening, during a break in the bombardments, Jane and I took a short walk to the corner of Monireth and Mao Tse Tung Boulevards, a major intersection. A half-dozen boys were happily watching the skirmishes from afar. One of them excitedly made the two-handed motion of a machine gunner. Then he asked us for money. Poverty is never far away in Phnom Penh. When a shell exploded behind some nearby buildings, we flinched. But the boys just laughed— they were used to this.

Although the artillery and mortar fire were intense, the shooting was confined to specific targets—Ranariddh's strongholds—and the fusillades were brief: a burst, then a lull. This was a coup, an intimidation strategy to scare the other side into giving up; it wasn't all-out warfare. One of the targets was the heavily guarded villa of Ranariddh's military chief, Nhiek Bun Chhay. Joe Cochrane, a reporter for *The Cambodia Daily*, briefly got through to him. "Can't talk now," the general said. "I'm busy. I'm busy fighting."

Fearing for their lives, royalist officials took refuge in hotels and safe houses, and residents began evacuating their homes. From our 13th-floor window, Jane and I watched people flee on foot, in cars, on motorbikes; some were pushing carts filled with their belongings. Cambodians have a lot of experience at this.

In France, Ranariddh called Hun Sen's charges a "pretext" for a coup and demanded that he be punished. Meanwhile, the prince's father, King Sihanouk, who was receiving medical attention in Beijing, appealed for a cease-fire and peace talks. Hun Sen responded tersely, saying, "It is too late," and calling Ranariddh *chao prey*—"thief in the jungle." The Khmer Rouge radio was also active—but too late. Khieu Samphan, a member of the movement's inner circle, announced the results of the deal with Ranariddh. Without mentioning the prince or his political party, Khieu Samphan said that the Khmer Rouge now recognized Cambodia's constitution, and that their political wing wished to participate in elections, which they had previously boycotted and tried to disrupt.

The next morning we left the Inter-Continental and went over to the Hotel Cambodiana, which was farther from the fighting, but it was full. With a little baksheesh, however, a room was found. Outside, fires were multiplying, mostly in the western quarter of the city and farther out, by the airport, huge black plumes of smoke darkened the sky.

By evening, Hun Sen's superior numbers had prevailed. Ranariddh's soldiers surrendered by hanging white cloths on the walls of his villa and party headquarters. Several of the prince's military leaders had already fled the capital, and warrants were issued for their arrest. Soon royalists were disarmed and Hun Sen's soldiers were looting the airport, completely ransacking it—the passenger terminal, the lounges, the duty-free shop. "There's nothing left," said the airport director. "There are no lights. No technicians. Only soldiers."

The fighting was over in the morning. The sun was out and the city, for a time, looked shiny.

By afternoon, looting had spread to the city, and almost all of it was done by Hun Sen's soldiers. On the airport road, they were pillaging car showrooms, auto-parts stores, warehouses, electronics shops, and some homes. At Prince Ranariddh's villa, soldiers were taking anything they could find: a jade vase, a refrigerator, a VCR, a set of golf clubs, a television, even a case of canned corned beef. Occasionally, civilians moved in and grabbed what was left. Everyone else just stood on the sidewalk, grimly watching the rampage. Cambodians were never fond of this army, which had a reputation for extortion and other banditry, but now they didn't trust it at all.

As I watched, I was struck by how similar the feel and look of these troops were to those of the Khmer Rouge guerrillas who entered Phnom Penh in 1975. Except for the different uniforms—camouflage fatigues and boots instead of black pajamas and rubber sandals—their demeanors were the same: icy, fierce, closed off.

Late in the day, four countries—Thailand, Singapore, Malaysia, and Australia—announced plans to evacuate their nationals by air. Perhaps they had been watching the hyperbolic television reports. One example came from CNN's John Raedler, who reported that some of the fire damage looked "like Hiroshima after the bomb." Later, an American engineer watching the exodus sighed, "This evacuation was ordered by CNN."

That same day, July 7, one of Ranariddh's chief advisers, Ho Sok, was shot dead after being seized by Hun Sen's security police. In the days ahead, additional Ranariddh supporters were arrested or killed; sometimes their eyes were gouged out or their bodies were burned to prevent identification. "They're literally incinerating the evidence," said a human-rights official.

Royalist officials were sleeping in different places every night. By day, they looked for ways to get their families out of the country. Human-rights workers protected as many as possible, but they could do only so much. "He will kill them one by one," one of my Cambodian acquaintances said of Hun Sen. "He learned well from his brother Pol Pot."

At this point, nasty allegations began to circulate that Ambassador Quinn had known of the coup in advance, and that he'd refused to help Ranariddh supporters, even those with American passports. "It's an absolute disgrace the way Western embassies have reacted," said one experienced human-rights official. "We've begged them to open their gates for people who are clearly targeted for persecution, and the Americans, the Australians, flatly said no." These charges—leveled by overworked, overstressed rights workers—were unfair.

Like every other diplomat in Phnom Penh, Quinn had been following the coup rumors for months, and he'd been warning Washington that the situation was headed for a violent blowup. But he strongly denied he had been tipped off, and there's no evidence that he knew when the coup would happen or what form it would take.

As for talk that the American Embassy had turned away desperate Ranariddh supporters, the State Department had given Quinn firm instructions that no sanctuary or visas could be granted without advance approval from Washington. So when Ranariddh supporters asked him for protection, Quinn was caught in the middle. Ultimately, though, he sided with those in danger. "In the end," he told his staff, "we're going to be judged as human beings. If people come to our door in imminent danger, we're going to let them in. We can't allow ourselves to wake up in the morning and have people lying dead on the doorstep."

As it turned out, such a situation was largely avoided. Some Ranariddh supporters were escorted—in embassy cars—to the Hotel Cambodiana. And later, after receiving a frantic call from a Ranariddh official trapped near the airport, Quinn slapped an American flag on his car's fender, got in, and drove out to rescue the man, who couldn't be found. (He eventually turned up safely at the Cambodiana.) "Since I've been ambassador," Quinn said, "no person has been turned away who was in danger and asked for help. And no person will be."

Diplomatic sources said Quinn had grown disillusioned with the disengaged, often feckless Prince Ranariddh. Quinn disputed that he was a Hun Sen supporter, but thought that the prime minister could, despite his anti-democratic tendencies, be an effective leader.

"Quinn understands that Hun Sen can be a thug, but doesn't condemn him as a dictator," said a diplomat who supports the ambassador. "He sees him also as a leader strong enough to get things done."

By Tuesday, July 8, the number of "extrajudicial killings" had risen to more than 40, and hundreds of Cambodians had been arrested. Some of Ranariddh's soldiers were tortured, and human-rights workers were hiding at-risk Cambodians and shepherding them to the airport. Some of my Cambodian friends said it felt a bit like the Pol Pot days. "It's already begun," said one. "People are being careful about what they say, looking over their shoulders. You cannot tell the neighbors what you think."

Foreigners were fleeing in droves, and a kind of temporary panic set in. Commercial flights had been suspended, so people left on planes flown by charter services, which charged double the normal fares. Eventually, 6,000 of the city's 8,000 expatriates left. Most will probably come back. Nonetheless, Cambodians routinely gathered at the departure gates and sadly watched the foreigners fly away.

Several foreign-investment projects were put on hold, and some countries, including the United States, temporarily suspended government aid. In Washington's case, that's about $40 million a year. (Washington also reduced its 61-person embassy staff to 20, citing an "uncertain security situation.") All told, foreign-government aid to Cambodia is about $350 million to $400 million a year—half the national budget. A significant reduction could unhinge the country's economy.

At the airport, while surveying the looting damage, Jane and I ran into Al Rockoff, a freelance photographer who lives in Cambodia. Rockoff was a friend and colleague of mine when the Khmer Rouge seized Phnom Penh in 1975. (He was played by John Malkovich in *The Killing Fields*.) Now he needed a ride to check on two tanks destroyed in a fierce battle he'd witnessed two days earlier. As usual, he described the scene breathlessly, almost without punctuation. "Both tanks were Hun Sen's—they're T-55s, Soviet or Chinese. Came into Sihanoukville two years ago on a ship to Mozambique with 80 other pieces. The first tank had no idea, turned down a side road right into the teeth of an oncoming royalist tank. The Hun Sen driver was hit just below the face. He was vaporized. The turret commander was hit low. He'll probably lose both legs. The second tank was knocked out about an hour later. I don't know the casualties there. If I was the tank commander, I'd have moved 10 degrees to the right . . ."

After Rockoff got out of the car, he grinned, said, "Hey, just like the bad old days, huh?" and loped off.

Another friend from the 70s was also in town: Jon Swain, a correspondent for *The Sunday Times*. (He was played by Julian Sands in the film.) We met on my first night back, at the atmospheric Foreign Correspondents Club. Nothing like this place existed back then. It was a sweet reunion; we hadn't seen each other in eight years. Predictably, we talked about how things had changed in Cambodia, mostly for the worse. The city's charm was gone, we agreed, replaced by big, ugly glass buildings.

We also talked about Pol Pot, the reason we were back in Cambodia. Swain recalled his interview with one of the dictator's brothers, Saloth Nhep, a farmer who lives up in Kompong Thom Province. Saloth Nhep hadn't heard from his brother in decades; until he saw a photo of him in 1978, he had no idea that his brother was the despicable Pol Pot. Saloth Nhep was still angry, since his family had suffered under Khmer Rouge rule just like everyone else. "My brother does not deserve to live," he told Swain. "If he is captured, then every Cambodian should be given a razor blade and allowed to make one cut."

It didn't work out that way. When Pol Pot finally appeared at his show trial this summer, his personal safety seemed assured. In fact, much about the trial had been orchestrated, including the press coverage. The only reporter invited in was Nate Thayer, a writer for the *Far Eastern Economic Review*, who had been pursuing Pol Pot for years. (He was also allowed to take a cameraman.) Ultimately, though, Thayer was not allowed to ask Pol Pot any questions. A day after the trial, Thayer sold the videotape to *Nightline* for a reported $650,000.

Perhaps the most interesting thing about the tape was what we didn't see. Clearly, Pol Pot was not being tried for the deaths of perhaps two million Cambodians, only for killing Son Sen and his family. The Khmer Rouge were not really acknowledging their genocide: they were merely getting rid of a leader whose evil reputation was impeding their political makeover. With Pol Pot gone, they believed, their campaign to oust Hun Sen could resume in earnest.

Also missing from the trial were Nuon Chea, known as Brother Number Two, and Ta Mok, known as the Butcher. Both shared Pol Pot's complicity in the Cambodian holocaust. These two almost certainly arranged the trial, perhaps hoping that Pol Pot's punishment would mollify the public and save their own lives. A senior Khmer Rouge military official at the trial said that, although Ta Mok and Nuon Chea are quite old, they are still consulted on all important Khmer Rouge matters.

Since the show trial, the United States and other countries have pressed Hun Sen to capture Pol Pot and turn him over to an international tribunal. By doing this, they say, Hun Sen would restore his credibility and make amends for the violent coup. This is an odd diplomatic pressure play, for if Washington and the other major powers had wanted to bring Pol Pot to justice they could have mounted a "snatch" operation at any time in the 1980s, when he was at his sanctuary in Thailand.

The current chaos is not just a bad patch for Cambodia. It's the by-product of 30 years of war and madness and guns. Cambodia has become an anarchic, anything-goes playland for every sort of criminal activity—a mecca for those who wish to exploit some of the poorest, most vulnerable people in the world.

In a single week during my visit, the newspapers reported on a pattern of police torture in Battambang, Cambodia's second-largest city; an American tourist who was mugged and shot dead in Phnom Penh; and a 53-year-old Canadian man convicted of sex trafficking in young boys (his sentence: four months). Meanwhile, AIDS is approaching epidemic proportions—100,000 are infected. And the country's primitive health-care system can do little to stop the epidemic.

"Sick politics, rotten politics," says one of my Cambodian friends. "That's what's ruining everything."

The economy, meanwhile, is at the mercy of foreign companies, those equal-opportunity exploiters. One of the best jobs an average Cambodian can hope to find is in the garment industry, making clothes for Montgomery Ward or the Gap. Garment workers earn about $40 a month, but it takes at least $150 a month to live at subsistence level in Phnom Penh.

Some Asia experts believe that Cambodia's future depends on which corporate and military interests Hun Sen decides to embrace. The future may also hinge on how well the prime minister holds off the ancient expansionist desires of Thailand and Vietnam.

It's not clear what would satisfy Washington and the other major powers—countries that created the unworkable system they now condemn. These countries talk about the need for a free and open society, with independent courts, well-trained lawyers, a healthy press, and a commitment to human rights. In fact, some of these institutions and traditions had been slowly developing over the past several years, but now their future is uncertain. (Witness *The Cambodia Daily*, a feisty, independent little paper with a staff of 16 young Westerners training 30 Khmers.) And a new leadership group had just begun forming when Hun Sen's power grab set it back dramatically.

The prospects for the Phnom Penh government are equally bleak. Hun Sen isn't popular enough to win a free election, so more strongman tactics are likely. Then again, one knowledgeable Western diplomat thinks the prime minister could be talked into sharing power and accepting a pluralistic system—but only if he is allowed to keep control of a significant portion of the nation's military and security forces.

And the Khmer Rouge? Marginalized by defections, attrition, and a loss of aid from China, they are no longer a military threat to Phnom Penh. But they are still a piece of the puzzle—even with Pol Pot out of the picture and perhaps gravely ill. The guerrillas continue to hold chunks of Cambodia—perhaps 15 percent of it—as their private fiefdoms. As long as they do, Cambodia will remain a torn country—and will find it painfully difficult to exorcise the ghost of Pol Pot.

Author's Note: Pol Pot, Cambodia's Hitler, died ignominiously in April 1998, at age eighty-three, in a shack deep in the country's northern jungle. He was being held there under a life sentence of house arrest by the remnants of his own extremist group, the Communist Khmer Rouge. They held a show trial in a clearing in that jungle and charged him with ordering the murder of his right-hand man, Son Sen (and his entire family), who had reportedly been negotiating some kind of clemency deal with the Phnom Penh government.

There was not a word in the charges about the nearly two million Cambodians—almost a quarter of the population—whose deaths the Khmer Rouge were responsible for under Pol Pot's command. He died not long after his trial. There were rumors that he may have been poisoned. He was cremated quickly on a pile of discarded tires and broken furniture.

The trial most Cambodians wanted to see, after the Vietnamese army drove the Khmer Rouge out of power and into the jungle in 1979, was a war crimes tribunal. Thirty years late, a pale version of such a trial is now (2009) being held in Phnom Penh. Five members of Pol Pot's leadership group have been charged.

As I write this note (January 8, 2010), no one has yet been convicted.

Under the trial's softened rules the severest sentence that can be imposed is life imprisonment. There is no death penalty.

Once again the neglected little country of Cambodia did not receive proper world respect and attention.

CHAPTER SIX

The Cover-Up of U.S. POWs Left Behind in Vietnam

HOW JOHN MCCAIN BURIED INFORMATION ON AMERICAN PRISONERS ABANDONED BY WASHINGTON

Author's Note: I have been writing about the missing U.S. POWs since the 1990s, when John McCain bonded with John Kerry and Dick Cheney to bury the voluminous evidence that hundreds had been left behind in Indochina. Kerry was chairman then of a special Senate committee created, supposedly, to get at the truth. McCain was the most powerful member on the panel. Cheney was the Pentagon chief.

The lengthy investigative piece I have chosen to present here is representative of my larger body of POW work. The detailed evidence in this piece has never been refuted. With the election of Barack Obama, the scandal has endured across eight presidencies. And the national press is still too scared to tackle the issue.

September 18, 2008, The Nation Institute (nationinstitute.org)

John McCain, who has risen to political prominence on his image as a Vietnam POW war hero, has, inexplicably, worked very hard to hide from the public stunning information about American prisoners in Vietnam who, unlike him, didn't return home. Throughout his Senate career, McCain has quietly sponsored and pushed into federal law a set of prohibitions that keep the most revealing information about these men buried as classified documents. Thus the war hero who people would logically imagine as a determined crusader for the interests of POWs and their families became instead the strange champion of hiding the evidence and closing the books.

Almost as striking is the manner in which the mainstream press has shied from reporting the POW story and McCain's role in it, even as the Republican Party has made McCain's military service the focus of his presidential campaign. Reporters who had covered the Vietnam War turned their heads and walked in other directions. McCain doesn't talk about the missing men, and the press never asks him about them.

The sum of the secrets McCain has sought to hide is not small. There exists a telling mass of official documents, radio intercepts, witness depositions, satellite photos of rescue symbols that pilots were trained to use, electronic messages from the ground containing the individual code numbers given to airmen, a rescue mission by a special forces unit that was aborted twice by Washington—and even sworn testimony by two Defense secretaries that "men were left behind." This imposing body of evidence suggests that a large number—the documents indicate probably hundreds—of the U.S. prisoners held by Vietnam were not returned when the peace treaty was signed in January 1973 and Hanoi released 591 men, among them Navy combat pilot John S. McCain.

MASS OF EVIDENCE

The Pentagon had been withholding significant information from POW families for years. What's more, the Pentagon's POW/MIA operation had been publicly shamed by internal whistleblowers and POW families for holding back documents as part of a policy of "debunking" POW intelligence even when the information was obviously credible.

The pressure from the families and Vietnam veterans finally forced the creation, in late 1991, of a Senate Select Committee on POW/MIA Affairs. The chairman was John Kerry. McCain, as a former POW, was its most pivotal member. In the end, the committee became part of the debunking machine.

One of the sharpest critics of the Pentagon's performance was an insider, Air Force Lieut. Gen. Eugene Tighe, who headed the Defense Intelligence Agency (DIA) during the 1970s. He openly challenged the Pentagon's position that no live prisoners existed, saying that the evidence proved otherwise. McCain was a bitter opponent of Tighe, who was eventually pushed into retirement.

Included in the evidence that McCain and his government allies suppressed or sought to discredit is a transcript of a senior North Vietnamese general's briefing of the Hanoi politburo, discovered in Soviet archives by an American scholar in 1993. The briefing took place only four months before the 1973 peace accords. The general, Tran Van Quang, told the politburo members that Hanoi was holding 1,205 American prisoners but would keep many of them at war's end as leverage to ensure getting war reparations from Washington.

Throughout the Paris negotiations, the North Vietnamese tied the prisoner issue tightly to the issue of reparations. They were adamant in refusing to deal with them separately. Finally, in a February 2, 1973, formal letter to Hanoi's premier, Pham Van Dong, Nixon pledged $3.25 billion in "postwar reconstruction" aid "without any political conditions." But he also attached to the letter a codicil that said the aid would be implemented by each party "in accordance with its own constitutional provisions." That meant Congress would have to approve the appropriation, and Nixon and Kissinger knew well that Congress was in no mood to do so. The North Vietnamese, whether or not they immediately understood the double-talk in the letter, remained skeptical about the reparations promise being honored—and it never was. Hanoi thus appears to have held back prisoners—just as it had done when the French were defeated at Dien Bien Phu in 1954 and withdrew their forces from Vietnam. In that case, France paid ransoms for prisoners and brought them home.

In a private briefing in 1992, high-level CIA officials told me that as the years passed and the ransom never came, it became more and more difficult for either government to admit that it knew from the start about the unacknowledged prisoners. Those prisoners had not only become useless as bargaining chips but also posed a risk to Hanoi's desire to be accepted into the international community. The CIA officials said their intelligence indicated strongly that the remaining men—those who had not died from illness or hard labor or torture—were eventually executed.

My own research, detailed below, has convinced me that it is not likely that more than a few—if any—are alive in captivity today. (That CIA briefing at the agency's Langley, Virginia, headquarters was conducted "off the record," but because the evidence from my own reporting since then has brought me to the same conclusion, I felt there was no longer any point in not writing about the meeting.)

For many reasons, including the absence of a political constituency for the missing men other than their families and some veterans' groups, very few Americans are aware of the POW story and of McCain's role in keeping it out of public view and denying the existence of abandoned POWs. That is because McCain has hardly been alone in his campaign to hide the scandal.

The Arizona senator, now the Republican candidate for President, has actually been following the lead of every White House since Richard Nixon's and thus of every CIA director, Pentagon chief and national security advisor, not to mention Dick Cheney, who was George H. W. Bush's defense secretary. Their biggest accomplice has been an indolent press, particularly in Washington.

MCCAIN'S ROLE

An early and critical McCain secrecy move involved 1990 legislation that started in the House of Representatives. A brief and simple document, it was called "the Truth Bill" and would have compelled complete transparency about prisoners and missing men. Its core sentence reads, "[The] head of each department or agency which holds or receives any records and information, including live-sighting reports, which have been correlated or possibly correlated to United States personnel listed as prisoner of war or missing in action from World War II, the Korean conflict and the Vietnam conflict, shall make available to the public all such records held or received by that department or agency."

Bitterly opposed by the Pentagon (and thus McCain), the bill went nowhere. Reintroduced the following year, it again disappeared. But a few months later, a new measure, known as "the McCain bill," suddenly appeared. By creating a bureaucratic maze from which only a fraction of the documents could emerge—only records that revealed no POW secrets—it turned the Truth Bill on its head. The McCain bill became law in 1991 and remains so today. So crushing to transparency are its provisions that it actually spells out for the Pentagon and other agencies several rationales, scenarios and justifications for not releasing any information at all—even about prisoners discovered alive in captivity. Later that year, the Senate Select Committee was created, where Kerry and McCain ultimately worked together to bury evidence.

McCain was also instrumental in amending the Missing Service Personnel Act, which had been strengthened in 1995 by POW advocates to include criminal penalties, saying, "Any government official who knowingly and willfully withholds from the file of a missing person any information relating to the disappearance or whereabouts and status of a missing person shall be fined as provided in Title 18 or imprisoned not more than one year or both." A year later, in a closed House-Senate conference on an unrelated military bill, McCain, at the behest of the Pentagon, attached a crippling amendment to the act, stripping out its only enforcement teeth, the criminal penalties, and reducing the obligations of commanders in the field to speedily search for missing men and to report the incidents to the Pentagon.

About the relaxation of POW/MIA obligations on commanders in the field, a public McCain memo said, "This transfers the bureaucracy involved out of the [battle]field to Washington." He wrote that the original legislation, if left intact, "would accomplish nothing but create new jobs for lawyers and turn military commanders into clerks."

McCain argued that keeping the criminal penalties would have made it impossible for the Pentagon to find staffers willing to work on POW/MIA matters. That's an odd argument to make. Were staffers only "willing to work" if they were allowed to conceal POW records? By eviscerating the law, McCain gave his stamp of approval to the government policy of debunking the existence of live POWs.

McCain has insisted again and again that all the evidence—documents, witnesses, satellite photos, two Pentagon chiefs' sworn testimony, aborted rescue missions, ransom offers apparently scorned—has been woven together by unscrupulous deceivers to create an insidious and unpatriotic myth. He calls it the "bizarre rantings of the MIA hobbyists." He has regularly vilified those who keep trying to pry out classified documents as "hoaxers," "charlatans," "conspiracy theorists" and "dime-store Rambos."

Some of McCain's fellow captives at Hoa Lo prison in Hanoi didn't share his views about prisoners left behind. Before he died of leukemia in 1999, retired Col. Ted Guy, a highly admired POW and one of the most dogged resisters in the camps, wrote an angry open letter to the senator in an MIA newsletter—a response to McCain's stream of insults hurled at MIA activists. Guy wrote, "John, does this [the insults] include Senator Bob Smith [a New Hampshire Republican and activist on POW issues] and other concerned elected officials? Does this include the families of the missing where there is overwhelming evidence that their loved ones were 'last known alive'? Does this include some of your fellow POWs?"

It's not clear whether the taped confession McCain gave to his captors to avoid further torture has played a role in his postwar behavior in the Senate. That confession was played endlessly over the prison loudspeaker system at Hoa Lo— to try to break down other prisoners—and was broadcast over Hanoi's state radio. Reportedly, he confessed to being a war criminal who had bombed civilian targets. The Pentagon has a copy of the confession but will not release it. Also, no outsider I know of has ever seen a non-redacted copy of the debriefing of McCain when he returned from captivity, which is classified but could be made public by McCain.

All humans have breaking points. Many men undergoing torture give confessions, often telling huge lies so their fakery will be understood by their comrades and their country. Few will fault them. But it was McCain who apparently felt he had disgraced himself and his military family. His father, John S. McCain

II, was a highly regarded rear admiral then serving as commander of all U.S. forces in the Pacific. His grandfather was also a rear admiral.

In his bestselling 1999 autobiography, *Faith of My Fathers*, McCain says he felt bad throughout his captivity because he knew he was being treated more leniently than his fellow POWs, owing to his high-ranking father and thus his propaganda value. Other prisoners at Hoa Lo say his captors considered him a prize catch and called him the "Crown Prince," something McCain acknowledges in the book.

Also in this memoir, McCain expresses guilt at having broken under torture and given the confession. "I felt faithless and couldn't control my despair," he writes, revealing that he made two "feeble" attempts at suicide. (In later years, he said he tried to hang himself with his shirt and guards intervened.) Tellingly, he says he lived in "dread" that his father would find out about the confession. "I still wince," he writes, "when I recall wondering if my father had heard of my disgrace."

He says that when he returned home, he told his father about the confession, but "never discussed it at length"—and the admiral, who died in 1981, didn't indicate he had heard anything about it before. But he had. In the 1999 memoir, the senator writes, "I only recently learned that the tape . . . had been broadcast outside the prison and had come to the attention of my father."

Is McCain haunted by these memories? Does he suppress POW information because its surfacing would rekindle his feelings of shame? On this subject, all I have are questions.

Many stories have been written about McCain's explosive temper, so volcanic that colleagues are loathe to speak openly about it. One veteran congressman who has observed him over the years asked for confidentiality and made this brief comment: "This is a man not at peace with himself."

He was certainly far from calm on the Senate POW committee. He browbeat expert witnesses who came with information about unreturned POWs. Family members who have personally faced McCain and pressed him to end the secrecy also have been treated to his legendary temper. He has screamed at them, insulted them, brought women to tears. Mostly his responses to them have been versions of: How dare you question my patriotism? In 1996, he roughly pushed aside a group of POW family members who had waited outside a hearing room to appeal to him, including a mother in a wheelchair.

But even without answers to what may be hidden in the recesses of McCain's mind, one thing about the POW story is clear: If American prisoners were dishonored by being written off and left to die, that's something the American public ought to know about.

10 KEY PIECES OF EVIDENCE THAT MEN WERE LEFT BEHIND

1. In Paris, where the Vietnam peace treaty was negotiated, the United States asked Hanoi for the list of American prisoners to be returned, fearing that Hanoi would hold some prisoners back. The North Vietnamese refused, saying they would produce the list only after the treaty was signed. Nixon agreed with Kissinger that they had no leverage left, and Kissinger signed the accord on January 27, 1973, without the prisoner list. When Hanoi produced its list of 591 prisoners the next day, U.S. intelligence agencies expressed shock at the low number. Their number was hundreds higher. *The New York Times* published a long, page-one story on February 2, 1973, about the discrepancy, especially raising questions about the number of prisoners held in Laos, only nine of whom were being returned. The headline read, in part, "Laos POW List Shows 9 from US—Document Disappointing to Washington as 311 Were Believed Missing." And the story, by John Finney, said that other Washington officials "believe the number of prisoners [in Laos] is probably substantially higher." The paper never followed up with any serious investigative reporting—nor did any other mainstream news organization.

2. Two defense secretaries who served during the Vietnam War testified to the Senate POW committee in September 1992 that prisoners were not returned. James Schlesinger and Melvin Laird, both speaking at a public session and under oath, said they based their conclusions on strong intelligence data— letters, eyewitness reports, even direct radio contacts. Under questioning, Schlesinger chose his words carefully, understanding clearly the volatility of the issue: "I think that as of now that I can come to no other conclusion . . . some were left behind." This ran counter to what President Nixon told the public in a nationally televised speech on March 29, 1973, when the repatriation of the 591 was in motion: "Tonight," Nixon said, "the day we have all worked and prayed for has finally come. For the first time in twelve years, no American military forces are in Vietnam. All our American POWs are on their way home." Documents unearthed since then show that aides had already briefed Nixon about the contrary evidence.

    Schlesinger was asked by the Senate committee for his explanation of why President Nixon would have made such a statement when he knew Hanoi was still holding prisoners. He replied, "One must assume that we had concluded that the bargaining position of the United States . . . was quite weak. We were anxious to get our troops out and we were not going to roil the waters . . . " This testimony struck me as a bombshell. The *New York Times* appropriately reported it on page one but again there was no sustained follow-up by the *Times* or any other major paper or national news outlet.

3. Over the years, the DIA received more than 1,600 firsthand sightings of live American prisoners and nearly 14,000 secondhand reports. Many witnesses interrogated by CIA or Pentagon intelligence agents were deemed "credible" in the agents' reports. Some of the witnesses were given lie-detector tests and passed. Sources provided me with copies of these witness reports, which are impressive in their detail. A lot of the sightings described a secondary tier of prison camps many miles from Hanoi. Yet the DIA, after reviewing all these reports, concluded that they "do not constitute evidence" that men were alive.

4. In the late 1970s and early 1980s, listening stations picked up messages in which Laotian military personnel spoke about moving American prisoners from one labor camp to another. These listening posts were manned by Thai communications officers trained by the National Security Agency (NSA), which monitors signals worldwide. The NSA teams had moved out after the fall of Saigon in 1975 and passed the job to the Thai allies. But when the Thais turned these messages over to Washington, the intelligence community ruled that since the intercepts were made by a "third party"—namely Thailand— they could not be regarded as authentic. That's some Catch-22: The U.S. trained a third party to take over its role in monitoring signals about POWs, but because that third party did the monitoring, the messages weren't valid.

    Here, from CIA files, is an example that clearly exposes the farce. On December 27, 1980, a Thai military signal team picked up a message saying that prisoners were being moved out of Attopeu (in southern Laos) by aircraft "at 1230 hours." Three days later a message was sent from the CIA station in Bangkok to the CIA director's office in Langley. It read, in part, "The prisoners . . . are now in the valley in permanent location (a prison camp at Nhommarath in Central Laos). They were transferred from Attopeu to work in various places . . . POWs were formerly kept in caves and are very thin, dark and starving." Apparently the prisoners were real. But the transmission was declared "invalid" by Washington because the information came from a "third party" and thus could not be deemed credible.

5. A series of what appeared to be distress signals from Vietnam and Laos were captured by the government's satellite system in the late 1980s and early '90s.

(Before that period, no search for such signals had been put in place.) Not a single one of these markings was ever deemed credible. To the layman's eye, the satellite photos, some of which I've seen, show markings on the ground that are identical to the signals that American pilots had been specifically trained to use in their survival courses—such as certain letters, like X or K, drawn in a special way. Other markings were the secret four-digit authenticator numbers given to individual pilots. But time and again, the Pentagon, backed by the CIA, insisted that humans had not made these markings. What were they, then? "Shadows and vegetation," the government said, insisting that the markings were merely normal topographical contours like saw-grass or rice-paddy divider walls. It was the automatic response—shadows and vegetation. On one occasion, a Pentagon photo expert refused to go along. It was a missing man's name gouged into a field, he said, not trampled grass or paddy berms. His bosses responded by bringing in an outside contractor who found instead, yes, shadows and vegetation. This refrain led Bob Taylor, a highly regarded investigator on the Senate committee staff who had examined the photographic evidence, to comment to me, "If grass can spell out people's names and a secret digit codes [sic], then I have a newfound respect for grass."

6. On November 11, 1992, Dolores Alfond, the sister of missing airman Capt. Victor Apodaca and chair of the National Alliance of Families, an organization of relatives of POW/MIAs, testified at one of the Senate committee's public hearings. She asked for information about data the government had gathered from electronic devices used in a classified program known as PAVE SPIKE.

The devices were motion sensors, dropped by air, designed to pick up enemy troop movements. Shaped on one end like a spike with an electronic pod and antenna on top, they were designed to stick in the ground as they fell. Air Force planes would drop them along the Ho Chi Minh trail and other supply routes. The devices, though primarily sensors, also had rescue capabilities. Someone on the ground—a downed airman or a prisoner on a labor gang—could manually enter data into the sensor. All data were regularly collected electronically by U.S. planes flying overhead. Alfond stated, without any challenge or contradiction by the committee, that in 1974, a year after the supposedly complete return of prisoners, the gathered data showed that a person or people had manually entered into the sensors—as U.S. pilots had been trained to do—"no less than 20 authenticator numbers that corresponded exactly to the classified authenticator numbers of 20 U.S. POWs who were lost in Laos." Alfond added, according to the transcript, "This PAVE SPIKE intelligence is seamless, but the committee has not discussed it or released what it knows about PAVE SPIKE."

McCain attended that committee hearing specifically to confront Alfond because of her criticism of the panel's work. He bellowed and berated her for quite a while. His face turning anger-pink, he accused her of "denigrating" his "patriotism." The bullying had its effect—she began to cry.

After a pause Alfond recovered and tried to respond to his scorching tirade, but McCain simply turned away and stormed out of the room. The PAVE SPIKE file has never been declassified. We still don't know anything about those twenty POWs.

7. As previously mentioned, in April 1993, in a Moscow archive, a researcher from Harvard, Stephen Morris, unearthed and made public the transcript of a briefing that General Tran Van Quang gave to the Hanoi politburo four months before the signing of the Paris peace accords in 1973.

In the transcript, General Quang told the Hanoi politburo that 1,205 U.S. prisoners were being held. Quang said that many of the prisoners would be held back from Washington after the accords as bargaining chips for war reparations. General Quang's report added, "This is a big number. Officially, until now, we published a list of only 368 prisoners of war. The rest we have not revealed. The government of the USA knows this well, but it does not know the exact number . . . and can only make guesses based on its losses. That is why we are keeping the number of prisoners of war secret, in accordance with the politburo's instructions." The report then went on to explain in clear and specific language that a large number would be kept back to ensure reparations.

The reaction to the document was immediate. After two decades of denying it had kept any prisoners, Hanoi responded to the revelation by calling the transcript a fabrication.

Similarly, Washington—which had over the same two decades refused to recant Nixon's declaration that all the prisoners had been returned—also shifted into denial mode. The Pentagon issued a statement saying the document "is replete with errors, omissions and propaganda that seriously damage its credibility," and that the numbers were "inconsistent with our own accounting."

Neither American nor Vietnamese officials offered any rationale for who would plant a forged document in the Soviet archives and why they would do so. Certainly neither Washington nor Moscow—closely allied with Hanoi—would have any motive, since the contents were embarrassing to all parties, and since both the United States and Vietnam had consistently denied the existence of unreturned prisoners. The Russian archivists simply said the document was "authentic."

8. In his 2002 book, *Inside Delta Force*, retired Command Sgt. Major Eric Haney described how in 1981 his special forces unit, after rigorous training for a POW rescue mission, had the mission suddenly aborted, revived a year later and again abruptly aborted. Haney writes that this abandonment of captured soldiers ate at him for years and left him disillusioned about his government's vows to leave no men behind.

"Years later, I spoke at length with a former highly placed member of the North Vietnamese diplomatic corps, and this person asked me point-blank: 'Why did the Americans never attempt to recover their remaining POWs after the conclusion of the war?'" Haney writes. He continued, saying that he came to believe senior government officials had called off those missions in 1981 and 1982. (His account is on pages 314 to 321 of my paperback copy of the book.)

9. There is also evidence that in the first months of Ronald Reagan's presidency in 1981, the White House received a ransom proposal for a number of POWs being held by Hanoi in Indochina. The offer, which was passed to Washington from an official of a third country, was apparently discussed at a meeting in the Roosevelt Room attended by Reagan, Vice-President Bush, CIA Director William Casey and National Security Advisor Richard Allen. Allen confirmed the offer in sworn testimony to the Senate POW committee on June 23, 1992.

Allen was allowed to testify behind closed doors and no information was released. But a *San Diego Union-Tribune* reporter, Robert Caldwell, obtained the portion relating to the ransom offer and reported on it. The ransom request was for $4 billion, Allen testified. He said he told Reagan that "it would be worth the president's going along and let's have the negotiation." When his testimony appeared in the *Union-Tribune*, Allen quickly wrote a letter to the panel, this time not under oath, recanting the ransom story and claiming his memory had played tricks on him. His new version was that some POW activists had asked him about such an offer in a meeting that took place in 1986, when he was no longer in government. "It appears," he said in the letter, "that there never was a 1981 meeting about the return of POW/MIAs for $4 billion."

But the episode didn't end there. A Treasury agent on Secret Service duty in the White House, John Syphrit, came forward to say he had overheard part of the ransom conversation in the Roosevelt Room in 1981, when the offer was discussed by Reagan, Bush, Casey, Allen and other cabinet officials.

Syphrit, a veteran of the Vietnam War, told the committee he was willing to testify but they would have to subpoena him. Treasury opposed his appearance, arguing that voluntary testimony would violate the trust between the Secret Service and those it protects. It was clear that coming in on his own could cost Syphrit his career. The committee voted 7 to 4 not to subpoena him.

In the committee's final report, dated January 13, 1993 (on page 284), the panel not only chastised Syphrit for his failure to testify without a subpoena ("The committee regrets that the Secret Service agent was unwilling . . . "), but noted that since Allen had recanted his testimony about the Roosevelt Room briefing, Syphrit's testimony would have been "at best, uncorroborated by the testimony of any other witness." The committee omitted any mention that it had made a decision not to ask the other two surviving witnesses, Bush and Reagan, to give testimony under oath. (Casey had died.)

10. In 1990, Colonel Millard Peck, a decorated infantry veteran of Vietnam then working at the DIA as chief of the Asia Division for Current Intelligence, asked for the job of chief of the DIA's Special Office for Prisoners of War and Missing in Action. His reason for seeking the transfer, which was not a promotion, was that he had heard from officials throughout the Pentagon that the POW/MIA office had been turned into a waste-disposal unit for getting rid of unwanted evidence about live prisoners—a "black hole," these officials called it.

Peck explained all this in his telling resignation letter of February 12, 1991, eight months after he had taken the job. He said he viewed it as "sort of a holy crusade" to restore the integrity of the office but was defeated by the Pentagon machine. The four-page, single-spaced letter was scathing, describing the putative search for missing men as "a cover-up."

Peck charged that, at its top echelons, the Pentagon had embraced a "mind-set to debunk" all evidence of prisoners left behind. "That national leaders continue to address the prisoner of war and missing in action issue as the 'highest national priority' is a travesty," he wrote. "The entire charade does not appear to be an honest effort, and may never have been. . . . Practically all analysis is directed to finding fault with the source. Rarely has there been any effective, active follow through on any of the sightings, nor is there a responsive 'action arm' to routinely and aggressively pursue leads."

"I became painfully aware," his letter continued, "that I was not really in charge of my own office, but was merely a figurehead or whipping boy for a larger and totally Machiavellian group of players outside of DIA . . . I feel strongly that this issue is being manipulated and controlled at a higher level, not with the goal of resolving it, but more to obfuscate the question of live prisoners and give the illusion of progress through hyperactivity." He named no names but said these players are "unscrupulous people in the Government or associated with the Government" who "have maintained their distance and remained hidden in the shadows, while using the [POW] Office as a 'toxic waste dump' to bury the whole 'mess' out of sight." Peck added that "military officers . . . who in some manner have 'rocked the boat' [have] quickly come to grief."

Peck concluded, "From what I have witnessed, it appears that any soldier left in Vietnam, even inadvertently, was, in fact, abandoned years ago, and that the farce that is being played is no more than political legerdemain done with 'smoke and mirrors' to stall the issue until it dies a natural death."

The disillusioned colonel not only resigned but asked to be retired immediately from active military service. The press never followed up.

My Pursuit of the Story

I covered the war in Cambodia and Vietnam, but came to the POW information only slowly afterward, when military officers I knew from that conflict began coming to me with maps and POW sightings and depositions by Vietnamese witnesses.

I was then city editor of *The New York Times*, no longer involved in foreign or national stories, so I took the data to the appropriate desks and suggested it was material worth pursuing. There were no takers. Some years later, in 1991, when I was an op-ed columnist at *Newsday*, the aforementioned special Senate committee was formed to probe the POW issue. I saw this as an opening and immersed myself in the reporting.

At *Newsday*, I wrote thirty-five columns over a two-year period, as well as a four-part series on a trip I took to North Vietnam to report on what happened to one missing pilot who was shot down over the Ho Chi Minh trail and captured when he parachuted down. After *Newsday*, I wrote thousands more words on the subject for other outlets. Some of the pieces were about McCain's key role.

Though I wrote on many subjects for *Life*, *Vanity Fair* and *Washington Monthly*, my POW articles appeared in *Penthouse*, the *Village Voice* and APBnews.com. Mainstream publications just weren't interested. Their disinterest was part of what motivated me, and I became one of a very short list of journalists who considered the story important.

Serving in the army in Germany during the Cold War and witnessing combat firsthand as a reporter in India and Indochina led me to have great respect for those who fight for their country. To my mind, we dishonored U.S. troops when our government failed to bring them home from Vietnam after the 591 others were released—and then claimed they didn't exist. And politicians dishonor themselves when they pay lip service to the bravery and sacrifice of soldiers only to leave untold numbers behind, rationalizing to themselves that it's merely one of the unfortunate costs of war.

John McCain—now campaigning for the White House as a war hero, maverick and straight shooter—owes the voters some explanations. The press were long ago wooed and won by McCain's seeming openness, Lone Ranger pose and self-deprecating humor, which may partly explain their ignoring his record on POWs. In the numerous, lengthy McCain profiles that have appeared of late in papers like *The New York Times*, the *Washington Post*, and the *Wall Street Journal*, I may have missed a clause or a sentence along the way, but I have not found a single mention of his role in burying information about POWs. Television and radio news programs have been similarly silent.

Reporters simply never ask him about it. They didn't when he ran unsuccessfully for the Republican nomination in 2000. They haven't now, despite the fact that we're in the midst of another war—a war he supports and one that has echoes of Vietnam.

The only explanation McCain has ever offered for his leadership on legislation that seals POW files is that he believes the release of such information would only stir up fresh grief for the families of those who were never accounted for in Vietnam. Of the scores of POW families I've met over the years, only a few have said they want the books closed without knowing what happened to their men. All the rest say that not knowing is exactly what grieves them.

Isn't it possible that what really worries those intent on keeping the POW documents buried is the public disgust that the contents of those files would generate?

How the Senate Committee Perpetuated the Debunking

In its early months, the Senate Select Committee on POW/MIA Affairs gave the appearance of being committed to finding out the truth about the MIAs. As time went on, however, it became clear that they were cooperating in every way with the Pentagon and CIA, who often seemed to be calling the shots, even setting the agendas for certain key hearings. Both agencies held back the most important POW files. Dick Cheney was the Pentagon chief then; Robert Gates, now the Pentagon chief, was the CIA director.

Further, the committee failed to question any living President. Reagan declined to answer questions; the committee didn't contest his refusal. Nixon was given a pass. George H. W. Bush, the sitting President, whose prints were all over this issue from his days as CIA chief in the 1970s, was never even approached.

Troubled by these signs, several committee staffers began asking why the agencies they should be probing had been turned into committee partners and decision makers. Memos to that effect were circulated. The staff made the following finding, using intelligence reports marked "credible" that covered POW sightings through 1989: "There can be no doubt that POWs were alive . . . as late as 1989." That finding was never released. Eventually, much of the staff was in rebellion.

This internecine struggle continued right up to the committee's last official act—the issuance of its final report. The "Executive Summary," which comprised the first forty-three pages—was essentially a whitewash, saying that only "a small number" of POWs could have been left behind in 1973 and that there was little likelihood that any prisoners could still be alive. The Washington press corps, judging from its coverage, seems to have read only this airbrushed summary, which had been closely controlled.

But the rest of the 1,221-page report on POW/MIAs was quite different. Sprinkled throughout are pieces of hard evidence that directly contradict the summary's conclusions. This documentation established that a significant number of prisoners were left behind—and that top government officials knew this from the start. These candid findings were inserted by committee staffers who had unearthed the evidence and were determined not to allow the truth to be sugarcoated.

If the Washington press corps did actually read the body of the report and then failed to report its contents, that would be a scandal of its own. The press would then have knowingly ignored the steady stream of findings in the body of the report that refuted the summary and indicated that the number of abandoned men was not small but considerable. The report gave no figures but estimates from various branches of the intelligence community ranged up to 600. The lowest estimate was 150.

Highlights of the report that undermine the benign conclusions of the Executive Summary:

* Pages 207–209: These three pages contain revelations of what appear to be either massive intelligence failures or bad intentions—or both. The report says that until the committee brought up the subject in 1992, no branch of the intelligence community that dealt with analysis of satellite and lower-altitude photos had ever been informed of the specific distress signals U.S. personnel were trained to use in the Vietnam War, nor had they ever been asked to look for any such signals at all from possible prisoners on the ground.

The committee decided, however, not to seek a review of old photography, saying it "would cause the expenditure of large amounts of manpower and money with no expectation of success." It might also have turned up lots of distress-signal numbers that nobody in the government was looking for from 1973 to 1991, when the committee opened shop. That would have made it impossible for the committee to write the Executive Summary it seemed determined to write.

The failure gets worse. The committee also discovered that the DIA, which kept the lists of authenticator numbers for pilots and other personnel, could not "locate" the lists of these codes for Army, Navy or Marine pilots. They had lost or destroyed the records. The Air Force list was the only one intact, as it had been preserved by a different intelligence branch.

The report concluded, "In theory, therefore, if a POW still living in captivity [today], were to attempt to communicate by ground signal, smuggling out a note or by whatever means possible, and he used his personal authenticator number to confirm his identity, the US Government would be unable to provide such confirmation, if his number happened to be among those numbers DIA cannot locate."

It's worth remembering that throughout the period when this intelligence disaster occurred—from the moment the treaty was signed in 1973 until 1991—the White House told the public that it had given the search for POWs and POW information the "highest national priority."

* Page 13: Even in the Executive Summary, the report acknowledges the existence of clear intelligence, made known to government officials early on, that important numbers of captured U.S. POWs were not on Hanoi's repatriation list. After Hanoi released its list (showing only ten names from Laos—nine military men and one civilian), President Nixon sent a message on February 2, 1973, to Hanoi's Prime Minister Pham Van Dong, saying, "US records show there are 317 American military men unaccounted for in Laos and it is inconceivable that only ten of these men would be held prisoner in Laos."

Nixon was right. It was inconceivable. Then why did the President, less than two months later, on March 29, 1973, announce on national television that "all of our American POWs are on their way home"?

On April 13, 1973, just after all 591 men on Hanoi's official list had returned to American soil, the Pentagon got into step with the President and announced that there was no evidence of any further live prisoners in Indochina (this is on page 248).

* Page 91: A lengthy footnote provides more confirmation of the White House's knowledge of abandoned POWs. The footnote reads:

"In a telephone conversation with Select Committee Vice-Chairman Bob Smith on December 29, 1992, Dr. Kissinger said that he had informed President Nixon during the 60-day period after the peace agreement was signed that US intelligence officials believed that the list of prisoners captured in Laos was incomplete. According to Dr. Kissinger, the President responded by directing that the exchange of prisoners on the lists go forward, but added that a failure to account for the additional prisoners after Operation Homecoming would lead to a resumption of bombing. Dr. Kissinger said that the President was later unwilling to carry through on this threat."

When Kissinger learned of the footnote while the final editing of the committee report was in progress, he and his lawyers lobbied fiercely through two Republican allies on the panel—one of them was John McCain—to get the footnote expunged. The effort failed. The footnote stayed intact.

* Pages 85–86: The committee report quotes Kissinger from his memoirs, writing solely in reference to prisoners in Laos: "We knew of at least 80 instances in which an American serviceman had been captured alive and subsequently disappeared. The evidence consisted either of voice communications from the ground in advance of capture or photographs and names published by the Communists. Yet none of these men was on the list of POWs handed over after the Agreement."

Then why did he swear under oath to the committee in 1992 that he never had any information that specific, named soldiers were captured alive and hadn't been returned by Vietnam?

* Page 89: In the middle of the prisoner repatriation and U.S. troop-withdrawal process agreed to in the treaty, when it became clear that Hanoi was not releasing everyone it held, a furious chairman of the Joint Chiefs of Staff, Admiral Thomas Moorer, issued an order halting the troop withdrawal until Hanoi complied with the agreement. He cited in particular the known prisoners in Laos.

The order was retracted by President Nixon the next day. In 1992, Moorer, by then retired, testified under oath to the committee that his order had received the approval of the President, the national security advisor and the secretary of defense. Nixon, however, in a letter to the committee, wrote, "I do not recall directing Admiral Moorer to send this cable."

The report did not include the following information: Behind closed doors, a senior intelligence officer had testified to the POW committee that when Moorer's order was rescinded, the angry admiral sent a "back-channel" message to other key military commanders telling them that Washington was abandoning known live prisoners. "Nixon and Kissinger are at it again," he wrote. "SecDef and Sec-State have been cut out of the loop." In 1973, the witness was working in the office that processed this message. His name and his testimony are still classified. A source present for the testimony provided me with this information and also reported that in that same time period, Moorer had stormed into Defense Secretary Schlesinger's office and, pounding on his desk, yelled, "The bastards have still got our men." Schlesinger, in his own testimony to the committee a few months later, was asked about—and corroborated—this account.

* Pages 95–96: In early April 1973, Deputy Defense Secretary William Clements "summoned" Dr. Roger Shields, then head of the Pentagon's POW/MIA Task Force, to his office to work out "a new public formulation" of the POW issue; now that the White House had declared all prisoners to have been returned, a new spin was needed. Shields, under oath, described the meeting to the committee. He said Clements told him, "All the American POWs are dead." Shields said he replied, "You can't say that." Clements shot back, "You didn't hear me. They are all dead." Shields testified that at that moment he thought he was going to be fired, but he escaped from his boss's office still holding his job.

* Pages 97–98: A couple of days later, on April 11, 1973, a day before Shields was to hold a Pentagon press conference on POWs, he and Gen. Brent Scowcroft, then the deputy national security advisor, went to the Oval Office to discuss the "new public formulation" and its presentation with President Nixon.

The next day, reporters right off asked Shields about missing POWs. Shields fudged his answers. He said, "We have no indications at this time that there are any Americans alive in Indochina." But he went on to say that there had not been "a complete accounting" of those lost in Laos and that the Pentagon would press on to account for the missing—a seeming acknowledgment that some Americans were still alive and unaccounted for.

The press, however, seized on Shields' denials. One headline read, "POW Unit Boss: No Living GIs Left in Indochina."

* Page 97: The POW committee, knowing that Nixon taped all his meetings in the Oval Office, sought the tape of that April 11, 1973, Nixon-Shields-Scowcroft meeting to find out what Nixon had been told and what he had said about the evidence of POWs still in Indochina. The committee also knew there had been other White House meetings that centered on intelligence about live POWs. A footnote on page 97 states that Nixon's lawyers said they would provide access to the April 11 tape "only if the Committee agreed not to seek any other White House recordings from this time period." The footnote says that the committee rejected these terms and got nothing. The committee never made public this request for Nixon tapes until the brief footnote in its 1993 report.

McCain's Catch-22

None of this compelling evidence in the committee's full report dislodged McCain from his contention that the whole POW issue was a concoction by deluded purveyors of a "conspiracy theory." But an honest review of the full report, combined with the other documentary evidence, tells the story of a frustrated and angry President, and his national security advisor, furious at being thwarted at the peace table by a small, much less powerful country that refused to bow to Washington's terms. That President seems to have swallowed hard and accepted a treaty that left probably hundreds of American prisoners in Hanoi's hands, to be used as bargaining chips for reparations.

Maybe Nixon and Kissinger told themselves that they could get the prisoners home after some time had passed. But perhaps it proved too hard to undo a lie as big as this one. Washington said no prisoners were left behind, and Hanoi swore it had returned all of them. How could either side later admit it had lied? Time went by and as neither side budged, telling the truth became even more difficult and remote. The public would realize that Washington knew of the abandoned men all along. The truth, after men had been languishing in foul prison cells, could get people impeached or thrown in jail.

Which brings us to today, when the Republican candidate for President is the contemporaneous politician most responsible for keeping the truth about this matter hidden. Yet he says he's the right man to be the Commander-in-Chief, and his credibility in making this claim is largely based on his image as a POW hero.

On page 468 of the 1,221-page report, McCain parsed his POW position oddly: "We found no compelling evidence to prove that Americans are alive in captivity today. There is some evidence—though no proof—to suggest only the possibility that a few Americans may have been kept behind after the end of America's military involvement in Vietnam."

"Evidence though no proof." Clearly, no one could meet McCain's standard of proof as long as he is leading a government crusade to keep the truth buried.

To this reporter, this sounds like a significant story and a long overdue opportunity for the press to finally dig into the archives to set the historical record straight—and even pose some direct questions to the candidate.

CHAPTER SEVEN

The Bush Doctrine in Iraq

THE WAR PLANNED YEARS BEFORE 9/11 BY CHENEY AND CO.
October 15–21, 2003, Village Voice

If some wishful Americans are still hoping President Bush will acknowledge that his imperial foreign policy has stumbled in Iraq and needs fixing or reining in, they should put aside those reveries. He's going all the way—and taking us with him.

The Israeli bombing raid on Syria October 5 was an expansion of the Bush policy, carried out by the Sharon government but with the implicit approval of Washington. The government in Iran, said to be seeking to develop a nuclear weapon, reportedly expects to be the next target.

No one who believes in democracy need feel any empathy toward the governments of Syria and Iran, for they assist the terrorist movement, yet if the Bush White House is going to use its preeminent military force to subdue and neutralize all "evildoers" and adversaries everywhere in the world, the American public should be told now. Such an undertaking would be virtually endless and would require the sacrifice of enormous blood and treasure.

With no guarantee of success. And no precedent in history for such a crusade having lasting effect.

People close to the president say that his conversion to evangelical Methodism, after a life of aimless carousing, markedly informs his policies, both foreign and domestic. In the soon-to-be-published *The Faith of George W. Bush* (Tarcher/Penguin), a sympathetic account of this religious journey, author Stephen Mansfield writes (in the advance proofs) that in the election year 2000, Bush told Texas preacher James Robison, one of his spiritual mentors, "I feel like God wants me to run for president. I can't explain it, but I sense my country is going to need me. . . . I know it won't be easy on me or my family, but God wants me to do it."

Mansfield also reports, "Aides found him face down on the floor in prayer in the Oval Office. It became known that he refused to eat sweets while American troops were in Iraq, a partial fast seldom reported of an American president. And he framed America's challenges in nearly biblical language. 'Saddam Hussein is an evildoer. He has to go.'" The author concludes, ". . . the Bush administration does deeply reflect its leader, and this means that policy, even in military matters, will be processed in terms of the personal, in terms of the moral, and in terms of a sense of divine purpose that propels the present to meet the challenges of its time."

Some who read this article may choose to view it as the partisan perspective of a political liberal. But I have experienced wars—in India and Indochina—and have measured their results. And most of the men and women who are advocating the Bush Doctrine have not. You will find few generals among them. They are, instead, academics and think-tank people and born-again missionaries. One must not entertain any illusion that they are only opportunists in search of power, for most of them truly believe in their vision of a world crusade under the American flag. They are serious, and they now have power at the top.

I believe that last week's blitz of aggressive speeches and spin by the president and his chief counselors removed all doubt of his intentions.

"As long as George W. Bush is president of the United States," Vice President Cheney told the friendly Heritage Foundation, "this country will not permit gathering threats to become certain tragedies." The president himself must tell us now what this vow entails.

The public relations deluge by Bush, Cheney, Secretary of State Colin Powell, National Security Adviser Condoleezza Rice, and Defense Secretary Donald Rumsfeld seemed to be aimed at denying any policy fumbles and insisting that the liberal press was ignoring the positive developments in Iraq.

Mr. Cheney, the president's usual attack dog, aimed his sharpest and most sneering words at those who offer dissent about the administration's foreign and economic policies. Perhaps seeking to stifle such criticism, he raised the specter of terrorists acquiring weapons of mass destruction that "could bring devastation to our country on a scale we have never experienced. Instead of losing thousands of lives, we might lose tens of thousands or even hundreds of thousands of lives in a single day of horror." His implication was that Saddam Hussein in particular had presented this threat—when virtually all the available intelligence shows that

Iraq's weapons programs had been crippled or drastically diminished by UN inspections and economic sanctions imposed after the first Gulf war in 1991.

But beyond all the distortions and exaggerations and falsehoods the Bush people engaged in to rally public support for the Iraq war, what I have never understood, from the 9/11 day of tragedy onward, is why this White House has not called on the American people to be part of the war effort, to make the sacrifices civilians have always made when this country is at war.

There has been no call for rationing or conservation of critical supplies, such as gasoline. There has been no call for obligatory national service in community aid projects or emergency services. As he sent 150,000 soldiers into battle and now asks them to remain in harm's way longer than expected, the president never raised even the possibility of reinstating the military draft, perhaps the most democratizing influence in the nation's history. Instead, he has cut taxes hugely, mostly for affluent Americans, saying this would put money into circulation and create jobs. Since Bush began the tax cutting two and a half years ago, 2.7 million jobs have disappeared.

All this I don't understand. If it's a crisis—and global terrorism surely is—then why hasn't the president acted accordingly? What he did do, when he sent out those first tax rebate checks, was to tell us to go shopping. Buy clothes for the kids, tires for the car—this would get the economy humming. How does that measure up as a thoughtful, farsighted fiscal plan?

In effect, George Bush says, believe in me and I will lead you out of darkness. But he doesn't tell us any details. And it's in the details where the true costs are buried—human costs and the cost to our notion of ourselves as helpers and sharers, not slayers. No one seems to be asking themselves: If in the end the crusade is victorious, what is it we will have won? The White House never asked that question in Vietnam either.

. For those who would dispute the assertion that the Bush Doctrine is a global military-based policy and is not just about liberating the Iraqi people, it's crucial to look back to the policy's origins and examine its founding documents.

The Bush Doctrine did get its birth push from Iraq—specifically from the outcome of the 1991 Gulf war, when the U.S.-led military coalition forced Saddam Hussein's troops out of Kuwait but stopped short of toppling the dictator and his oppressive government. The president then was a different George Bush, the father of the current president. The father ordered the military not to move on Baghdad, saying that the UN resolution underpinning the allied coalition did not authorize a regime change. Dick Cheney was the first George Bush's Pentagon chief. He said nothing critical at the time, but apparently he came to regret the failure to get rid of the Baghdad dictator.

A few years later, in June 1997, a group of neoconservatives formed an entity called the Project for the New American Century (PNAC) and issued a Statement of Principles. "The history of the 20th Century," the statement said, "should have taught us that it is important to shape circumstances before crises emerge, and to meet threats before they become dire." One of its formal principles called for a major increase in defense spending "to carry out our global responsibilities today." Others cited the "need to strengthen our ties to democratic allies and to challenge regimes hostile to our interests and values" and underscored "America's unique role in preserving and extending an international order friendly to our security, our prosperity and our principles." This, the statement said, constituted "a Reaganite policy of military strength and moral clarity."

Among the 25 signatories to the PNAC founding statement were Dick Cheney, I. Lewis Libby (Cheney's chief of staff), Donald Rumsfeld (who was also defense secretary under President Ford), and Paul Wolfowitz (Rumsfeld's No. 2 at the Pentagon, who was head of the Pentagon policy team in the first Bush presidency, reporting to Cheney, who was then defense secretary). Obviously, this fraternity has been marinating together for a long time. Other signers whose names might ring familiar were Elliot Abrams, Gary Bauer, William J. Bennett, Jeb Bush, and Norman Podhoretz.

Three years and several aggressive position papers later—in September 2000, just two months before George W. Bush, the son, was elected president—the PNAC put military flesh on its statement of principles with a detailed 81-page report, "Rebuilding America's Defenses." The report set several "core missions" for U.S. military forces, which included maintaining nuclear superiority, expanding the armed forces by 200,000 active-duty personnel, and "repositioning" those forces "to respond to 21st century strategic realities."

The most startling mission is described as follows: "Fight and decisively win multiple, simultaneous major theater wars." The report depicts these potential wars as "large scale" and "spread across [the] globe."

Another escalation proposed for the military by the PNAC is to "perform the 'constabulary' duties associated with shaping the security environment in critical regions."

As for homeland security, the PNAC report says, "Develop and deploy global missile defenses to defend the American homeland and American allies, and to provide a secure basis for U.S. power projection around the world. Control the new 'international commons' of space and 'cyberspace,' and pave the way for the creation of a new military service—U.S. Space Forces—with the mission of space control."

Perhaps the eeriest sentence in the report is found on page 51: "The process of transformation, even if it brings revolutionary change, is likely to be a long one, absent some catastrophic and catalyzing event—like a new Pearl Harbor."

Apparently for the neoconservative civilians who are running the Iraq campaign, 9/11 was that catalyzing event—for they are now operating at full speed toward multiple, simultaneous wars. The PNAC documents can be found online at newamericancentury.org.

In the end, the answers lie with this president and later maybe with Congress and the American voters. Is he so committed to this imperial policy that he is unable to consider rethinking it? In short, is his mind closed? And if so, how many wars will he take us into?

These are not questions in a college debate, where the answers have no consequences. When a president's closest advisers and military planners are patrons of a policy that speaks matter-of-factly of fighting multiple, simultaneous, large-scale wars across the globe, people have a right to be told about it.

In his new book, *Winning Modern Wars*, retired general Wesley Clark, a candidate for the Democratic presidential nomination, offered a window into the Bush serial-war planning. He writes that serious planning for the Iraq war had already begun only two months after the 9/11 attack, and adds:

"As I went back through the Pentagon in November 2001, one of the senior military staff officers had time for a chat. Yes, we were still on track for going against Iraq, he said. But there was more. This was being discussed as part of a five-year campaign plan, he said, and there were a total of seven countries, beginning with Iraq, then Syria, Lebanon, Libya, Iran, Somalia and Sudan. . . . I left the Pentagon that afternoon deeply concerned."

A five-year military campaign. Seven countries. How far has the White House taken this plan? And how long can the president keep the nation in the dark, emerging from his White House cocoon only to speak to us in slogans and the sterile language of pep rallies?

A REPORTER'S ITCH TO RETURN TO THE ACTION—AND THE MADNESS
March 25, 2003, Village Voice

It is a paradox of war that some people who have lived through its slaughter and madness never lose the itch to go back and live through it again. Some soldiers feel the pull, lured by memories of the intense bonding. Medical professionals and relief workers feel it too, still carrying the images of the wounded they saved and lost. And some reporters also have the craving because war is life's most primal story. I, for one, still hear the siren call.

One modifying remark: Most people who have survived war have little or no or minus desire to relive the experience. Second, I really can speak only about reporters, for it's the only skin I have.

Why have I chosen to write about this phenomenon of attraction to war? We journalists so rarely explain ourselves to our audience perhaps in fear of letting you see, heaven forbid, our fallibility that a gulf has widened between us and the public. I thought a little self-examination might help people better understand what they'll be seeing and reading in the days of war ahead.

First, though you probably already know this, a lot of the people reporting on the war have no firsthand experience with it, especially those working from air-conditioned television studios an ocean and continent away from the fighting. Probably they should begin their reports with some kind of ignorance acknowledgment, but no matter, they are harmless if you hit the mute button. Reporters in the war zones are, for the most part, quite different. Some are new at it, as we all were, but they won't be innocent for long. War vastly speeds up the initiation process. Clears the mind of flotsam too. Journalists are already among the allied casualties.

My own initiation happened in Laos in 1970. The Laotian government flew a small foreign press group by helicopter to a tiny, half-abandoned town with dirt streets that was essentially encircled by the Communist Pathet Lao. After touring the town we returned to the makeshift airstrip to fly back to Vientiane. Several townspeople were waiting there, hoping to escape with us. As the chopper revved up, they rushed for it. I was blithely standing off, taking pictures of the scene. Then a puff of dirt and smoke suddenly kicked up 50 yards to the left of the chopper. I kept clicking. Another puff went up 50 yards to the right of it. I realized my colleagues were screaming at me. I ran hard and jumped on, with the aircraft two feet off the ground. I learned that day about the military art of "bracketing" a target. The two "puffs" were aiming rounds fired from mortars in the surrounding hills; the next one presumably would have landed in the middle on the helicopter.

I learned two other things that day as well. One was that not all people, including journalists, behave well under stress. As I was dashing toward the helicopter, an aged and wispy Laotian woman was struggling to climb on. A reporter already on board kicked out with his combat boots and tried to dislodge her.

Others lifted her aboard. She clutched my hand through the entire flight, and when we set down in Vientiane, she knelt and kissed the tarmac. The rest of us never discussed the incident with the reporter in combat boots.

The day's other lesson was the adrenaline rush that comes after you emerge alive from an incident that could just as easily have killed you. After this happens to you a few times, subconscious notions of immortality may begin to rattle around in your psyche.

Beyond the adrenaline high that fuels this news-gathering drive, there are other motivations, such as career advancement and the urge to beat the competition to a story or at least out-report them. After all, if a conflict involves American troops or interests, rightly or wrongly that war will likely be the biggest story around, since the United States is now the world's dominant nation. All these factors narcissistic and self-referential as they are help explain the draw that war can be.

I always know when the itch is at peak levels because, even when I'm in denial about it, my phone will ring and an old colleague with the fever will be on the other end. It began happening early last week, as the attack on Iraq approached. Norman Lloyd, the best combat cameraman I've ever known, needed to talk just as I did. We tiptoed slowly up to the subject, which was how we felt not being there. Disoriented, we agreed. More than a little irrelevant. So far away from the scene of the story. Norman is still covering stories, for CBS's 60 Minutes. But not combat. "I know I could go if I wanted to," he said, "but then," here he broke into laughter, "then I think about my knees and whether they could still handle jumping down from tanks."

Friday afternoon in the Voice office, as I was writing this piece, people gathered around a television set to watch the opening air blitzkrieg of Baghdad, a mesmerizing, death-delivering son et lumière spectacle. All of this came to us live and in color, with a little box at the bottom of the screen flashing the latest stock figures from Wall Street. The figures seemed to rise with each explosion and plume of flame.

So why the reporter's urge to be near that carnage? I can only tell you that after a reporter has tasted the war experience and acknowledged to himself that many of the reasons he gets gratification from it are narcissistic, he may still discover deeper reasons for keeping at it. This may sound corny, even naive, but a reporter can come honestly to believe in the importance of delivering the full face of war—families decimated, bent refugees walking in endless streams, children orphaned, uplifting acts of honor and friendship, unspeakable acts of cruelty and depravity, bravery, betrayal, human lives saved by Samaritans, human beings lying in pieces from explosive projectiles. People should have to look upon all of that.

If ours is truly a democracy, the people should be told and shown—even if they wish to turn their eyes away—exactly what is being waged in their name. No sugarcoating. No sanitizing. Just a faithful picture of the wild convulsion that is war.

So far, the Pentagon's about-face decision this time to allow journalists to accompany battle units is a vast improvement over the sequestered and censored conditions of the first Gulf War in 1991. America is seeing war almost in the raw, and while the pictures and words are often unsettling, they may be helpful in the new world of scariness to our coming-of-age.

INDEX

ABOUT THE AUTHOR

When Sydney Schanberg decided to remain in Cambodia and cover the fall of that country to the fanatical Communist Khmer Rouge in April 1975, his main consideration was staying with the story he had been reporting in *The New York Times* for the previous five years—how America pushed its war in Vietnam into this small neighboring country and consumed it. His daily dispatches were written with cinematic detail, often throughout the night, and following perilous daytime visits to the scenes of battles or bombings. For his account of the war and the disaster of Cambodia, he received the Pulitzer Prize for international reporting "at great risk," as well as the George Polk Award and numerous other distinguished journalism prizes. The Academy Award–winning film *The Killing Fields*, which brought the Cambodian tragedy to worldwide attention, was based on Schanberg's experience in the final days of the country's collapse, when he was forced to leave behind his Cambodian colleague Dith Pran. The highly personal story of his search for Pran—who was feared lost in the brutal chaos imposed after the takeover by the genocidal Khmer Rouge regime—was first published in *The New York Times Magazine* in January 1980 and solidified Schanberg's reputation as one of the premier war correspondents of the twentieth century.

However, Cambodia and Vietnam were not Sydney Schanberg's only exposure to armed conflict. On overseas assignment for *The Times* in 1971—as bureau chief in New Delhi during the Indira Gandhi years—he went to the front lines of the war for independence in Bangladesh and reported that clash between the Indian and Pakistani armies and the ethnic cleansing that preceded it. After leaving Asia, Schanberg went back to the paper's home office, where he was promoted to Metropolitan Editor. He returned to writing in 1981 on the Op-Ed page, producing *The Times*'s first opinion column about New York—exposing abuses of power, government corruption, and special treatment for the city's power elite. *The Times* discontinued the column four years later.

Schanberg then left *The Times* after twenty-six years and moved on to *New York Newsday*, where he also wrote an opinion column, until the paper's demise in 1995. Since then he has done investigative journalism at APBNews.com, written press criticism for the *Village Voice*, and devoted an academic semester to the State University of New York at New Paltz, as the initial fellow of the James H. Ottaway Sr. Visiting Professorship. Schanberg continues to write about international affairs, press issues, and the fate of American POWs still unaccounted for in Vietnam.

Sydney Schanberg was born in Clinton, Massachusetts, and attended Harvard College. He divides his time between New York City and a house in the woods at New Paltz, in the Hudson Valley.

Beyond the Killing Fields—the first anthology of his major writings on war and its consequences—spans four decades. It includes the conflicts in Bangladesh, India, Vietnam, Cambodia, and Iraq as well as the original articles on which *The Killing Fields* film was based.

ABOUT THE EDITOR

Robert Miraldi is an award-winning newspaper reporter and author. His 2004 book *The Pen Is Mightier: The Muckraking Life of Charles Edward Russell* (Palgrave) received the Frank Luther Mott Award as best journalism book in America. He has taught journalism at SUNY New Paltz for twenty-nine years.